Josias L. Porter

Science and Revelation

a series of lectures in reply to the theories of Tyndall, Huxley, Darwin, Spencer, etc

Josias L. Porter

Science and Revelation
a series of lectures in reply to the theories of Tyndall, Huxley, Darwin, Spencer, etc

ISBN/EAN: 9783337888206

Printed in Europe, USA, Canada, Australia, Japan

Cover: Foto ©Andreas Hilbeck / pixelio.de

More available books at **www.hansebooks.com**

SCIENCE AND REVELATION:

A Series of Lectures

IN REPLY TO

THE THEORIES

OF

TYNDALL, HUXLEY, DARWIN, SPENCER,

ETC.

WILLIAM MULLAN.

NEW YORK:
SCRIBNER, WELFORD & ARMSTRONG.
1875.

PREFACE.

THESE lectures owe their origin to certain proceedings connected with the meeting of the British Association in Belfast in the autumn of 1874. In his opening address, the President thought fit to assail some of the most important principles of religion, whether natural or revealed. In that address, and in some others subsequently delivered, the facts of science were presented as antagonistic to the claims of every form of religion which recognises the existence of a personal God ; and although the wonders of nature were disclosed, the hand of God was ignored.

Whilst courtesy and precedent forbade any protest at the time, it was felt by many, and more especially by those resident in Belfast, that such teaching should not be permitted to pass unchallenged. The paramount importance of the questions at issue, the literary and scientific prestige of the men by whom these strange doctrines were propounded, the injurious influence which such deliverances were calculated to exercise on some minds, and the strong desire expressed by many honest and earnest believers in the sacred Scriptures that these adverse theories should be thoroughly analysed, suggested the necessity of an elaborate defence of the fundamental truths so wantonly impugned ; and at a meeting of ministers, held shortly afterwards, the programme of the lectures now published was arranged.

These lectures will speak for themselves, for the men who delivered them, and for those Divine truths which they so ably and eloquently expound. They will be found clear, logical, and conclusive. Each subject is thoroughly

sifted.   The *facts* of science are admitted, whilst the inferences of the *savans* are disputed.   The respective territories
of science and religion are distinctly defined ; and whilst
the conflicting theories of these philosophers—some materialistic, some idealistic, and others rationalistic—are brought
out as demoralising, and often mutually destructive ; the
harmony ever subsisting between true philosophy and true
religion ; the moral beauty of Christianity, and its adaptation
to the wants and wishes of our common humanity ; and the
being and wisdom and goodness of God as manifested in the
pages of inspiration, the works of creation, and the arrangements of providence, will be found unfolded with a freshness, a fulness, and a power highly creditable to the men by
whom the discussion is conducted, and to the Church which
they so well represent.

The lectures were delivered in the Presbyterian Church,
Rosemary Street, Belfast, during the past winter, and have
already received the favourable imprimatur of the public.
They have been heard with pleasure and profit by intelligent audiences, they have been sought for in pamphlet
form by tens of thousands ; and they are now issued in one
harmonious whole, and given to the Church and to the
world, with the earnest prayer that the perusal of the
volume may confirm many in the faith once delivered to
the saints, and produce in all who read it a loving and
intelligent allegiance to Him whom to know is life eternal.

WM. JOHNSTON,
Ex-Moderator of the General Assembly.

BELFAST, *March, 1875.*

CONTENTS.

SCIENCE AND REVELATION.

TO be able to define the exact province and limits of
each branch of knowledge under investigation, is one
of the best evidences of intellectual power and logical
training. Until the student can do so he is not a safe
guide. And farther, the man who, knowing the limits of
any particular branch, deliberately attempts, by alleged
deductions or specious theories, to pass beyond them, is, in
so far, unworthy of trust ; and his conclusions, even on other
points within his proper sphere, must be received with
caution, for a lax method of reasoning, when once indulged
in, has a tendency to become habitual. No matter how
profound a man may be in his knowledge of any one department, he is not thereby warranted in attempting to
make that knowlege a passport for theory and speculation,
nor for dogmatism in another department. It is of the very
essence of science that the mind form accurate conceptions
of what is submitted to it ; that it be able to draw round
each subject a clear line of demarcation, separating it from
all others, and making it stand out in its distinctive indivi-
duality. Then only will thought be restrained from what
is vague and indefinite, and rigidly confined to what is real
and true.

I admit that the several departments of knowlege in some
respects overlap each other, and that all have certain
mutual relations ; yet this fact does not tend to confuse the
boundaries of mathematics and psychology, or of science and
theology, as fields of research and thought ; nor does it
warrant the student of one department to intrude his views
and theories into another so as to overthrow its legitimate
deductions. No psychological belief, for example, can
affect a mathematical demonstration, and no theological

dogma can annul a fact of science ; but, on the other hand, psychology has a sphere in which mathematics has no place, and theology has a sphere into which science must not intrude. The method of investigation in each department is specifically different. The mathematician has a problem which he works out in accordance with certain fundamental axioms, until he arrives at a demonstration which cannot be disputed. The scientist examines natural objects through his senses ; his mind interprets the observations thus made, compares them, and frames generalisations to which he gives the name of " laws ;" and these, though never attaining the absolute certainty of mathematical demonstrations, are yet, as a rule, readily comprehended and accepted as facts of science. In the departments of psychology and natural theology a different method is followed, because the grand subjects with which they are concerned are, for the most part, presented directly to the mind, and not to the senses or the logical faculty. They can only be grasped and comprehended in their entirety by abstract thought and profound reflection—quickened and guided in the case of theology by Divine illumination. It consequently happens that minds trained to scientific research alone, and habitually occupied with the severe and exact demonstrations of geometry, or with the palpable forms of matter, encounter an almost insuperable difficulty when they attempt to enter the field of abstract thought. They cannot place the problems of metaphysics and theology under the microscope, nor can they apply to them the test of the mathematical axiom, and, therefore, they cannot always comprehend and will not receive them. And yet to those who are intellectually qualified for this higher department of knowledge, and thoroughly trained in it, the sublime truths which it embraces become as definite and as convincing as the truths of physical science. It is a well-known fact that " each man is strong in that he is trained in, weak in other regions—so much so, that often the objects there seem to him non-existent."*

* Shairp, " Culture and Religion," p. 80.

All this shows the necessity in these days of determining
the exact provinces, and defining the precise limits of
Science and Revelation. The attempts in times past,
and even yet on the part of the Church of Rome, to fetter
science by ecclesiastical shackles, have brought discredit
upon Christianity at large. We hear scientific men now com-
plaining loudly, but not very logically, that all theologians
are despots ; and they whine as if they were martyrs to
free thought. I would, therefore, warn all Christian men
not to betray, or give the appearance of betraying, any
opposition to science. Let us look upon it as a friendly
territory—a province of God's universe, where His foot-
steps can be traced by every unprejudiced scientific
observer, and where His wisdom can be seen by every
philosophic mind. But then, on the other hand, it is plain
to all educated men that science is at this moment committing the very error which it charges on theologians—it
is striving to invade the province of Revelation, and to
sweep away its most sublime doctrines, not by established
facts, but by crude theories and wild speculations. There
can be no peace between them until each is rigidly confined to its own sphere ; there they are in harmony, and
they mutually contribute to the solution of the highest
problems. As a theologian I have no desire to fetter
science. I willingly accord to it the utmost freedom, and
bid it " God speed" in its own field. There it does noble
service to my cause, enabling me to reason with the unerring rigour of logic from palpable manifestations of design
in every department of nature, to the existence of an Omnipotent Designer. But when science leaves its legitimate
field to assail Revelation ; or when the scientist, to use the
words of the distinguished president of the British Association, having reached the limits of experimental evidence,
attempts to prolong the vision backwards into the unknown, * so as to solve a problem which science cannot solve,
and thus to overthrow theological truth, then, as a theologian, and in the name of science itself, I place an arrest

* Tyndall, " Address," p. 56.

upon him as he would do upon me ; and if he will not desist, I shall ever feel it my duty to warn the public that his conclusions so arrived at, however skilfully framed and eloquently expressed, are no more worthy of belief than the splendid creations of a poet's fancy.   In this course of action I am virtually sustained by Professor Tyndall, who says —" The profoundest minds know best that Nature's ways are not at all times their ways, and that the brightest flashes in the world of thought are incomplete until they have been proved to have their counterparts in the world of fact.   .   .   .   His experiments constitute a body, of which his purified intuitions are, as it were, the soul."*

By science I here mean *Physical or Natural Science,* which has for its field the universe of matter, and which, by observation and experiment on its various parts and organisms, endeavours to gain a knowledge of the facts and phenomena of matter, with their relations and laws.   The field of science being the material universe, it follows that our knowledge of it must be obtained through the senses ; so that scientific evidence is evidence addressed to, and apprehended by, the senses ; so far, then, as science is concerned, the only knowledge we can obtain is through the senses, or through legitimate deductions from facts thus perceived.

In investigating the province of science I shall proceed as follows :—I shall critically examine the attempts made by scientists to solve certain great problems which naturally force themselves upon the attention of thoughtful men in every age.—I. The origin of matter and of the existing material universe.   II. The origin of life.   III. The origin of species.   IV. The origin of mind ; and, connected with it, the conceptions formed by mind of a God and of a future state.   I shall then turn to Revelation, sketch its purpose, and define its province.   The field before me is, as you may see, a very wide one ; it is a field, too, which embraces most momentous questions, bearing alike on time and eternity, on man's happiness here and on

* " Fragments of Science," p. 111.

his state hereafter. It is difficult to treat it at all within the scope of a single lecture ; and I can only promise to give you, with as much clearness as is in my power, the results of anxious thought and laborious research, extending at intervals over many years.

One point I think it right to notice at the outset, because much has been made of it. Professed scientists complain that their conclusions are criticised by many who have never examined nature for themselves, who have never conducted a single investigation, physiological, chemical, or anatomical ; and they denounce, in no measured terms, such presumptuous criticisms. The charge is plausible, but not very logical. Let me show this in a sentence. The scientist, by his researches, long, minute, laborious, and complicated, establishes certain facts. He explains these facts in intelligible language, so that all, scientific and non-scientific alike, can understand them. Then he proceeds to deduce from them conclusions with regard, say, to the origin of matter, or the origin of life, or the origin and nature of mind. Now, I take his facts as established and explained by himself; and I maintain that I am as competent to examine and test the accuracy of the general conclusions he professes to deduce from them as he is. It is not practical science which is here required, it is logic ; and scientific men cannot lay claim to a monopoly of this gift. So then, in prosecuting my critical examination, I shall not attempt to enter the domain of the professional student of nature. I shall simply accept his observations and demonstrations ; not his theories, however, nor his speculations, nor his guesses, but those phenomena which he has established by observation ; and then I shall place them side by side with the conclusions to which they are supposed to lead, and submit the whole to a searching logical analysis. Surely this is not presumption ; and if fairly carried out, no real scientist will venture to take exception to it.

I.—The Origin of Matter and of the Existing Material Universe.

The teachings of scientists on matter and the material universe are not uniform ; were they so they would have much greater weight. Nearly every scientific man has a theory of his own, which he propounds with all authority, not to say dogmatism ; and it so happens that these theories are, for the most part, inconsistent with each other—and indeed in some cases mutually destructive. Democritus, a Greek sage, who lived about B.C. 400, propounded a theory of the structure and origin of the material universe, which he appears to have derived from Leucippus, its founder. It was substantially adopted by the Latin poet Lucretius, whose prime object in adopting it was thereby to banish from the mind of man all idea of a creating and superintending deity. It has received its latest development or exposition in the address of Professor Tyndall before the meeting of the British Association in Belfast. Its leading principles are as follows :—Matter is eternal ; it has two characteristics—1. Quantitative relations, which are original ; 2. Qualitative, which are secondary and derived ; and thus the distinction between matter and mind is abolished. Matter consists ultimately of atoms, which were at first distributed through empty space ; the atoms are homogeneous in quality, but heterogeneous in form ; motion is the eternal and necessary consequence of the original variety of atoms in the vacuum ; the atoms are impenetrable, and, therefore, offer resistance to one another ; all existing forms—the stars, the planets, the earth, plants, animals, mind itself—evolved from these atoms ; the process of evolution began by the atoms striking together, and the lateral motions and whirlings thus produced were the beginnings of worlds ; the varieties of things depend on the varieties of their constituent atoms ; the first cause of all existence is necessity, that is, the necessary succession of cause and effect. To this succession they gave the name "chance," as opposed to the "mind" (νοῦς) of Anaxagoras.* There are many differences in details among atomic philosophers, but the leading principles are embodied in the foregoing propositions. Many of the modern atomists admit that matter was created, as I shall show in the sequel.

As this theory is now put forward in the name of science, we naturally ask—What are its scientific proofs? We cannot admit theories. They have no weight in our present critical investigation. And first—What proof is advanced that matter is eternal? There is none; and from the nature of the case there can be none. All that science can prove is, that matter has existed so long as man has existed to observe it. We all admit this; and farther science cannot possibly go. To affirm that it is eternal is a pure assumption, which has no logical connection with observed facts. Herbert Spencer rightly says that the eternity, or self-existence, of matter is unthinkable; and he argues, with true philosophic insight, that "the assertion that the universe is self-existent does not really carry us a step beyond the cognition of its present existence; and so leaves us with a mere re-statement of the mystery."† And, besides, while science cannot advance one step towards the proof of the eternity of matter, some of the most eminent scientific men of the present age affirm that this atomic theory affords the strongest proof of the existence of a Creator. At the meeting of the British Association in 1873, Professor Clerk Maxwell said, "We are unable to ascribe either the existence of the molecules or any of their properties to the operation of any of the causes which we call natural." On the other hand, the exact equality of each molecule to all others of the same kind gives it, as Sir John Herschel has well said, "the essential character of *a manufactured article*." And in the seventeenth century, the celebrated French philosopher and mathematician, Gassendi, enunciated views substantially the same. So much then for the teaching of science as to the eternity of matter.

* Tyndall, "Address," p. 4. Brandis, *Geschichte*, i., p. 293, sq.
† "First Principles," p. 32.

But we now return to the atoms.   Democritus, following
Leucippus, held that they were originally scattered throughout empty space, and that they combined in obedience
to mechanical laws.   Empedocles, a Sicilian philosopher
of the same age, could not believe this possible, and he
suggested that the atoms possessed original and elementary
powers or sensations, some of love and some of hate, and
that influenced by these sensations they combined or separated.   Lucretius conceived the atoms falling eternally
through space, and their interaction throughout infinite
time forming the worlds ; it was a truly poetic conception,
worthy of its author.   Professor Clerk Maxwell supposes
the atoms to have been originally created, and endowed
with certain powers, under the guidance of which they
gradually evolved those complex forms now presented to
the eye of the observer ; and Tyndall, though he speaks with
hesitation, appears to think that the material atoms possess
some inherent energy or life ; and hence he discerns in
"molecular force the agency by which both plants and
animals are built up," though he does not tell us whence
this molecular force has come.

I do not profess to reconcile these discordant theories ;
nor is it necessary for my purpose, even were it possible.
My sole object is to submit them to the test of scientific
proof.   As to the atoms themselves, they have never yet
been discovered.   Scientists have searched for them ; the
highest powers of the microscope, and the utmost skill of
the chemist, have been tried in vain.   " Loschmidt, Stoney,
and Sir William Thomson have sought to determine the
sizes of the atoms, or rather to fix the limits between which
their sizes lie,"* and they have failed.   Their very existence,
then, is a theory—a theory, too, which has no logical connection with any observed fact.   And besides, the idea of
an atom is inconceivable, or, as Herbert Spencer would say,
it is unthinkable.   To conceive of a piece of matter, having
necessarily, because it is matter, length and breadth, and
yet being indivisible, is an absurdity.   And if we adopt the

* Tyndall, "Address," p. 26.

view of Faraday, that atoms are "centres of force," the difficulty remains. A centre of force must be either material or immaterial ; if material, the absurdity is as before ; if immaterial, then no aggregate of the immaterial could form the material universe. Science is thus completely at fault regarding these imaginary atoms.

And when we proceed to test the atomic theory in its development, difficulties and absurdities accumulate at every stage. It is held that atoms, whether eternal or "manufactured articles," whether inert or gifted with love and hate, or possessing inherent potency, have arranged themselves, by chance friction and spontaneous interaction, throughout the infinite past, into those forms of wondrous beauty, and delicate and complicated mechanism, which we now see in every part of the universe, and which appear to be guided by wise laws, and adapted to wise ends. What is the scientific proof of this theory? There is none, and there can be none. No scientist professes to have seen atoms building up worlds. The nature of the theory places it beyond the range of science, away in the infinite past. And farther, the theory of matter arranging itself spontaneously into systems governed by exact law, and organisms exhibiting the most exquisite design, is not only unsupported by scientific observation, but is opposed to the whole analogy of scientific observation. Spontaneous action is, as Huxley rightly says, action without a cause, which is unscientific and impossible. It is impossible to conceive of a change taking place without a cause, and action necessarily involves change, so that spontaneity in matter is an absurdity.* It is not one of those physical theories which, as Tyndall says, lies beyond experience, but is yet derived by a process of abstraction from experience. No process of abstraction can derive from experience a thing which is contrary to experience. Take as an illustration of the impossibility of conceiving mere matter capable of evolving an object familiar to us all, the structure of the eye ; and I here borrow the words of one of the most distinguished of living

* See H. Spencer, " First Principles," p. 32.

naturalists, Professor Pritchard :—"From what I know, through my own speciality, both from geometry and experiment, of the structure of the lenses of the human eye, I do not believe that any amount of evolution extending through any amount of time, could have issued in the production of that most beautiful and complicated instrument, the human eye. The most perfect, and at the same time the most difficult, optical contrivance known is the powerful achromatic object-glass of a microscope ; its structure is the long unhoped-for result of the ingenuity of many powerful minds, yet in complexity and in perfection it falls infinitely below the structure of the eye. Disarrange any one of the curvatures of the many surfaces, or distances, or densities of the latter ; or, worse, disarrange its incomprehensible self-adaptive powers, the like of which is possessed by the handiwork of nothing human, and all the opticians in the world could not tell you what is the correlative alteration necessary to repair it, and, still less, *to improve it, as a natural selection is presumed to imply.*"*

Tyndall himself is, in the end, forced to admit that the structure of the universe around us is an " insoluble mystery ;"† and Huxley, after placing the dogma of atheistic materialism in its strongest light, says, " The materialistic position that there is nothing in the world but matter, force, and necessity, is as utterly devoid of justification as the most baseless of theological dogmas."‡ This with him is, of course, the acme of incredibility and absurdity. So I am content to leave the theory of atomic materialism in the position thus assigned to it.

Here again we see that the solution of the grand problem of the origin of the universe is beyond the range of science. And, besides, the inferential teaching of science is not exhausted in this negative result. It reveals in nature everywhere the existence of *force*. However far its observations extend back, that force cannot be eliminated. It

* Paper read at Brighton, Oct. 8th, 1874.
† " Address," p. 58.
‡ " Lay Sermons," p. 144.

is involved in the movement of a grain of sand as fully as
in the circling of the spheres ; and if science here attempt
to pass beyond the range of sense, and to theorise about
force existing in atoms, we follow it and say—You are but
shifting the mystery ; and we press the natural question—
What put the force in the atoms ? Whence came it ? Thus
we drive the scientist back and back through every province of his own legitimate domain ; we drive him back, too,
through those regions of hazy theory and dim speculation,
in which he loves to expatiate, until at last, by an inexorable logic, we compel him to admit an author of force—
the Great First Cause. Tyndall has virtually admitted this
in a lecture delivered at Manchester only a few days ago.
I ask special attention to his words, which conclude a long
argument on force :—" In my ignorance of it all, I have
asked myself whether there is no power, being, or thing, in
the universe whose knowledge of that of which I am so
ignorant is greater than mine.   I have asked myself, can it
be possible that man's knowledge is the greatest knowledge
—that man's life is the highest life ?   My friends, the *profession of that atheism with which I am sometimes so lightly
charged would, in my case, be an impossible answer to the
question.*"*

II.—THE ORIGIN OF LIFE.

The origin of life is a still deeper problem than the preceding, and it is at present occupying the thoughts of the
first scientists of the age.   Huxley, Owen, and Darwin may
be regarded as the leading men, at least in England, in
physiological observation.   Tyndall follows in their wake ;
and Herbert Spencer is the philosopher who, systematising
their observations and deducing from them general principles, endeavours, by a recondite biology, to trace life to
its source and to reveal its cause.   I shall try to show you
the line of argument, and to test its scientific accuracy.
And here again let me remind you that I do not profess to

* " Crystalline and Molecular Forces," p. 12.

enter the laboratory or the dissecting-room ; nor do I care
to follow Professor Huxley in his curious and cruel experiments on animal organisms ; I accept his own established
facts, and my only duty is to put to the test of a rigorous
logic the conclusions drawn from them.

In attempting to discover the origin of life, the eye of the
professional physiologist is naturally turned to the germ in
which the life-power, if I may so speak, lies, and in which
it begins to develop ; the ultimate object being to ascertain
how it springs into operation, and what is its cause.
Huxley's description is very graphic, and I must give it in
full :—"Examine the recently-laid egg of some common
animal, such as a salamander or a newt. It is a minute
spheroid in which the best microscope will reveal nothing
but a structureless sac, enclosing a glairy fluid, holding
granules in suspension. But strange possibilities lie dormant in that semi-fluid globule. Let a moderate supply of
warmth reach its watery cradle, and the plastic matter undergoes changes so rapid and yet so steady and purpose-like
in their succession, that one can only compare them to those
operated by a skilled modeller upon a formless lump of clay.
As with an invisible trowel, the mass is divided and sub-
divided into smaller and smaller portions, until it is reduced
to an aggregation of granules not too large to build withal
the finest fabrics of the nascent organism. And then, it is
as if a delicate finger traced out the line to be occupied by
the spinal column, and moulded the contour of the body ;
pinching up the head at one end, and the tail at the other,
and fashioning flank and limb into due salamandrine proportions, in so artistic a way, that, after watching the process hour by hour, one is almost involuntarily possessed by
the notion, that some more subtle aid to vision than an
achromatic would show the hidden artist, with his plan
before him, striving with skilful manipulation to perfect his
work." And then, to sum up the entire results of his scientific observations, he adds :—"What is true of the newt is
true of every animal and of every plant ; the acorn tends
to build itself up again into a woodland giant such as that

from whose twig it fell ; the spore of the humblest lichen reproduces the green or brown incrustation which gave it birth ; and at the other end of the scale of life, the child that resembled neither the paternal nor the maternal side of the house would be regarded as a kind of monster. . . . . It is the first great law of reproduction, that the offspring, tends to resemble its parent or parents."*

But what light does all this throw upon the origin of life ? None. Quite true, Huxley adds, " Science will some day show us how this law is a necessary consequence of the more general laws which govern matter." But this is just a gratuitous theory, a prophecy, in fact, springing from Mr. Huxley's foregone opinion, and having no logical connection with his scientific observations. The fact is, his observations tend to a widely different conclusion. They show us the guiding power which that mysterious entity we call life exercises upon matter, moulding it at will into forms of exquisite beauty and wide diversity ; they show us that life cannot be a unit, that is, a thing of one essence and type, emanating from matter ; for, were it so, then its operations upon matter would be uniform, and there would be but one class of organisms in the universe. Or, suppose we admit, with Herbert Spencer, that the life-principle is modified to meet the requirements of its environments, then the nature of the full-grown animal could never be predicted, as that would depend on the environments, which accident might entirely change. On the contrary, Huxley's researches prove that there are essentially distinct types of life, though they all seem to have the same elementary material basis ; and that each type operates upon matter—the very same matter—with such irresistible guiding potency as to build it up into forms exactly corresponding to the parent stock. Science cannot in this respect control it, it can only observe it. Matter—all life's visible environment—can do nothing except supply what may be called the raw material. Life guides the moulding and building in entire independence alike of man and of matter ; and all scientific observation

* " Lay Sermons," pp. 261. 262.

proves that life—pre-existing life—is absolutely necessary to the building up of animal organisms.

But scientists have tried to go deeper, and we must follow them. The material germ or *protoplasm*, as it is now technically termed, has been subjected to the keen scrutiny of the microscope, and the searching analysis of the chemist. Its constituent elements have been discovered and described. Huxley says, " All the forms of protoplasm which have yet been examined contain the four elements, carbon, hydrogen, oxygen, and nitrogen, in very complex union."* In whatever form it appears, " whether fungus or oak, worm or man," its elements are the same ; and when life in it becomes extinct, it " is resolved into its mineral and lifeless constituents."† It is admitted that carbon, hydrogen, oxygen, and nitrogen are lifeless bodies ; and that they all exist previous to their union ; " but when they are brought together," says Huxley, " under certain conditions they give rise to protoplasm, and this protoplasm exhibits the phenomena of life."‡ Would it not, at first sight, appear from these words as if science had at length succeeded in solving the grand mystery of the origin of life. It knows all the elements of protoplasm ; and there is no lack of them in nature. They exist everywhere around us. " With my own hands," writes Professor Pritchard, " a quarter of a century ago, I obtained all the elements which I found in an egg and in grains of wheat out of a piece of granite and from the air which surrounded it, element for element. It has been one of the most astonishing and unexpected results of modern science that we can unmistakably trace these very elements also in the stars."§ So, then, the elements are known, and are at hand ; science can put them together ; and Professor Huxley says, " I can find no intelligible ground for refusing to say that the properties of protoplasm"—that is, of course, life—" result from the nature and disposition of its molecules."‖ Yet he cannot produce life from those materials. Science here utterly fails. Its

---

* " Lay Sermons," p. 130. † *Ibid*, p. 131. ‡ *Ibid*, p. 135.
§ Paper read at Brighton. ‖ " Lay Sermons," p. 138.

field, alike of potency and of knowledge, is at this point shut in by an impassable barrier. Huxley confesses that *pre-existing living matter* is absolutely requisite to the development of the phenomena of life, and he admits that its influence "is something quite unintelligible;" while Pritchard affirms that "no chemist, with all his wonderful art, has ever yet witnessed the evolution of a living thing from those lifeless molecules of matter and force."*

So far, then, as science is concerned, we are as remote as ever from the solution of the problem of the origin of life. Scientists have tried to produce life from its so-called physical basis, but every trial has been a failure. They have tried also to trace it to its origin; but they have only been able to observe its phenomena—they cannot reach its source, nor can they reveal its nature. They see motion and development in the living protoplasm; but these are the effects of a life already existing, not the essence or principle of life itself. Herbert Spencer describes life as "a continuous adjustment of internal relations to external relations;" but this Delphian utterance, if it have any meaning at all, can only refer to the phenomena of life; it does not touch its essence, nor does it throw one ray of light upon its origin. That the life is inherent in, or evolved by, matter is inconceivable, for the living protoplasm often dies, and then, though all the material elements are still there, development ceases at once; the power which moulds and builds has gone mysteriously as it came, and no human agency can again vitalise the dead mass, which now obeys the ordinary laws of matter, and is resolved into its mineral constituents. "The living body resists the chemical agencies that are ready to attack it; the dead body at once succumbs to these agencies." Life is the power which moulds and builds up organisms, and preserves the matter of which they are composed from the dissolving force of the ordinary laws to which mere matter is subject. The teaching of science, therefore, is, that life is something apart from matter; but what it is—whence it comes and whither it

* Paper read at Brighton.

B

goes—science cannot tell. Its operation on matter is
wonderful. It guides the chemical forces already existing,
so as to arrange inert matter into shapes of the most exquisite proportions, and organisms of the most delicate and
complicated mechanism—all of which are entirely distinct
from those normal forms which the constituent elements
would assume, if uncontrolled by the life-principle. And
then again, when the life departs, the very matter in which
it existed, and which it moulded with such mystic power
into bodies of matchless grace and beauty, speedily becomes
a mass of loathsome rottenness, and dissolves into its original elements. Professor Huxley is, in the end, forced to
admit all this, when he speaks of the " living protoplasm"
which preserves and builds up organic forms, and the
" dead protoplasm" which is resolved into its mineral constituents ; but he tries to save his favourite theory by
affirming—not in accordance with, but in spite of logical
sequence—that the phenomena presented by protoplasm,
living or dead, are its properties ;* and that all vital action
may be said to be the result of the molecular forces of the
protoplasm which displays it. How, I ask, can vital action
be the result of molecular forces alone, when, according to
the Professor's own admission, the influence of pre-existing
living matter is shown by scientific observation to be
necessary to vital action ? The vital action is clearly the
result, not of molecular forces, but of the life-principle operating on the protoplasm. In denying this, Huxley sacrifices his logic to his theory ; and he would do well thoughtfully to read Tyndall's striking words :—" There is in the
true man of science a wish stronger than the wish to have
his beliefs upheld—namely, the wish to have them true.
And the stronger wish causes him to reject the most
plausible support, if he has reason to suspect that it is vitiated by error. Those to whom I refer as having studied
this question, believing the evidence offered in favour of
spontaneous generation to be thus vitiated, cannot accept
it. They know full well that the chemist now prepares

* " Lay Sermons," p. 137.

from inorganic matter a vast array of substances which were some time ago regarded as the sole products of vitality. They are intimately acquainted with the structural power of matter as evidenced in the phenomena of crystallisation ; they can justify, scientifically, their belief in its potency, under the proper conditions, to produce organisms ; but in reply to your question they will frankly admit their inability to point to any satisfactory experimental proof that life can be developed save from demonstrable antecedent life."* Tyndall's final conclusion is contained in these words :—" In fact, the whole process of evolution is the manifestation of a Power absolutely inscrutable to the intellect of man. As little in our days as in the days of Job can man by searching find this Power out. Considered fundamentally, then, it is by the operation of an insoluble mystery that life on earth is evolved."†

This is enough for my purpose. The limits of the province of science are here drawn definitely by the President of the British Association. Science shows that life is an entity, a power, apart from and above matter, but that in its essence it eludes the keen eye of the philosopher ; that it cannot be discovered by the researches of the physiologist ; that it will not emanate from the retort of the chemist, however skilfully he arrange and manipulate the elements of its physical basis ; that, in fact, it lies hid among those sublime mysteries of nature which human wisdom utterly fails to penetrate, and which the Infinite Wisdom of the Great Creator can alone reveal to the yearning spirit of His faithful creatures. The whole teachings of science are, so far as they can go, in harmony with that simple but sublime record—" And the Lord God formed man of the dust of the ground, and breathed into his nostrils the breath of life ; and man became a living soul."‡

* " Address," &c., p. 56.
† " Address," p. 57.
‡ Gen. ii. 7.

III.—THE ORIGIN OF SPECIES.

Darwin is the apostle of the doctrine of development, though the idea was broached long before his day. To the naturalist, Darwin's book on " The Origin of Species" is one of the most important contributions to modern science ; to the logician, it is an utter failure. As a scientific observer, an acute, laborious, skilful, profound student of nature, Darwin has perhaps no equal ; but his reasoning faculty seems to have been completely overwhelmed by the force of one preconceived idea. The range of his research has been wonderful ; he has roamed over the world to sift and amass materials ; he has recorded the results with a lucidity that leaves nothing to be desired ; and yet one can, with perfect logical consistency, admit the whole of his observed facts, and reject the whole of his theories. He has a strange way of overlooking what logicians call the middle term ; that is, the connecting link between the fact established by scientific observation, and the conclusion which he professes to deduce from it. Professor Huxley—whom Tyndall characterised, and rightly too, as Darwin's ablest interpreter— virtually acknowledges this when he says, "that notwithstanding the clearness of the style, those who attempt fairly to digest the book find much of it a sort of intellectual pemmican—a mass of facts crushed and pounded into shape, rather than held together by the ordinary medium of an obvious logical bond." Yet he attempts, in his own peculiar way, to account for this, and in some measure to remove its damaging force. "From sheer want of room," he suggests, " much has to be taken for granted which might readily enough be proved ; and hence, while the adept, who can supply the missing links in the evidence from his own knowledge, discovers fresh proof of the singular thoroughness with which all difficulties have been considered and all unjustifiable supposition avoided, at every re-perusal of Mr. Darwin's pregnant paragraphs, the novice in biology is apt to complain of the frequency of what he fancies is gratuitous assumption." *

Well, I presume Professor Huxley himself is not a novice in biology. I have no doubt he would lay claim—and, in fact, he does lay claim—to be an adept of sufficient skill to supply any missing link, when possible ; yet even he does not hesitate, in the end, to admit that Darwin's theory of the origin of species is only "a hypothesis."† It has not, therefore, in Huxley's estimation, any real scientific basis.

My limits forbid an attempt to analyse Darwin's whole theory ; I can only glance at one or two leading points. The essence of his theory is, that all forms of life, from the humblest zoophyte up to man, have evolved from one primordial germ. His theory, while it may admit a primal act of creation, yet sets aside the Bible narrative, and assigns to man a common parentage with the monkey and the worm. The line of proof is, that species may be originated by selection; that natural causes are competent to exert selection ; and that the most remarkable phenomena exhibited by the distribution, development, and mutual relations of species, can be shown to be deducible from the general doctrine of their origin, combined with the known facts of geological change ; "and that, even if all these phenomena are not at present explicable by it, none are necessarily inconsistent with it."‡

It will be easily seen that the crucial point is the first. We naturally ask—What are the proofs of this startling assertion that species may be originated by selection ? Does it rest on any sound scientific basis ? Have we evidence that any distinct species has been originated ? I have not space to examine Darwin's observed facts. I admit their accuracy ; but I deny that any or all of them satisfy the requirements of logic, as proofs of the truth of his theory. No man has ever seen a species originated. The impossibility of submitting the theory to a scientific test is admitted, for the process is relegated away into the infinite

* "Lay Sermons," p. 257.　† Ibid, p. 295.　‡ Ibid, p. 293.

past. Thus Darwin writes, "Nature grants vast periods of time for the work of natural selection." Again, "The chief cause of our natural unwillingness to admit that one species has given birth to another and distinct species is, that we are always slow in admitting any great change of which we have not seen the intermediate steps. The mind cannot possibly grasp the full meaning of a hundred million of years. It cannot add up and perceive the full effects of many slight variations accumulated during almost an infinite series of generations." All this, and there is much in the book of a like character, is very striking and very original; but any one can see that it is not scientific. Science has its basis in observation; and the things here mentioned are all outside the field of observation. The facts which Darwin's own observations establish are insignificant modifications of race, most of them under man's guiding skill, and which confessedly tend to disappear again when man withdraws and nature resumes its sway. In fact, it appears to me that the fundamental error in Darwin's reasoning is, his accepting slight variations of race as a proof of transmutation of species.

Darwin draws largely upon an infinite past. Countless ages form the basis of his theory. Without these, development could not have reached its present stage. But Sir Wm. Thompson, one of the greatest of our natural philosophers, "has dissipated all speculation regarding an infinite series of life-forms, by proving that they could not extend over millions of millions of years; because, assuming that the heat has been uniformly conducted out of the earth, as it is now, it must have been so intense within a comparatively limited period, as to be capable of melting a mass of rock equal to the bulk of the whole earth."* What would have become of Darwin's half-developed animals under such circumstances?

It may possibly be said that I am no scientist, and that, therefore, my opinion on this point is worthless. I should not wonder if some person with a great name, or with no name

* Frazer, "Blending Lights," p. 4.

at all, would charge me with presumption, in attempting to criticise such a book as "The Origin of Species." Now, while maintaining that I am just as competent to test the character and soundness of a logical sequence as any scientist—and that is the sole point here at issue—I am, at the same time, in order to avoid the possibility of cavil, content to adopt the conclusion of one whose scientific eminence will not be questioned. Professor Huxley says:—"After much consideration, and with assuredly no bias against Mr. Darwin's views, it is our clear conviction that, as the evidence stands, it is not absolutely proven that a group of animals, having all the characteristics exhibited by species in nature, has ever been originated by selection, whether artificial or natural."* This is clear, and ought to be conclusive. I could say nothing more damaging to Mr. Darwin's theory. Another distinguished scientist, M. Flourens, strikes at the very root of the theory in a single sentence— "Natural selection is only nature under another name . . . it is nature personified ; that is, nature endowed with the attributes of God."† I conclude, therefore, that Darwin totally fails in his attempt, by science, "to banish the belief in the continued creation of new species."

One other point in Darwin's theory I must notice. In answer to the question, How do groups of species arise? he says—"From the struggle for life. Owing to this struggle for life, any variation, however slight and from whatever cause proceeding, if it be in any degree profitable to an individual of any species, in its infinitely complex relations to other organic beings and to external nature, will tend to the preservation of that individual, and will generally be inherited by its offspring. The offspring, also, will thus have a better chance of surviving ; for, of the many individuals of any species which are periodically born, but a small number can survive. I have called this principle, by which each slight variation, if useful, is preserved, by the term Natural Selection, in order to mark its relation to

* "Lay Sermons," p. 295.
† See "The Darwinian Theory Examined," p. 135.

man's power of selection."* The essence of this theory is, that all the wonderful adaptations which we find in the physical structure of the various species of animals, to the conditions in which they are placed, to the work they have to do, to the wants they have to supply, have sprung from a long and fortuitous sequence of natural events, to which Mr. Darwin gives the scientific name, Natural Selection. If this be true, then the most beautiful and complex organs of animals—the heart and veins, the nervous system, the human hand, the eye, the mind itself, with all its wondrous faculties—have been constructed, not by the infinite wisdom of an Almighty Creator, adapting every part and organ and faculty, with requisite skill, to the office it was designed to fill; but from a medley of blind chance, countless blunders, and innumerable minute accidental modifications, which occurred in the struggle for existence during myriads of past ages. The fish was not designed for the water; the bird was not designed to fly; the ear was not designed for hearing; the eye was not designed for seeing; all these, says Darwin, are just the fortuitous products of organised matter pushing its way at random, and after incalculable instances of trial and failure, during incalculable ages, at last hitting on what was best.†

And what is the evidence on which he bases this theory, which to every thoughful man must, at first sight, appear incredible? Nothing short of actual observation of the whole alleged process could, in such a case, satisfy the requirements of science, or make the theory even credible. There has been no such observation, and no such observation is possible, because the process of development is supposed to have extended over an "almost infinite series of generations." It thus lies outside the province of science, and has therefore no claim upon the belief of scientific men. Darwin himself only advances it as a theory. "By the theory of natural selection," he says, "all living species have been connected with the parent species of each genus, by

* "Origin of Species." p. 61.
† See "The Darwinian Theory Examined." p. 286.

differences not greater than we see between the varieties of the same species in the present day."* And here, as it seems to me, is the fundamental logical fallacy which takes away its basis even as a theory. He argues from the existence of slight varieties in the same species to the entire transmutation of species. The former is admitted on all hands ; the latter has no logical connection with it, and is, besides, opposed to scientific observation. Yet Professor Huxley records his conviction that Darwin's theory has given a " death-blow" to teleology ; that is, to the grand doctrine of design in nature. Huxley's critique on this point is inimitable. I do not believe there is anything comparable to it in the whole range of literature. To do it justice, I must give it in full and in his own words :—" The teleological argument runs thus : an organ or organism is precisely fitted to perform a function or purpose ; therefore it was specially constructed to perform that function. In Paley's famous illustration, the adaptation of all the parts of the watch to the function or purpose of showing the time, is held to be evidence that the watch was specially contrived to that end ; on the ground, that the only cause we know of, competent to produce such an effect as a watch which shall keep time, is a contriving intelligence adapting the means directly to that end.

" Suppose, however, that anyone had been able to show that the watch had not been made directly by any person, but that it was the result of the modification of another watch which kept time but poorly ; and that this again had proceeded from a structure which could hardly be called a watch at all, seeing that it had no figures on the dial, and the hands were rudimentary ; and that, going back and back in time, we came at last to a revolving barrel as the earliest traceable rudiment of the whole fabric. And imagine that it had been possible to show that all these changes had resulted, first, from a tendency of the structure to vary indefinitely ; and, secondly, from something in the surrounding world which helped all variations

* " Origin of Species," p. 281.

in the direction of an accurate time-keeper, and checked all those in other directions ; then it is obvious that the force of Paley's argument would be gone. For it would be demonstrated that an apparatus thoroughly well adapted to a particular purpose might be the result of a method of trial and error worked by unintelligent agents, as well as of the direct application of the means appropriate to that end, by an intelligent agent.

"Now, it appears to us that what we have here, for illustration's sake, supposed be done with the watch, is exactly what the establishment of Darwin's theory will do for the organic world."*

Well, if Paley's argument remain in force until we are able to produce "a developed watch," my impression is it will last a long time ; and if Darwin's theory must wait for support until that watch be discovered, then the process of proof will reach at least as far into the future as the process of the evolution of species reaches into the past. True, Professor Huxley puts his evolved watch forward as a supposition ; but is it not monstrous to propound such a supposition in the name of science ? It reads more like a broad joke from a corner in " Punch" than an extract from a scientific lecture. Professor Huxley is an unsparing antagonist. He uses every weapon which irony and ridicule and vituperation can furnish to overwhelm his opponents. He exposes with unmitigated contempt every weak point, real or fancied, in their reasoning. He does not hesitate to question the motives, especially of Christian men, and to charge them with downright dishonesty. I recommend him in future to store up all these special gifts of his for home use, because I feel convinced that no writer, lay or clerical, ancient or modern, so richly deserved their full and concentrated force, as the author of the theory of a deloped watch.

Teleology remains in its high seat, absolutely unmoved by theories which one can only rightly describe, in the graphic words of Carlyle, as "diluted insanity." We have heard

* " Lay Sermons," pp. 301-2.

Huxley's opinion; but how very differently men of the highest scientific attainments interpret the observations of Darwin may be seen from the following eloquent words recently uttered by Professor Pritchard :—"I know of no greater intellectual treat—I might even call it moral— than to take Mr. Darwin's most charming work on the 'Fertilisation of Orchids,' and his equally charming and acute monograph on the Lythrums, and repeat, as I have repeated, many of the experiments and observations therein detailed. The effect on my mind was an irresistible impulse to uncover and bow my head, as being in the too immediate presence of the wonderful prescience and benevolent contrivance of the UNIVERSAL FATHER. And I think such, also, would be the result on the convictions and the emotions of the vast majority of average men. I think the verdict would be that no plainer marks of contriving will exist in a steam-engine, or a printing-press, or a telescope." Design in nature can be seen by every unprejudiced man who observes nature, or who thoughtfully studies the recorded observations of others. Every fresh discovery in physiology ; every searching glance of the scientist into the wonderful mechanism of the animal frame ; every minute inspection of the marvellous adaptation of insect organisms to the complicated structure of flowers ; in a word, every new achievement of the scientific mind in exploring the vast domain of nature, reveals more clearly, and establishes more firmly, the presence everywhere, and in everything, of an infinitely powerful and infinitely wise designing Mind. Unseen by human eye, undiscoverable by scientific observation in the mystery of its working, we yet discern the impress and recognise the beneficent control of that Infinite Mind in earth and sea and sky.

IV.—THE ORIGIN OF MIND, AND THE CONCEPTIONS FORMED BY IT OF GOD AND OF A FUTURE STATE.

This is the highest problem with which science has ventured to grapple ; and even the most daring of scientists

approach it with feelings akin to awe. Democritus, as we
have seen, held that the soul consists of fine, smooth, round
atoms, like those of fire. Huxley says, "Even those manifestations of intellect, of feeling, and of will, which we rightly
name the higher faculties, are not excluded from this
classification, inasmuch as to everyone but the subject of
them, they are known only as transitory changes in the
relative positions of parts of the body."* In another place
he says somewhat more clearly, "And what do we know of
that 'spirit' over whose threatened extinction by matter a
great lamentation is arising, except that it is also a name
for an unknown and hypothetical cause, or condition, of
states of consciousness? In other words, matter and spirit
are but names for the imaginary substrata of groups of
natural phenomena."† Tyndall is a little more explicit
when he thus writes:—"Not alone the mechanism of the
human body, but that of the human mind itself—emotion,
intellect, will, and all their phenomena—were once latent in
a fiery cloud." All this reads like "Material Atheism." I
am not alone in this opinion. But as the language is somewhat hazy, and as Tyndall and Huxley seem indignant that
they should be charged with holding such a dogma, I leave
them to explain their meaning, and to give to the world
their scientific creed in intelligible language. One thing,
however, is clear : whatever view of the origin and nature of
the human mind the words of each are intended to give,
they do not attempt to establish it by scientific evidence.
It is confessedly outside the legitimate province of science.
No observation has ever yet reached, or can ever reach, the
development of a fiery cloud into emotion, intellect, will,
and all the phenomena of the human mind. It is a daring
theory, and nothing more. Tyndall himself seems to shrink
from it in moments of thoughtfulness, when fancy is restrained by judgment—"What baffles and bewilders me, is
the notion that from those physical tremors things so utterly
incongruous with them as sensation, thought, and emotion
can be derived ;" and then he puts the problem in its true

* "Lay Sermons," p. 122.   † *Ibid*, p. 143.

light in a single sentence : " You cannot satisfy the human understanding in its demand for logical continuity between molecular processes and the phenomena of consciousness. This is the rock on which materialism must inevitably split whenever it pretends to be a complete philosophy of life."* Herbert Spencer is right in asserting that of the substance of mind nothing is known, or can be known, by science. Even the faculties of the mind are outside the field of science ; for we get our knowledge of them, not through the senses, but by introspection or consciousness. Science looks outward for its proofs, psychology inward. It is quite true that the phenomena of mind are exhibited to all, except the individual himself, in one way or another through a material medium, and are apprehended by the senses ; yet, in the case of the individual himself, they are apprehended in a different way. Consciousness alone, therefore, has direct access to the mind ; and it is the ultimate source of all mental knowledge. So, then, science can throw no light on the great problem now before us.

But, besides, it is by mind the scientist obtains his knowledge of nature. The senses are only the material avenues through which the mind apprehends physical phenomena. The senses observe, but to the observations thus made must be added primary beliefs or intuitions, ere any intelligible interpretation, even of the simplest phenomena, can be given. It is from intuition we derive our knowledge of the reality of the external world and everything in it ; for sensation is only the apprehension by the mind of an impression made on the sensorium, and it is the mind itself which intuitively forms the conception of the reality of the object that made the impression. So, in like manner, from intuition we get our knowledge of the properties of matter, such as weight, extension, and force ; it is by intuition we form comparisons ; and it is from intuition we obtain our ideas of cause and effect. The senses, on whatever object exercised, and though aided by the utmost experience of the physicist, and the utmost precision of instruments, merely

* " Address," p. 33.

make certain impressions on the mind ; and those impressions must be interpreted by our intuitions ere they can be
of use in science. So then, affer all, our primary beliefs,
or the intuitions of our mind, form the foundation of all
scientific reasoning. Dr. Carpenter, in his address as President of the British Association in 1872, set this matter in
its true light. " Even in astronomy, the most exact of the
sciences, we cannot proceed a step without translating the
actual phenomena of nature into intellectual representations
of those phenomena."*   It is this great fact which lies at
the foundation of all those differences which exist among
scientists themselves.†   The minds of some are warped by
theories ; others entertain strange views regarding primary
beliefs ; and consequently their interpretation of the very
same natural phenomena differ as widely as the poles.
Darwin, for instance, interprets certain observed phenomena
so as to support his theory, that all the species of animals
are derived from one primordial germ ; while Professor
Kölliker, a German naturalist of equal eminence, interprets
the same phenomena in a way totally different.‡   A more
remarkable illustration is the following :—Rude flint im-
plements have been found in gravel-beds in France. It has
been argued with great force that, because they exhibit
evidence of design, they must have been formed by human
hands, though their age is believed to extend thousands of
years beyond the Mosaic period. But some members of
the very same school of science, who point to these flints as
triumphant refutations of the Bible, refuse to recognise any
evidence of design in the structure of plants and animals,
because thereby they would be compelled to acknowledge
the existence of a God. I have not time to dwell upon this
instructive phase alike of scientific scepticism and credulity ;
but there can be no doubt we have here, in the fact that the
individual mind is the interpreter of all natural phenomena,
the fruitful source of many of those errors which have ap-

* " Report," p. 73.
† See Tyndall, " Crystalline and Molecular Forces," p. 7.
‡ Huxley, " Lay Sermons," p. 300.

peared under the name of science, as well as of those wild
theories which have not even a shadow of logical connection
with scientific observations.

There is one point to which I must ask attention ere I
close this part of my subject. Among our primary beliefs
is that of "cause and effect," and, what is embodied in it,
"force." Believing in these, we must carry them back and
back, until at length, compelled by an inexorable logic, we
believe in a First Cause, the primal origin of force. Herbert
Spencer enunciates the same truth with much clearness :—
" We cannot think at all about the impressions which the
external world produces on us, without thinking of them as
caused ; and we cannot carry out an inquiry concerning
their causation, without inevitably committing ourselves to
the hypothesis of a First Cause."* Science, of itself, does
not reveal, because it cannot reach, that First Cause ; but
science reveals phenomena which, being rightly interpreted,
lead by sound logical sequence to a belief in that First Cause.
Here, then, is borderland between Science and Revelation.

And farther, the mind which, as we have seen, embodies
those primary beliefs that constitute the foundation of all
scientific reasoning, has other beliefs, equally definite, connected intimately with the doctrine of a Great First Cause,
or, to speak plainly, of God. There is in the mind of every
man, from the rudest savage to the most gifted philosopher,
the belief that he is dependent on some superior Being ;
that he owes allegiance to Him ; that there is a moral law ;
that we are responsible for obedience or disobedience to it ;
and that there is a future state. This latter especially we
cannot quench. Do what we will, reason as we will, our
higher nature looks away onward with earnest, irrepressible,
unceasing yearning, to immortality in another sphere. The
belief is brought out dimly, but beautifully, by Tennyson :—

> " Thou wilt not leave us in the dust :
> Thou madest man, he knows not why ;
> He thinks he was not made to die ;
> And thou hast made him ; thou art just.

* " First Principles," p. 37.

> " We have but faith ; we cannot know :
>   For knowledge is of things we see ;
>   And yet we trust it comes from Thee,
> A beam in darkness : let it grow."

Science opens no field to which these beliefs belong, or in which they can find a resting-place. Science cannot satisfy them. It leaves us in the dark, helpless and hopeless, on those very points which, constituted as we are, with yearning affections and boundless aspirations, are of supremest importance. That very theory of " the survival of the fittest," propounded with so much learning and ingenuity by Darwin, is here completely at fault ; for it would represent a series of beliefs to have been developed in the mind which are yet useless and deceptive. No power of genius, no perverse skill of sophistry, can ever, even seemingly, reconcile these beliefs with any theory of evolution ; for if this be the ultimate result of the latest combinations of atoms, if this be all nature has done or can do for us, then this ultimate result is human life without adequate motive, " affections with no object sufficient to fill them, hopes of immortality never to be realised, aspirations after God and godliness never to be attained ; and thus, too, myriads of myriads of other nebulæ may still be the potentials of delusions, and their outcomes the kingdom of despair."*

But a sounder and a higher philosophy gives far other teaching. It tells man that those grand intuitions were not implanted in vain. It leads him to look beyond the material universe for the satisfaction of his profoundest thoughts and the realisation of his most earnest longings. It sees, exhibited in one form or another, by every nation, tribe, and family of mankind, a feeling of dependence on some One greater than man, and of moral obligation to some One holier than man. This feeling appears with the earliest development of consciousness, and it grows and strengthens with our mental vigour. We cannot repress it ; and the mind which is forced to interpret the impressions

* Pritchard. " Address at Brighton."

received through the senses, as proofs of the reality of a material world, is in like manner forced to interpret the intuitions of dependence and moral obligation, as proofs of the reality of a spiritual world. And thus " in the universal consciousness of innocence and guilt, of duty and disobedience, of an appeased and offended God, there is exhibited the instinctive confession of all mankind, that the moral nature of man, as subject to a law of obligation, reflects and represents the moral nature of a Deity by whom that obligation is imposed."*

We now see the legitimate province of science, in which it reigns supreme, and beyond which it cannot pass. Science observes, compares, and classifies natural phenomena. It lays the whole material universe open to the mind. It reveals the constituent elements of rude matter, and the plan in which its multitudinous combinations are effected. It shows the wondrous structure of vegetable and animal organisms, and the evidences of design in them all. It unfolds the mechanism of the heavens, and the sublime simplicity of those laws which guide the stars in their spheres. It indicates, besides, a harmony and a unity pervading nature, adapting each particle of matter—each insect, plant, and animal—each planet, star, and constellation—to its own place, and making it fulfil its own mission in the grand scheme of the Universe. It shows that nothing is defective, nothing redundant. Scientific investigation tends to establish the fact of oneness of design and plan in everything. And thus, as one of the greatest of living naturalists tells us, we are led to the culminating point of man's intellectual interpretation of nature—his recognition of the unity of the Power of which her phenomena are the diversified manifestations.†

All nature's phenomena, wherever and however observed, direct towards a Supreme Designer and Lawgiver, whose existence is also recognised, as we have seen, in the primitive instincts of universal humanity. We hail Science,

* Mansell, " Bampton Lectures," p. 113.
† Carpenter, " Presidential Address."

C

therefore, as a most powerful ally ; we bid her God-speed in her vast field of research. But we see at the same time that it is not within the province of science to solve any of those great problems which I have mentioned. They lie beyond her ken. The dogma of materialism which, it has been supposed, science confirms, utterly fails to answer the questions put by the philosophic mind, or to satisfy the longings of the human heart. Tyndall himself has been obliged to confess the fact. With touching pathos he says; in the preface to the expurgated edition of his now famous " Address" :—" I have noticed, during years of self-observation, that it is not in hours of clearness and vigour that this doctrine (of material atheism) commends itself to my mind ; that in the presence of stronger and healthier thought it ever dissolves and disappears, as offering no solution of the mystery in which we dwell, and of which we form a part." These remarkable words, the results evidently of much and even painful reflection, convey a solemn warning to all students and teachers of science. They show the folly of reckless speculation, the futility of dogmatic assertion, and the danger of attempting to prolong the vision backward beyond the well-defined line of rigid observation. They show, too, the absolute necessity of calm, thoughtful, exhaustive investigation, ere we venture to suggest a doubt, or propound a theory, which would have the tendency to unsettle earnest minds, or overthrow cherished beliefs.

V.—THE PROVINCE OF REVELATION.

Little time now remains to me for considering the *Province of Revelation.* Fortunately, lengthened discussion is here unnecessary, for the Bible is its own best exponent. The one grand purpose of Revelation is to communicate to man those truths, a knowledge of which prepares him for a full discharge of his duties in life, and for an entrance into the kingdom of heaven. Scientific teaching does not come within the province of revelation. It is true, however—and the fact should not be lost sight of—that revealed truth touches on scientific truth at many points ; and in all such cases, while we are not to expect from Revelation pure scientific treatment, we are warranted in looking for strict accuracy. God's truth, as revealed, can never be at variance with the phenomena of God's world. So, then, the theologian must not attempt to intrude his dogmas into the field of science, so as to stifle free thought, or limit independent and legitimate research. Free as the air we breathe, free as the light of heaven, must the scientist be left to prosecute his noble studies in the vast realms of nature.

Revelation does not give a scientific cosmology. That lies outside its province. But then, just where science stops short, unable to solve one of the grandest problems of nature—the origin of matter and of the material universe— Revelation steps in to supplement its teaching. Science, as we have seen, points to the great truth that there must be a Creator, though it cannot of itself reach to it ; Revelation confirms and crowns that truth with the simple and sublime declaration, " In the beginning GOD *created* the heaven and the earth."

Revelation does not treat systematically or philosophically of " force" and " motion ;" but it indicates that solution of their ultimate origin, in a living omnipotent Being, which the highest philosophy points to. We read in the first chapter of Genesis, " The Spirit of God *moved* upon the face of the waters"—representing, as it seems to me, that Almighty Being as the quickening principle of the Universe.

Revelation does not touch on geology ; but it leaves room for the fullest development of the successive strata of the earth's crust, even though it could be proven that millions of years had been occupied in their formation. " *In the beginning* God created the heaven and the earth." No date is given. The simple fact of *creation* is affirmed, in opposition to any idea of development or material atheism ; but myriads of ages may have intervened between that " beginning" and the creation of man. Then, again, the historical record of creation which follows seems to have a scientific basis, as if the writer, by a Divine prescience, had anticipated the results of modern research.   He tells us how the lowest forms of life were first made, and how there was a gradual progression up to man, the last and lord of all.

Revelation does not enter into the mysteries of molecular physics, or the development of the life-germ, or the way in which it operates on material organisms.   All these it relegates to science, whose function it is to investigate them. There is, however, one mystery which science cannot reach —the origin of life ; and here again Revelation makes a clear and full discovery.   That brief account of the creation of Adam, given in the second chapter of Genesis, assumes a new significancy when read in the light of the most recent discoveries of science.   Chemistry has demonstrated, as we have seen, that the whole constituent elements of our bodies —in fact, of all organised bodies—are identical with those in the material world around us ; and science, as we have also seen, indicates that the life-principle must be something entirely different from those material elements.   The record contained in Genesis is here in complete accord with science, so far as science can go :—"And the Lord God formed man *of the dust of the ground.*"   Had the writer of these remarkable words heard the recent statements of those eminent scientists, Professors Pritchard and Huxley, he could not have been more scientifically accurate.   Huxley says of the matter of our bodies, that it is "the clay of the potter ; which, bake it and paint it as he will, remains clay, separated by artifice, and not by nature, from the commonest brick or sun-dried clod."*   Again, the sacred writer records man's inevitable doom—"In the sweat of thy face shalt thou eat bread, *till thou return unto the ground: for dust thou art, and unto dust shalt thou return ;*" and Professor Huxley, all unconsciously no doubt, re-echoes the words of the inspired scientist—"Under whatever disguise it takes refuge—whether fungus or oak, worm or man—the living protoplasm ultimately dies and *is resolved to its mineral*

* " Lay Sermons," p. 129

and lifeless constituents."* And the sacred writer does not stop here. He goes on to add what science might infer, but could not reach, as to the origin and implanting of life itself—" The Lord God . . . . breathed into his nostrils the breath of life : and man became a living soul."†

Revelation gives no detailed or systematised account of the various species of animals that exist on the earth, nor does it profess to enter into questions of structure, descent, or development. All this is outside its province ; and it never interferes with the researches of the naturalist. It authoritatively declares a great general truth, however, which all the recondite theories of Darwin cannot over-throw, and which the profoundest studies of the physiologist tend to indicate and confirm—that each species was brought into existence by the distinct fiat of the Almighty Creator.

In approaching the highest problems which occupy human thought—the origin, duty, and destiny of man, and the existence and nature of God—Revelation becomes fuller and clearer. Where science utterly fails to satisfy our wants and aspirations, where philosophy sheds but a faint and flickering ray, Revelation shines with a greater than noon-day splendour. The origin of intellect and conscience, with all their mysterious conceptions of law, obligation, a future state, and a holy God, is embodied in one pregnant sentence—" So God created man *in His own image.*"‡ Here are revealed the essential personality and omnipotence of God ; and, as flowing from them, the personality, knowledge, self-consciousness, moral feeling, and immortality of man, who was made "in the image of God." Of these sublime truths, in all their wondrous development, Revelation be-comes the complete and sole exponent ; and every new phase of truth set forth by it—whether of law, or morals, or worship, or faith, or love,—finds such a responsive echo in our own deepest feelings and loftiest aspirations, that we instinctively bow before it as a message replete with the infinite wisdom of God. While science disappoints our

* " Lay Sermons," p. 131.   † Gen. ii. 7.   ‡ Gen. i. 27.

most momentous inquiries, while philosophy leaves an aching void in the human heart, Revelation fulfils all our wishes, and satisfies all our hopes.

By the testimony of some of the greatest men who have shed the lustre of genius upon the walks of science —Newton and Herschel, Guizot and Pritchard, Brewster and Chalmers—the Bible has been shown to be in full harmony with the facts of science. But it has a far higher claim upon our faith than even scientific testimony can give it. It develops an ethical code, purer and nobler than ever emanated from the schools of the world. It inspires man with a holy ardour, a self-denying, self-sacrificing love, such as philosophers never dreamt of. It reveals to the eye of faith that other world after which our higher nature longs. It shows us that the consciousness of immortality, which haunts us here like a dream, is not a delusion, but a glorious reality. It enables us to look through the gloomy vista of this earth's labours and sorrows, to another, where labour shall have its full reward, and sorrow shall be unknown. It shows, away beyond the tomb, a life, peaceful, happy, glorious, for which the life on earth, with its limitations and disappointments, its ceaseless struggles and unfulfilled desires, is only the school of preparation. It opens before us a sphere where the perfect knowledge after which we here vainly toil, and the perfect happiness after which we here as vainly strive, shall be fully and for ever realised. There is nothing in science or philosophy like this. There is no power in them to make man so wise, so useful, so holy. There is no discovery of science which can bring life and immortality to light. There is no scientific agency which can conquer death, and throw wide the gates of Paradise to the disembodied spirit. In breadth of true knowledge, in sublimity of discovery, in ennobling, quickening power, philosophy and science sink into complete insignificance before this grand Revelation of God.

Design in the Structure & Fertilisation of Plants.

Dr. MOORE, Glasnevin.

THE STRUCTURE, &c., OF PLANTS.

I.—INTRODUCTORY REMARKS.

DURING the latter half of the sixteenth century, John Ray, an English divine, wrote a discourse, as he calls it, in Latin, on "the wisdom of God manifested in the works of the creation;" and for his text he took the well-known 24th verse of the 104th Psalm—"O Lord, how manifold are Thy works! in wisdom hast Thou made them all." If I could to-night cull and translate freely from this book the arguments and observations which he so ably brings to bear on his subject, they would prove much more effectual and convincing than anything I can offer of my own accord. In the preface to the work, the author, in stating his reasons for writing it, mentions, first, that the belief in a Deity is the foundation of all religion; for he that cometh to God must believe that He is God. It is, therefore, a matter of the highest concernment to be firmly settled and established in a full persuasion of this main point. Now this must be demonstrated by arguments drawn from the light of nature and works of creation; for divinity, like all other sciences, proves not, but supposes its subjects, taking it for granted that, by natural light, men are sufficiently convinced of the being of a Deity. Secondly, not only to demonstrate the being of a Deity, but also to illustrate some of His principal attributes, as, namely, His infinite power and wisdom. The vast multitude of creatures—and those not only small, but immensely great—the sun, moon, and all the heavenly hosts, are effects and proofs of His almighty power. "The heavens declare the glory of God, and the firmament sheweth forth His handiwork." The admirable contrivance of all and each of them; the adapting all the parts of animals to their several uses ; the provision that is made for their sustenance, which is often taken notice of in Scripture—" The eyes of all wait upon Thee ; Thou givest them their meat in due season ; Thou openest Thy hand, and satisfieth the desire of every living thing ;"—their mutual subserviency to each other, and unanimous conspiring to promote and carry on the public good, are evident demonstrations of His sovereign wisdom. Such are some of the reasons given by this good man for undertaking the work I have mentioned, and wherein he so ably demonstrates the power, wisdom, and goodness of the Almighty. He also grapples with and condemns the Aristotelian hypothesis, which seems to have been to some extent prevalent in his time—namely, that the world was co-eternal with God ; also, the Epicurean hypothesis, that the world was made by a casual concurrence and cohesion of atoms ; and Descartes' assertion, in his " Principles of Philosophy," that the ends of God in any of His works are equally undiscovered by us.

II.—DESIGN AND ADAPTATION IN SEEDS, ROOTS, STEMS, AND LEAVES OF PLANTS.

As I am unable to illustrate the arguments of Ray on all the various topics mentioned, I think it will be more prudent for me to confine myself chiefly to the subject I am best acquainted with, and endeavour to show preconcerted design and infinite wisdom in the vegetable kingdom. In the outset, we must see and acknowledge the wisdom and power of God, in clothing the earth with such kinds of plants as are best adapted for the use of man and other animals which inhabit the different parts of the globe where these particular kinds are most required, and also in the power they possess of purifying the pestilential air breathed forth by animals, and produced by combustion into an atmosphere of life. Even in the almost universal colouring of plants, infinite wisdom is evinced, green being that colour on which the eye can longest look without tiring. We find a chemical substance diffused through the sap of nearly all plants—namely, chlorophyll, which, on being exposed to light, turns green.

In farther considering this matter, it may probably suit our purpose to take a brief review of the various organs of plants and their uses in the life of the individual, which will enable us to make remarks suitable to our subject on each. In following this plan, we shall commence with the seed, which contains the germ of the

Kidney Bean Germinating.
a Radicle.   *b* Plumule.   *c* Fleshy Cotyledons.

future plant. In this we may readily observe order and regulation, the work of some intelligent being, in furnishing sustenance for the young germ which is contained within the seed, either in the substance called albumen (but properly perisperm), or, when that is wanting, by large fleshy cotyledonary leaves. These support the young embryo until it germinates and extends its roots in the earth to draw nourishment therefrom. It has, however, been remarked that it is not when the seed bursts its coats, or the eggshell is broken by the young chick, or the animal is born, that life begins; for the seed, the embryo or fœtus, had a previous existence more or less independent of, or connected with the parent, according to species. We are unable, by the aid of the most powerful instruments, to perceive the moment when the first embryo cell receives that impress which has irrevocably determined the form which the perfect being is to assume within these narrow limits, · and which neither impregnation nor any other physical influence can make it exceed. And if life is once stopped, no force that is yet known can set it in motion again. In the case of seeds, it may remain dormant for a long succession of years, its action may be limited or imperceptible, until recalled into operation by the necessary amount of certain elements — namely, heat, moisture, and air, which are requisite for germination. We thus see how wisely the embryo of the plant is provided for, until germination takes place, when the root invariably strikes downwards to the earth and seeks darkness, while the stem is elevated and points towards the light, so that each may be in their proper spheres; and, as Dr. Lindley remarks, no known power has yet been found to overcome these tendencies. In the root we see evident design for the nourishment and support of the plant. In the first place it derives nourishment from the seed-leaves until it enters its proper element, where it is soon enabled to provide for itself, and support the individual depending on it. Thousands of mouths are soon opened to absorb the food from the

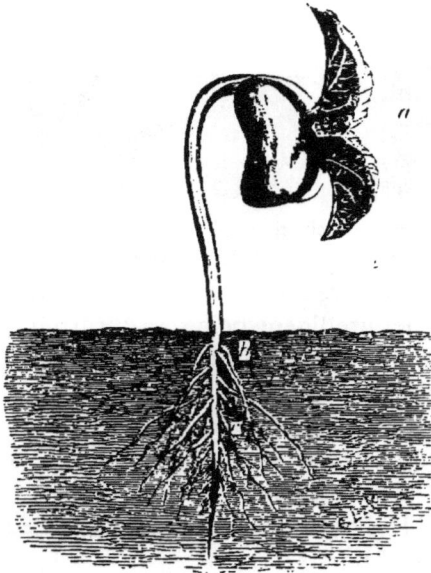

Plant Germinating.

a Plumule. with Cotyledon.
b Collet, line of junction between Stem and Root.
c Root.

earth, by the minute cellular hairs with which the roots of all plants are more or less covered ; though they are invisible to the naked eye, they are easily discovered by the aid of a simple lens or microscope. The young points of the rootlets are constantly receiving additions of new cellular matter to their extremities, which enables them to extend in every direction in search of food, and fix the individual to which they belong steadfastly to the earth. In countries which are subject to long droughts, the roots of plants frequently acquire a thick fleshy form, and assume various shapes, which enables them to withstand dryness for long periods, where plants with only fibrous roots would perish. These fleshy underground stems or roots, as they are sometimes called, often contain the nutritious substances which we feed on ; for example, the potato, arrow-root, yam, sweet potato, Tarro, &c. They sometimes contain fluids which quench the most burning thirst. In the natural progress of their growth, roots are constantly pushing forward, either vertically or horizontally, arriving gradually at fresh portions of soil from which the nutritive matters have not been absorbed ; and as a constant relation is preserved between the spreading of the branches and the spreading of the roots in various kinds of trees, the rain which falls on the tree drops from the leaves at the exact distances where the young spongioles of the rootlets

Tubercular Root of Dahlia.

are in greatest abundance ready to absorb it. We have here, as Dr. Roget observes, a striking instance of that beautiful correspondence which has been established between processes belonging to different departments of nature, and which are made to concur in the production of remote effects, that could never have been accomplished without these preconcerted and harmonious adjustments. Our admiration cannot fail to be excited when we contemplate the manner in which a large tree is chained to the earth by its powerful and widely-spreading roots. By the firm hold which they take of the ground, they produce the most effectual resistance to the force of the wind, which, acting on so large a surface as that presented by the branches covered with dense foliage, must possess an immense mechanical power. As the roots penetrate downwards into the earth to different distances, in order to procure the requisite nourishment, so the stem grows upwards for the purpose of obtaining for the leaves and flowers an ample supply of air and the influence of a brighter light, both of which are of the highest importance to vegetable life. We shall therefore pass from the roots to the stem, and briefly consider the latter in its anatomical and physiological characters. Here we find the gradual lengthening of the cellular structure into long tough tubes, called vascular tissue, as channels for the conveyance of the sap from the roots to its destination; and in the physical process of endosmotic action, by which the circulation of the sap is propelled through these capillary tubes, which also contain the necessary amount of air required for the process of vegetable life—all proving design and not chance. The lowly herb and the lofty tree grow in the same way, the difference being only in size and duration. The stems of the plants of a very large section of the vegetable kingdom are covered with a bark to protect them from outward injuries, and also to enable the physiological functions of life to be carried on. The very structure of this bark being composed of three distinct layers, each having its proper use, is suggestive of wisdom, by adaptation to an end or purpose. The form of the stem may also be taken into consideration In nearly all plants this form is cylindrical, angular-stemmed plants being of rare occurrence.

We may ask, Is there no design in this? Here we have the form known to engineers which has the greatest strength with the least resisting surface. On this account, it is said, the idea of the Eddystone lighthouse was suggested by the form of the stem of a palm tree. If the stems of trees had been square, in place of round, they could not have withstood the violent hurricanes they are often exposed to, without being blown down by the wind. The many æsthetic uses of the stems of plants I shall be obliged here to pass over, and next consider the leaves, which are the most important organs, both physiologically and morphologically. In no other part of the plant is design so strongly manifested as in the leaves. Were it only for the refreshing shade they afford, particularly in warm countries, we see how essential they are for our comfort and delight, circumstances which have been noticed from the remotest periods that any mention is made of trees. Hence that expression so often repeated from Scripture, " Every man sitting under his own vine and under his own fig tree." It would also seem that the ancients were in the habit of eating under trees, as appears from Abraham's entertaining the angels under a tree, and standing by them while they did eat, Gen. xviii. 8. It is, however, when we examine their wonderful mechanism that we can form a just appreciation of their adaptations to the functions they have to perform. To the naked eye, a leaf of a tree appears a solid body, contained within a skin or cuticle ; but to the vegetable anatomist it is known to consist of two distinct layers, soldered firmly together in life, but after death separable into two halves. Were this not the case, the functions of the elaboration of the sap which circulates through the stems to the leaves could not be carried on.

I cannot here enter into the physiology of these functions, but I shall briefly mention the apparatus by which they are principally effected. By looking at the leaf of a tree, it is seen to be traversed from the stalk to the apex, and from one margin to the other, by a wonderful contrivance of veins, which botanists designate as vascular tissue, appearing to the naked eye like the meshes of a net, the meshes being filled up with a softer substance called cellular tissue. It is these cords of vascular veins which give form to leaves, according as they spread from the strong central vein or midrib to the sides. If a small portion of the leaf be laid on the table of a microscope, and viewed through a half or quarter-inch lens, the marvellously beautiful structure will command our admiration.   Hundreds of small openings leading from the exterior to the interior of the leaf will be revealed, through which the vital functions of respiration and transpiration are carried on, in a manner somewhat analogous to similar functions as they are effected through the lungs of animals.   These stomates, as they are called, enable the plant, when acted on by solar light, to decompose the carbonic acid in the sap, and secrete solid carbon, which latter constitutes so large a portion of the vegetable structure.   It is by this action also that the vital air which supports animal life is chiefly purified.   One of the most beautiful provisions known in nature is, that the deleterious air breathed forth by animals is purified and rendered salubrious by plants ; if it were otherwise, the globe would become uninhabitable.   But, as Dr. Lindley observes, every leaf, every blade of grass—nay, the finest of those green silken confervoid threads which we see so abundantly floating in streams and pools of water—is incessantly occupied during daylight in effecting this most important change of pestilential air into an atmosphere of life.   In the greater number of plants these vital cells or stomates are mostly confined to the under surfaces of leaves, but in water-plants they are mostly on the upper surface ; were it otherwise, they could not perform the functions for which they are destined. Their numbers and size vary greatly in different kinds of plants, being sometimes as many as 70,000 to one square inch of the leaf.

Such being a brief statement of the apparatus in leaves for carrying on the life of the plant, he must indeed be a stolid individual who cannot perceive wisdom and design of the highest order in all this cohesion of atoms.   Again, how

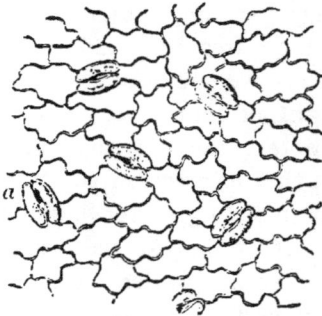

Section of Leaf, with Stomates.
a Stomates.

exquisitely beautiful and how manifold are the forms of
leaves. In the whole vegetable kingdom, no two different
species of plants have their leaves similar ; even in the same
individual, scarcely two leaves are exactly alike—some
larger, some smaller, and so on. It is not too much to
suppose that all this wonderful change of form and of
colouring was intended by the Creator to gratify and
please the senses of His creatures. Had there been only
one form of leaf, however beautiful that may have been, the
eye would have soon become wearied with beholding it.

III.—DESIGN AND ADAPTATION IN THE MORPHOLOGY OF LEAVES.

In considering the forms of leaves, we are led to one of
the principal topics of our subject—viz., what is termed the
morphology of leaves—which enables us to account for the
peculiar forms that these remarkable plants assume, which
have lately been designated carnivorous plants, and which
have caused so much amazement among the readers of the
" Graphic," arising from the curious representations of them
in that popular periodical. It is not only in this country
they have received marked attention, but also in America,
where admirably written articles have appeared in the
New York " Nation," and other newspapers published by
our transatlantic cousins, on insect-devouring plants, during
the early part of the present year, written chiefly by Professor Asa Gray, of Boston, U.S. Dr. Hooker, as you are all
aware, made this the subject of the opening address which he
delivered in this town last August to the biological section
of the British Association; and so admirably did he delineate
the peculiarities of these plants, that he kept one of the
most crowded audiences I ever was present in, almost spell-
bound during the whole course of his address. The two
gentlemen I have named have thrashed the subject pretty
well out, and consequently I shall not have much that is
novel to communicate to you this evening on it. Although
these plants have long been known to capture insects in

their morphologised leaves, it is to the researches of Mr. Darwin that we principally owe our knowledge of their carnivorous propensities, though that was pretty well ascertained by the Americans many years ago.

Regarding that most expert of fly-catchers, *Dionæa muscipula*, about which so much has been written and so little known until lately, Ellis, in his correspondence with Linnæus, describes the structure and action of its living trap. He notices that the power of irritability which caused the movement, making the trap to close, resided in the few bristles which are on the upper face of the leaves among the glands, which latter produce the bait for the unhappy insect that becomes its prey. From these exudes a sweetish liquid, which the animal is tempted to taste, and in doing so, touches those springs or bristles on the surface. The trap then instantly closes, and the spines either transfix the insect or fold it in their fatal embrace, as firmly as ever the legs of a rat were held in a trap, the ordinary kinds of which that are now used so nearly resemble the halves of the leaf of this plant. It has, however, been lately ascertained that the liquid secreted by the glands on the leaf does not appear until the trap has been closed on some unhappy insect, and has held it there for several hours. It is rather considered that insects are attracted to the trap by some peculiar odour emitted. Within one or two days after the capture has taken place, this liquid becomes abundant, macerating the body of the perished insect. Its analogy is not with water, but rather gastric juice, which, like the latter, has an acid reaction. I have long known those plants in a cultivated state, and have had many opportunities of observing them ; but it is only when the plant is vigorous and the

Leaf and Trap of
Dionæa.

a Leaf.
b Trap Appendage.

atmosphere warm that their trap movements are quick. When the leaves are weak or the conservatory cold where they are grown, the traps close very gradually ; but when the leaves are strong, and supplied with sufficient heat, the movement is instantaneous. According to the articles in the American newspapers which I have already alluded to, the nature of this liquid was first ascertained by Dr. Curtis, who had opportunities of making observations on the *Dionæa* in its native habitats. At times he found the entrapped insects enveloped in a mucilaginous consistence, which seemed to act as a solvent, the insect being more or less consumed by it. The observations made by Dr. Curtis were followed up by a Mr. Canby, who discovered that the fluid is always poured out around the captive insects in due time, if the leaf be in good condition and the prey suitable ; also, that it comes from the leaf itself, and not from the decompos-ing insect. He laid on the leaves bits of raw beef, and these, though sometimes rejected, were generally acted on like insects—the traps closed down tightly on the crumbs, which became covered over with the liquid, dis-solved mainly and absorbed by the leaves. He, however, gave the plant a fatal dyspepsia by feeding it with cheese. Most of the foregoing observations have been confirmed by that excellent observer, Mr. Darwin, who has for some years had the subject under his investigation, and who has found that the leaves of *Dionæa* absorbed particles of muscle and other animal matter, but were insensible to par-ticles of inorganic matter. In this we have indeed a subject for contemplation, and we may well be reverently led to ask ourselves, who gave this plant these remarkable peculiarities and propensities ? It will be found rather difficult to explain them on the evolution principle. It is, however, to be clearly understood that this digestive matter in the plant, dissolving the insects which it captures, is in no way identical with the action of the stomachs of animals in digesting their food ; it is only in some way analogous to that operation.

The American plant is not the only one which the Author of nature has endowed with the power of entrapping insects in a similar manner by the leaves. We have, in our bogs all over Ireland, plants belonging to the same natural family as the *Dionæa*, which catch insects also, though not so expertly. They are called "Sundews," in English, which name is derived from the beautiful glistening appearance the numerous glandular hairs on their leaves have when the sun shines brightly on them. Our bogs furnish three species, all of which capture various kinds of insects. They spread out from their base a circle of small leaves, the upper faces of which are beset with glands, and their margins are fringed with long stiff hairs, each tipped by a secreting gland, which produces, while in a vigorous state, a globule of clear liquid, like a drop of dew. A touch shows that the glistening drops are glutinous, as flies become aware to their cost, when they are tempted to alight and sip the liquid. A fly once entangled among those tenacious hairs begins a struggle to get free, but the more he struggles the more he becomes enwrapped among them. This was known to be the case by Roth, a German botanist of the last century, who states the telling fact, that not only the bristles with which the unfortunate insect has come first in contact, but also the surrounding ones, which had been at first widely-spreading, curved inward one by one, although they had not been touched, so as within a few hours to press their gelatinous tips likewise against the body of the captive insect. It is now supposed that it is through these surfaces some part of the animal matter is imbibed by the plant. Roth at that early period surmised that they were predaceous, having observed that the disc of the *Drosera* leaf often became concave and enveloped the prey. These circumstances, although mentioned so long ago, were either ignored or mostly forgotten, until they have again been verified and more light thrown on them by Mr. Darwin, who not only confirmed all Roth's observations, but also found that the bristly leaves responded equally to a bit of muscle or animal substance. Other independent observers have been working at the same class of phenomena in different parts of the world. In the American "Journal of Science," for November, 1871, some of the experiments of Mrs. Treat of New Jersey with these plants are noticed. These experiments were afterwards published in the December number of the American "Naturalist," from which we shall here transcribe. Mrs. Treat selected a particular day in July, when the leaves of the Sundew were unusually active; for, like those of *Dionæa*, they vary much by the state of the weather in the way of appetising. She writes as follows :—"At 10.15 a.m. of the same day, I placed bits of raw beef on some of the most vigorous leaves of *Drosera longifolia*. At 12.10, ten of the leaves had folded around the beef, hiding it from sight. At 11.30 on same day, I placed living flies on the leaves of *Drosera longifolia*. At 12.48, one of the leaves had folded entirely round its victim ; the other leaves had partially folded, and the flies had ceased to struggle. At 2.30; four leaves had each folded round a fly. I tried mineral substances, bits of dry chalk, magnesia, and pebbles. In twenty-four hours neither the leaves nor the bristles had made any move like clasping these articles. I then wet a piece of chalk in water, and in less than an hour the bristles were curving around it ; but they soon unfolded again, leaving the chalk free on the blade of the leaf." Parallel experiments made on the round-leaved Sundew *(Drosera rotundifolia)* gave similar results ; but when Mrs. Treat tried raw apple on the leaves, she found that although the bristles curved towards it, it took eleven hours before they touched it ; and they did not adhere to the apple so firmly as they did to the beef. More recent experiments have been made at the suggestion of Mr. Darwin, and it has been found that when a fly alights upon a leaf a little below its apex, or when a bit of crushed fly is there affixed, within a few hours the tip of the leaf bends at the point, and contracts and curves over or around the body in question ; and Mrs. Treat even found that when living flies were pinned at the distance of half-an-inch from the leaves, these in forty minutes had bent their tips per-ceptibly towards the flies, and in less than two hours reached them ! We may here remark that if these observations be really confirmed by future investigation, the leaves of these plants would seem to indicate purpose nearly as manifest as that of the spider's web. They, however, require to be carefully repeated. There are many other kinds of Sundews, which grow in different parts of the world, but chiefly in New Holland and at the Cape of Good Hope, all of which are armed with apparatus for catching insects, which they invariably do. One very remarkable and beautiful plant, which grows in Portugal, and belongs to the family of *Drosera*, though not a species of that genus, affords a fine example of its power for attracting and capturing small flies, &c. It is called *Drosophyllum lusitanicum*, and has long linear leaves, which are so closely beset with glandular hairs as to render them objects of great beauty, especially when viewed towards bright light. The number of insects this plant captures is so great as to render the leaves nearly black at times ; these insects do not consist of small flies only, but I have occasionally seen rather large moths sticking on them. Like the *Droseræ*, the glands adjacent to those on which the insect is caught bend towards the struggling creature, and entangle it the more.

The next group of curious plants which show design in their morphologised leaves are the *Sarraceniæ*, or "side-saddle plants," as they are sometimes called in this country. In America they are better known under the name of "huntsman's caps." In these there is no contractile action similar to that in the former group, but the construction of the trap is such as to make the capture of insects more certain. They were well explained by Dr. Hooker in his late lecture in Belfast, but some new facts have since been ascertained which warrant me in again referring to the matter.

The leaves of the *Sarraceniæ* are hollow, and form pitchers or trumpet-shaped tubes, containing liquid in which flies and other insects are trapped and drowned. They are all natives of America, and grow in bogs or low ground, so that they cannot be supposed to stand in need of water. In some of the kinds, the apex of the leaf is open, so that water and insects may drop in at once ; but in others the point of the leaf curves over the opening like a hood, and prevents the free access of water. The interior of the tubular leaves is closely beset with bristly hairs, which point in a downward direction to the base of the tube. This is particularly the case near the mouth; but farther down, near the base, they are either short or disappear altogether. The effect of this will be rendered apparent as we proceed in describing the manner insects are entrapped.

Like the *Dioneæ* and *Droseræ*, natural history facts connected with the *Sarraceniæ* were reported about the end of the last century, but they appeared so incredible, that they were either overlooked or forgotten, until the matter has been renewed lately. Dr. James Macbride of South Carolina, the early associate of Elliot, whom I have already mentioned as having been an active

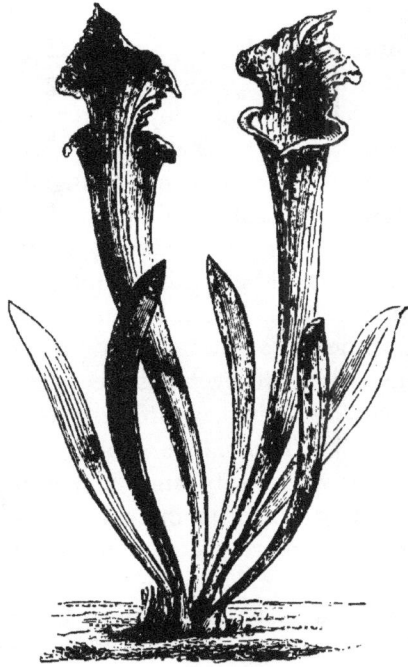

Sarracenia flava.

and voluminous correspondent of Linnæus, sent to Sir James Smith an account of his observations made on this subject in 1810, which was read to the Linnæan Society, London, in 1815, and published in Vol. XII. of their "Transactions." The observations relate chiefly to *Sarracenia adunca*, which is said to be the most efficient fly-catcher among them in its natural habitat, though certainly not so in cultivation, so far as my experience extends. The pitchers of the two large kinds, *S. flava* and *S. purpurea*, contain quadruple the quantity of dead flies and other insects that those of *Sarracenia variolaris (adunca)* contain. Dr. Macbride in

B

this communication states, that "in the month of May, June, or July, when the leaves of these plants perform their extraordinary functions in the greatest perfection, if some of them be removed to a house and fixed in an erect position, it will soon be perceived that flies are attracted by them. These insects immediately approach the hollow tubes of the leaves, and, leaning over their edges, appear to sip with eagerness something from their internal surfaces. In this position they linger, but at length, allured, as it would seem, by the pleasure of taste, they enter the tubes. The fly, which has thus changed its situation, will be seen to stand unsteadily ; it totters for a few seconds, and falls to the bottom of the tube, when it is either drowned or attempts in vain to ascend against the points of the hairs in the tube. In a house much infested with flies, the entrapment goes on so rapidly, that a leaf is filled in a few hours, and it becomes necessary to add water, the natural quantity being insufficient to drown the imprisoned insects." The cause which attracts flies is evidently a sweet viscid substance resembling honey, secreted by, or exuding from the internal surface of the tube. From the margin, where it commences, it does not extend lower than one-fourth of an inch. The falling of the insect is wholly attributable to the downward or inverted pointing of the hairs lining the inner surface of the leaf, till, at or quite near the surface covered by the bait, they are no longer perceptible to the naked eye, or to the most delicate touch. It is here that the fly cannot take a hold sufficiently strong to support itself, but falls.

Farther evidence on this curious and interesting subject has lately been afforded by Dr. Mellichamp, who, Dr. Hooker remarked, is now resident in the district where Dr. Macbride made his observations. He has investigated the fluid which is found at the bottom of the tubes, and satisfied himself that it was really secreted. It is described as being mucilaginous, but leaving in the mouth a peculiar astringency. Although he does not attribute any true digestive power to this fluid, he found it had a remarkable

anæsthetic effect upon flies immersed in it.   He states that
a fly when thrown into water is very apt to escape, as the
fluid seems to run from its wings, but it never escapes from
the *Sarracenia* secretion.   Ants seem to fall victims oftener
than flies, as their decomposing bodies, according to Dr.
Mellichamp's observation, form the principal bulk of the
mass found in these pitchers.   One remarkable fact is
mentioned by that gentleman—namely, that he never
found the honey bee or other *melliferæ* about these plants.
So far as I can recollect, my observations on those under
cultivation would lead me to corroborate Dr. Mellichamp.
I never observed our honey-making bee approach the
Sarraceniæ or *Nepenthes* in our conservatories ; nor did I
ever find their dead bodies in the pitchers, though I have
often found the bodies of wasps in great abundance in them,
and have seen these insects enter.   More recent observations
might lead us to suppose that all this beautiful arrangement
and adaptation may be necessary, and wisely designed, for
keeping up certain links in the chain of insect life.   Although
fatal to nearly all of that tribe which approach the lure
held out for them, there are yet some species which are
proof against its siren influences, and oblige these plants,
either directly or indirectly, to support them.   One, a little
glossy moth, which has at present received from the Americans the trivial name of the *Sarracenia* moth, is stated to
live and breed in the pitchers.   It is said to walk with
perfect impunity over their inner surface, which proves
treacherous to many other insects.   It is often found in
pairs within these pitchers soon after they open in the early
part of the season, or about the end of April.   The female
lays her eggs singly near the mouth of the pitchers, and the
young *larva*, from the moment of hatching, spins for itself a
carpet of silk, and very soon closes up the mouth of the
pitcher, by drawing the rims together, and covering them
with a delicate gossamer-like web, which effectually debars
all outside intruders.   It then frets the leaf within, com-
mencing under the hood, and feeding downwards on the
cellular tissue, leaving only the epidermis.   As it proceeds,

the lower part of the pitcher, above the putrescent insect collection, becomes packed with ochreous excrementitious droppings ; and by the time the worm has attained its full size, the portion of the pitcher above these droppings gene-rally collapses. A small woodcut of this insect and its *larva* may be seen in the number of " Nature" for October 8, with the article in question copied from the New York " Tribune."

The second species is a more invariable living accom-paniment to the *Sarraceniæ* mentioned. It is a legless grub, about the size of the base of a goose quill, which riots among the putrid insect remains, and when fed to repletion, bores through the leaf just above the petiole, and burrows in the ground. Here it contracts to the pupa state, and in a few days issues as a large two-winged fly. These two species are stated to be the only insects of any size yet known to invade these death-dealing traps. The only other species which seems at home in the leaf is a small mite.

Along with the *Sarraceniæ*, I have yet to notice, in this part of our subject, another very remarkable plant, which has also morphologised leaves adapted for capturing insects. It is the Californian "side-saddle plant," *Darling-tonia Californica*, named in honour of Dr. Darlington of Pennsylvania, and belonging to the same natural family of plants as the *Sarraceniæ*. In it the leaves all rise from the base, the adult ones varying from a foot to 18 inches long in strong plants. They are tubular, the tube gradually tapering downwards, and singularly twisted on the axis ; arched and vaulted at the summit into a sac, about the size of a hen's egg, on the under side of which is an orifice opening into the hollow tubular cavity of the pitcher. Over this cavity are two long highly-coloured lobes, which Dr. Torrey, in describing this plant, very aptly compares to the lop ears of some varieties of rabbit. This attractive flag, which is no doubt suspended and designed for attracting insects, is smeared with a honied sweet exudation on the inner surface (as may be seen from the specimen on the table), and was first noticed by Professor Asa Gray ; thus a farther lure is provided for effecting the end for which these peculiar pitchers are formed.

Dr. Hooker, in the observations he made on this plant, stated that, "on looking at the flowering plant, he was struck with a remarkable analogy between the arrangement and colouring parts of the leaf and of the flower, the petals of the flower being nearly of the same colour as the flap of the pitcher, and between each pair of petals is a hole formed by a notch on the side of the two opposite petals, leading to the stamens and pistil." This we also observed in the flower of a plant which blossomed in the Glasnevin gardens last May. The hypothesis that the coloured parts of flowers are designed for attracting insects to assist in fertilisation, while feeding themselves on the pollen and nectar, is well exemplified in this instance. The petals remain fixed round the stigma, while in the meantime, during three or four days, the anthers burst within, and are liable to lose their effect unless assisted by insects. " It is here conceivable," Dr. Hooker observes, " that this marvellous plant lures insects to its flowers for one object, and feeds them while it uses them to fertilise itself; but when that is accomplished, some of its benefactors are lured to its pitchers for feeding it." If such be the case, surely no man with ordinary reasoning powers, whatever his belief may be, can deny design of the highest order in this instance.

We have still another group of beautiful and highly interesting plants, whose leaves are marvellously morphologised for capturing insects and holding water—the *Nepenthes*. Some of the pitchers belonging to species in this group are among the most beautiful and curiously formed organs in the whole vegetable kingdom, though considered by botanists less complicated than those of *Sarraceniæ*. Difference of opinion still exists among those who are best informed on the subject, regarding the parts of the leaf thus changed into the pitcher form, which we cannot further allude to here. We shall only remark respecting them, that although great variety of form may be observed in the pitchers of the different species, it is always the same parts of the leaf

that are changed.   These pitchers are tubular, with a lid at
their apex, which more or less covers the mouth of most
kinds ; but in some, the mouth is quite open, and the lid, in
place of bending over the mouth, bends backward.   The
pitcher is furnished with a thickened corrugated rim, which,
Dr. Hooker observes, serves three purposes : it strengthens

Nepenthes distillatoria.

the mouth and keeps it distended ; it secretes honey for
attracting insects into the funnel-shaped tube in which it
terminates ; and is, in some kinds, beset with a row of
incurved hooks, that are occasionally strong enough to prevent even a small bird from escaping, if it has the temerity
to enter these large pitchers in search of water or insects.
The under side of the lid and rim of the pitchers is provided with honey-secreting glands in great abundance.
These parts are more highly coloured than the other parts
of the pitchers, which it is reasonable to suppose is a design
for attracting insects to them.   The interior of the pitchers,
though not beset with stiff retrorse bristles like the interior
of the tubes of *Sarracenia*, nevertheless proves as fatal a trap
to the unwary insect which is lured into them as that
of the latter.   The interior of the pitcher affords no foothold for insects, which drop to the bottom and are drowned

in the fluid, or become stupefied, so as to be unable to escape. One of the curious phases of these pitchers is, that fluid is secreted in them before the lid opens, and when it is as closely sealed over as it is possible to be. In this state the pitchers can be turned upside-down, without a drop of the fluid escaping.* To test the digestive powers of *Nepenthes*, Mr. Darwin and Dr. Hooker put white of egg, raw meat, fibrine, and cartilage in the pitchers, which, they state, had a surprising and evident action on them. After twenty-four hours' immersion, the edges of the cubes of white of egg are eaten away, and the surface gelatinised. Fragments of meat are rapidly reduced, and pieces of fibrine weighing several grains dissolve and disappear in two or three days. I have often been amazed at the large quantities of dead bodies of insects, in a half-decomposed state, some of those pitchers occasionally contain. In one instance I emptied a pitcher, and counted in it the remains of ninety-one ants, sixteen wasps, four large blue flies, one cockroach, five earwigs, and seven wood-lice, besides a putrid mass of the dead bodies of these creatures which could not be distinctly recognised.

The *Nepenthes* are all natives of the warmer parts of the Old World, and chiefly inhabit the islands in the Indian archipelago, though some extend to New Holland. One of the New Holland pitcher-leaved plants, *Cephalotus folli-cularis*, affords another instance of those singularly-formed organs for holding water. It is smaller than any of the *Nepenthes* ; but for beauty of form and elegance of construction, it is not surpassed by any of the other pitcher-leaved plants. Its pitchers are hollow, and have their covering-lids exactly similar to some of those of the *Nepenthes*, though

---

* Dr. Voelcker's experiments prove that the water is a true secretion of the plant, and not obtained from without. When he dipped litmus paper in the water taken from an unopened pitcher, the paper turned red, thus proving the presence of an acid or an acid salt. When heated, it gave out a slight smell of boiled apples, and on being analysed, it was found to contain small quantities of malic and citric acids.—Voelcker "On the Chemical Composition of the Fluid of the Acidia of *Nepenthes*," *Trans. of Bot. Soc. of Edinburgh*, Vol. III., p. 233.

they are not otherwise botanically related to them. This
plant is only found in one quarter of the globe, near King
George's Sound, Western Australia. I might add many
more examples which evidently show design in the form
of their leaves; but having already dwelt on this topic at
too great a length, I shall now speak of the flower itself.

IV.—DESIGN AND ADAPTATION IN THE MORPHOLOGY
OF THE FLOWERS.

The flower, in all its beauty and captivating loveliness, consists only of leaves, changed or morphologised so as to effect
most important purposes in the economy of the plant—
namely, the production of seed and the continuation of its
kind on the face of the earth. In stating a fact which is now
an axiom in vegetable physiology, I do not mean that the
parts which form the flower were ever real leaves and became
changed, but they are the true analogues of leaves, and
frequently change back to leaf-like organs. "This doctrine,
which was dimly apprehended by the great Linnæus,
was initiated by a German botanist, Caspar Frederic Wolf;
and again independently, in successive generations, by the
poet Göethe and by the elder De Candolle; but it was not,
until lately, well understood. The botanists of Göethe's day
could not see any sense or practical application to be made
of the proposition that the parts of a blossom answer to
leaves; and so the study of homologies had long to wait."
—*Garden.* Even now it is somewhat repulsive to our
senses to be told, when we eat an apple, pear, or orange, that
we are eating altered leaves; yet such is true. Every step we
take in considering this matter shows infinite wisdom and
design. After the proper organs of nutrition of the plant
have been perfected, it puts on a different aspect, and begins
to prepare for reproduction. The large leaves become
smaller, and somewhat altered in appearance; the part on
which the flowers are produced, shows itself, and elongates;
the individual flower-buds follow; these, in the greater
number of plants, are placed in the axil of a bract or small

altered leaf, which covers and protects them when young. As they advance and begin to swell out, a further protecting covering is observable in the outer whorl of changed leaves—

the calyx, which in turn protects the more tender parts while they are immature; next, the second whorl of protecting covering—the corolla, which is generally considered by those unacquainted with botanical science to be the flower *par excellence;* but it is only a portion of it, and has

a Calyx.   c Stamens.
b Corolla.   d Pistils.

its duties to fulfil in the economy of reproduction. We have already noticed that the highly-coloured parts of leaves of plants, and also the blossoms, are supposed to be principally designed for attracting insects to them. Now these creatures are very sensitive to perfumes, which in most instances lead them to their prey; and it is from the corolla and nectariferous glands, situated on it, or near it, that the

perfumes of flowers are chiefly emitted. We here see that the corolla has two offices assigned to it—the protecting of the more essential organs of reproduction, the stamens and pistils, while they are in a young state, and the displaying gay colours for attracting insects; as well, no doubt, as to please and gratify mankind, and to adorn and beautify the external world—thus leading us to look with thankfulness and adoration to

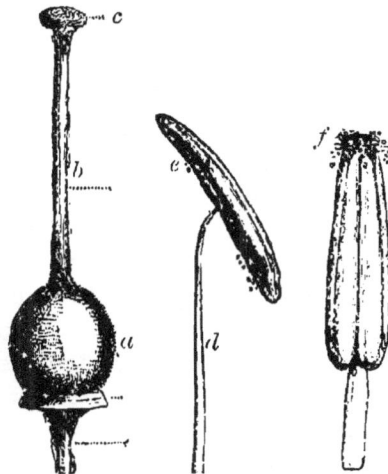

Pistil.
a Ovarium.
b Style.
c Stigma.

Stamens.
d Filament.
e Anther.
f Pollen.

the great God of the Universe through His manifold
works. These two important coverings, calyx and corolla,
are not, however, essential to all plants for reproduction,
as there are a considerable number which bear seeds
abundantly with the aid of only one of them, the calyx—
some without this aid altogether. The parts which are
truly essential are the two inner rows of altered leaves, the
stamens and pistils ; and the manner which they operate
for the production of seeds is often very wonderful, and
surely beyond the realm of chance.

V.—DESIGN AND ADAPTATION IN THE FERTILISATION OF PLANTS.

At the late meeting of the British Association in Belfast,
I doubt not that many of you will remember the interesting lecture given by Sir John Lubbock on " Common wild
flowers considered in relation to insects," when he showed
the many beautiful and mechanical contrivances which they
possess for their fertilisation.   This curious subject has been
well attended to by our painstaking and thoughtful friends
the Germans.   In a book published last year at Leipzig, by
Dr. Herman Muller, under the title of " Die Refruchtung
der Blumen durch Insecten," it is well and cleverly handled.
Numerous and excellent woodcuts of the parts of the flowers
noticed are given, and their construction explained ; also
the parts of insects are figured, which together show the
immense field of observation the author has travelled over.
We shall only be able to make a few brief observations on
this extensive subject, in order to show design in the formation of the stamens and pistils for fertilisation.   This matter,
like that which we have been discussing on insect-catching
plants, was known and written on with considerable ability
at the end of the last century ; but in a similar manner was
allowed to remain in oblivion, until disentombed by Mr.
Darwin.   Sprengel, in an early work on the subject, had
observed how necessary it was that insects should visit plants,

in order to transfer the pollen of the stamens of one flower to that of another ; but he did not fully comprehend its great importance. It frequently happens that the pistils in flowers ripen before the stamens, and become incapable of fertilisation when the pollen is ripe ; but insects visiting the plant, and feeding from one flower to another, carry the pollen on their head or shoulders to other flowers, by which means they are fertilised. This we noticed during the present summer in one of the conservatories of Glasnevin, in a very beautiful plant belonging to the family of Gentians—*Lisianthus Russelianus*, which has protandrous stamens. The pollen grew in large masses on the anthers, and was visited by flies and humble bees, which constantly became more or less besmeared with it when feeding, and carried it to the pistils prepared to receive it, after their own stamens had become effete. By the aid of insects, nearly every flower became fertilised, and produced seeds.

With regard to the corolla, the supposition is that one of its uses is to attract insects to the flower. As an exemplification of this, I may mention the singular fact that those plants which flower at night, and remain open only one night, have principally white flowers, which we may conjecture is designed for attracting night moths and other night-feeding insects to them. The splendid night-blooming Cactus, *Cereus grandiflorus*, affords a good example. The flowers of this plant begin to expand about eight o'clock in the evening, and by ten o'clock are fully opened. They are of a creamy white colour, with hundreds of stamens in each flower, and the delicious perfume emitted fills the whole conservatory in which they are cultivated with a spicy kind of odour. By the first dawn of morning, they are partially or nearly closed, and they never open again. If they are fertilised artificially, or perchance by insects, they close up quickly ; but if not fertilised, they remain partially open during a portion of the following morning. This species was, for many years, supposed to be the only night-flowering kind of Cactus ; but amongst the numerous plants introduced into our gardens and conservatories within the last quarter of a century, there has been a fair proportion of the Cactus tribe, including a number of night-flowering kinds, the flowers of which are all white. I do not know a single instance of a purple, red, or yellow Cactus which is night-flowering, though in no other genus of plants are those brilliant colours more conspicuous than in the day-flowering species of it. The perfume in most of the night-flowering kinds is also strong and agreeable. In these instances we have, no doubt, design displayed, both in the colouring of the flowers and perfume emitted from them, for the attraction of insects. Again, we have a number of flowers which smell sweetly and powerfully by

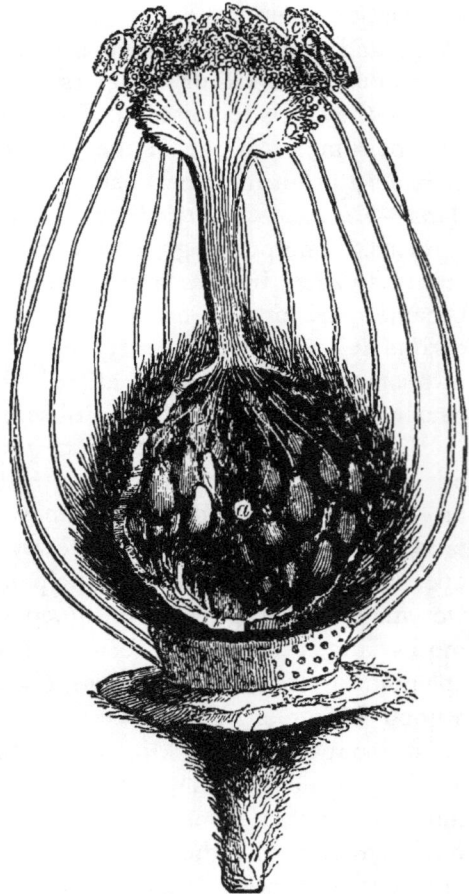

a Ovarium. *b* Pistils. *c* Stamens.

night, but have little or no perfume during the day; and these for the most part have dull, greyish-coloured flowers. This occurs among a considerable number of orchids, but a more familiar example may be found in the old-fashioned "night-smelling Stock," *Cheiranthus tristis*, with which many of us have long been familiar, though it is not now so frequently met with in gardens as it formerly was. I may mention another plant, at one time rather a favourite in our conservatories, which only opens its flowers and emits its perfume at night— namely, the *Nycterinia lychnidea :* its habit is denoted by its generic name. During the day the sepals and petals incurve so as nearly to meet and close up the flower; but at sundown they expand widely, and show the pretty white blossoms, which are very agreeably perfumed.

There are many instances that might be adduced, showing design for fertilisation among plants which have the stamens in one individual and the pistils in another, and which are called by botanists diœcious or diclinous. I shall mention one very remarkable case—viz., *Valisneria spiralis,* a plant which grows in fresh-water rivers, and is not uncommon in many parts of Southern Europe. The flowers in the male or staminiferous plant are extremely minute, white, and of a globular form, and are sessile on a conical-formed rachis, the whole being enclosed, while young, in a spathe or sheath, which latter splits open into two or three pieces when mature, thus allowing the little flowers to detach them- selves from the rachis on which they were seated, and rise by their natural buoyancy to the surface of the water, where the three-parted calyx expands, and permits the pollen to escape from the anthers of the stamens. The female or pistiliferous flowers are quite different from those of the staminiferous. Each of the former is enclosed in a tubular spathe, attached simply to the end of a very long, slender, spirally-twisted stalk, which uncoils more or less according to the depth of the water, so as to allow the flower to float on the surface, where it expands and is fertilised by the float- ing pollen of the numerous male flowers coming in contact with its stigmas.

We have yet to notice design in the structure of flowers, connected with their fertilisation by the aid of insects. The large family of the orchidaceous plants has been made a special study by Mr. Darwin, who considers that none of the flowers in this numerous section is fertilised by its

own stamens, but rather by the pollen of other flowers,
aided by insects.   The arguments and reasons he brings
forward to support his views are certainly ingenious and
original.   No doubt his theory is correct in the main, but
we have seen the flowers of orchids produce seed in our
conservatories during the winter months, when flying
insects were not visible.   The peculiar structure and
forms of the flowers of this remarkable genus, along with
the beautiful colours which adorn them, give them an interest which is not attached to any other family of plants
at the present time.   Many of them are fac-similes of bees,
flies, spiders, moths, locusts, and even small birds.   In many
of them their flowers are so grotesque in form, that it is
no longer with the vegetable kingdom they can be compared, but their resemblance must be sought in the animal
world.   For the most part they do not grow in the earth
like other plants, but attach themselves to the bark of
trees, taking their support from the bodies they adhere to,
yet they are not nourished by them ; hence they are called
epiphytes, not parasites.   In the flowers of all this tribe the
stamens are seated on the pistillum, and their pollen—or
pollinia, as it is called—is different in consistence from that
of nearly all other flowers, being viscid, soft, and col-
lected together in little masses attached to short stalks or
caudicles.   These pollinia are enclosed in a slender envelope
or cap, which ruptures transversely on being touched, thus
exposing the viscid masses.   When the enveloping cap,
which often resembles the head of an insect or bird, is removed, the pollinia are often irritable and spring forward,
attaching themselves by their viscid surface to the body
which causes the irritation to take place.   The nectar-gland
is within the flower, and cannot be reached by an insect
until it pushes its head inward, and thrusts forth its proboscis
towards the gland.   By this action, the head of the creature
and its proboscis come in contact with the pollen masses,
which adhere to them, owing to their viscid nature, and
are carried to the next flower the insect visits ; being thus
brought in contact with its pistillum, the latter is fertilised

by the pollen of a different flower.   I have frequently seen
bees flying about from flower to flower with a number
of those pollen bodies attached to their head, shoulders,
and proboscis.   In none of the kinds is this wonderful
design and contrivance more conspicuous than in the
"lady-slipper" plants, the genus *Cypripedium*, the species of
which have the pollen masses rather differently fixed from
those of most of the other kinds of *Orchidaceæ*.   They are in
two separate sets, so that in the Linnæan system this genus
was placed in a different order of the class *Gynandria*—
namely, the second order *Diandria ;* the others being in the
first order, *Monandria*.   In some of the species of this genus
the top of the rostellum, which in many of the other kinds
forms an appearance like a little head, is here flattened out and
coloured, so that insects may readily alight on it ; near the
base of it are two apertures, one on each side, in which the
pollen masses are placed in such a manner as to render it
nearly impossible for an insect to enter without carrying
them away on its head or shoulders ; and there is no other
way it can reach the honey, except through one or other of
those two apertures.   The honey-gland in some species is
surrounded with viscid hairs which entangle small insects that
enter, and hold them fast until they perish.   I have counted
from twelve to fifteen of their dead bodies lying among the
hairs of one flower of *C. Schlimii*.   In the irritability of the
stamens, design might be shown in many cases, a few of
which may suffice for our present purpose.   In one genus
of plants—namely, *Stylidium*—the column of fructification
is curiously placed.   The stigma is at the apex of a long
ovary-like body, which is articulate or jointed at its base ;
the two anthers are sessile, close to the stigma, and placed
one on each side of it.   This long ovary body is reflexed,
and hangs almost directly head-downwards ; but the instant it is touched by any insect, or designedly, it throws
a somersault by the aid of the articulation at its base, and
in so doing, hits against the body which caused it to jerk
forward, and thus scatters the pollen and fertilises the stigma.
    Our common barberry affords another instance of this

phenomenon. The stamens in the barberry flowers lie
back in the cavities of the petals of the corolla, away from
the pistillum, so that the pollen would be lost if discharged
while they are in that state ; but their irritable filaments,
on being touched on their inner faces by insects in search
of honey, move forward one after the other in regular succession, and discharge their pollen on the pistillum, or on
any insect that may be near at the time, thus giving the
flowers a double chance of being fertilised naturally and
by the aid of insects. The stamens in the North American
Kalmias act similarly, and are highly irritable. I might
farther show design in the formation of flowers, as well as
in the behaviour of plants after fertilisation had been effected
and the seeds ripening ; but having already observed
on all the parts of the plant *seriatim*, I shall only remark, in conclusion, how unerringly the pollen tubes penetrate the stigma, and, overcoming all obstacles, direct their
course to the small opening in the ovule, through which
alone they can enter to effect the fertilisation of the embryo
cells. In this one might be led to suppose it nearly an act
of consciousness. We thus see in the important phenomena of reproduction, not only unmistakable instances of
design manifested, but indications of vitality, especially
when the reproduction of some of the lower tribes of cellular
plants is taken into consideration. In all nature, the simplicity of her works is not less remarkable than their
perfection, and their acting harmoniously to accomplish
whatever end they are destined for in the boundless conceptions of the Creator. We shall therefore conclude by
again quoting from the sweet Psalmist of Israel, " O Lord,
how manifold are Thy works ! in wisdom hast Thou made
them all : the earth is full of Thy riches."

An Examination of Herbert Spencer's Biological Hypothesis.

REV. PROFESSOR WATTS.

SPENCER'S BIOLOGICAL HYPOTHESIS.

A S stated by himself, Mr. Spencer's aim in his elaborate treatise on biology, "is to set forth the general truths of biology, as illustrative of, and as interpreted by, the laws of evolution : the special truths being introduced only so far as is needful for elucidation of the general truths." For aid in the execution of this task, Mr. Spencer acknowledges his indebtedness to Professor Huxley and Dr. Hooker, who not only supplied him with information where his own was deficient, but also looked through the proof-sheets, pointing out errors of detail into which he had fallen ; or, as he expresses it in the preface to his second volume, furnished him with valuable criticisms, and took the trouble of checking the numerous statements of fact on which the arguments proceed. .

The candour of Mr. Spencer in this acknowledgment of his dependence upon others for information, and of his indebtedness for correction and criticism, is only equalled by his polemic chivalry in his review of Professor Owen's theory of the vertebrate skeleton. He prefaces his strictures by the following confession :—" We confess that nearly all we know of this department of biology" (the bony structure of the vertebrata), " has been learnt from his lectures and writings. We pretend to no independent investigations, but merely to such knowledge of the phenomena as he has furnished us with. Our position, then, is such that, had Professor Owen simply enunciated his generalisations, we should have accepted them on his authority. But he has brought forward evidence to prove them. By so doing, he has tacitly appealed to the judgment of his readers and hearers —has practically said, ' Here are the facts ; do they not warrant these conclusions ?' And all we propose to do, is to consider whether the conclusions are warranted by the facts brought forward."

The position here assumed is not only just, but generous. It is just, in that the reviewer judges of Professor Owen's conclusions from the facts adduced in their support; it is generous, in that he holds himself in readiness to accept Professor Owen's generalisations on his own authority, without any proof whatever. It is, of course, to be presumed that this profession of generosity is to be accepted with all the abatements demanded by the interests of science. Science cannot afford to be generous, and it is peculiarly unscientific, as it is unphilosophical and unwise, to accept generalisations on the mere authority of any man.

The chief object of these references to Mr. Spencer's relation to the facts with which he deals in his work on biology, is to vindicate the class to which he belongs from the charge of presumption, in undertaking to judge of the warrantableness of the conclusions which scientists have deduced from the phenomena of nature. Mr. Spencer confesses that he is not a scientist in the ordinary acceptation of the term. He is not a chemist ; he is not an astronomer ; he is not a physiologist ; he is not a molecular or atomic physicist ; he does not profess to be a geologist or a botanist ; but he, nevertheless, claims the right of judging of the conclusions arrived at by the foremost of the practical investigators in these departments of the wondrous phenomena of nature. If a man come forth out of any of these departments with his conclusions, and refer, in proof of their validity, to facts, Mr. Spencer will meet him with all the courtesy and grace of a knight-errant ; but he will give him to understand that he must face him in a logical tournament before he has earned his scientific spurs. He will trust him as a witness of what he has seen with the telescope or miscroscope, or of what has been revealed to him under the torture of the crucible, or the stroke of the hammer, or the all but atom-disclosing radiance of the electric beam ; but as soon as he passes from testimony to inference, he will apply to his conclusions tests furnished, not by the laws of matter, but by the laws of mind, to which, by the very fact of his attempt at inference, he has appealed.

What Mr. Spencer has done in his review of Professor Owen, theologians claim the right to do in his own case. "All they propose to do is to consider whether his conclusions are warranted by the facts brought forward "— facts, be it observed, which he, like themselves, has merely at second-hand. In estimating his work on biology, they raise no other questions than he himself has raised in his treatment of the works of others. They simply ask what are his conclusions, and what are the facts to which he appeals in support of them?

In general terms, his conclusions may be characterised by the one word evolution. The term biology means simply the science of life, and Mr. Spencer's hypothesis, on which he has built up this system of biology developed in these two volumes, is evolutionary. The term evolutionary is here employed advisedly, because of the equivocalness of the term evolution. As evolution simply signifies the process of evoking, or rolling out, something already existing, at least in its elements (which is more than Mr. Spencer admits), it has been employed by parties differing widely both in regard to the agencies and instruments by which the process of evolvement or evocation, has been effected, or conducted. A man who holds that the present order of things—embracing the orderly arrangements of the universe, and the fauna and flora of our earth—has been evoked or evolved from previously created, or previously existing, suitable material, by the skill and power of an infinitely wise and an infinitely powerful Architect, may, nevertheless, be called an evolutionist. Or a man may entertain the crude notions of a Democritus or a Lucretius, recently eulogised before the British Association, and regard the existing order as evolved from atoms equipped with hooks and claws, and be none the less entitled to rank as an evolutionist; or he may differ from Lucretius as much as a modern worker in the domain of molecular physics differs from a man absolutely destitute of the rudest appliance of

the laboratory, and yet belong to this wide-reaching
category.   Democritus and Lucretius, Dr. Erasmus Darwin
and Lamarck, Mr. Charles Darwin and Professor Huxley,
Dr. Tyndall and Mr. Herbert Spencer, theist and atheist,
believers in a personal God, and those who, stripping God
of the attribute of personality, would identify Him with
nature, and deny that He possesses any independent ante-
mundane or extramundane life—may all, so far as the signi-
fication of the term is concerned, be designated evolutionists.
In a word, the term is equivocal, and therefore misleading,
until it is defined.   It may be used to designate a general
class, but only where the design is to express the very
general notion, that those embraced under the class agree
in holding that the present order of things is the outcome,
whether by natural or supernatural agency, of previously
existing states of matter.   As soon as it is proposed to treat
of an evolutionary hypothesis, it is demanded alike by per-
spicuity and honesty, that it be differentiated from others
bearing the same general class-name.

Mr. Spencer's hypothesis differs from all the evolutionary
hypotheses which, as far as I am aware, have hitherto been
broached.   He is not, it is scarcely necessary to say, a
Lucretian, and he is not a Darwinian of the type of Dr.
Erasmus Darwin, or Lamarck, or even of Mr. Charles
Darwin.   He rejects every theory which might militate in
any way against the assumption that mind has nothing to
do, either directly or indirectly, with the evolutionary
process ; and therefore he will not admit that there exists
in organisms even a primordial impulse impelling them to
unfold into more heterogeneous forms.   Had he been in the
vicinity of Professor Tyndall on the occasion of his recent
Manchester recantation, when he admitted that "everywhere throughout our planet we notice this tendency of the
ultimate particles of matter to run into symmetric forms,"
and affirmed that "the very molecules seem instinct with a
desire for union and growth," he would have warned him
that he was treading on the margin of very dangerous con-
cessions, and would have informed him that, not "tendency

to unfold," but "liability to be unfolded,"* is the present position of the advanced thinkers of the evolutionary school. Nor is he satisfied even with this safeguard against the intrusion of mind. He is careful to add, as a qualifying clause, that even this "liability to be unfolded" arises from the actions and reactions of organisms and their fluctuating environments." His hypothesis may be termed the mechanical-genesis hypothesis. Adaptation becomes, in his hands, "direct equilibration;" and Mr. Darwin's "natural selection" is translated into "indirect equilibration." But whilst he criticises, or rejects, or modifies, all previous scientific hypotheses, the chief design of his work is to overthrow the Scripture doctrine of special creations. Singling out this doctrine, which he entitles a hypothesis, he says—"Either the multitudinous kinds of organisms that now exist, and the still more multitudinous kinds that have existed during past geologic eras, have been from time to time separately made ; or they have arisen by insensible steps, through actions such as we see habitually going on. Both hypotheses," he adds, "imply a cause. The last, certainly as much as the first, recognises this cause as inscrutable. The point at issue," he alleges, "is how this inscrutable cause has worked in the production of living forms. This point, if it is to be decided at all, is to be decided only by the examination of evidence. Let us inquire which of these antagonistic hypotheses is most congruous with established facts."†

It will be seen from this statement that Mr. Spencer admits a cause, but holds this cause to be inscrutable. In this he claims agreement with what he is pleased to designate the creation hypothesis, which he rejects. Now this is not a fair account of the views of his opponents in regard to the ultimate cause. Creationists do not regard the ultimate cause as inscrutable. They do hold that the ultimate cause cannot be known to perfection ; but this is a very different thing from holding that they know nothing whatever about that cause.

* " Principles of Biology," Vol. 1., pp. 430-1.   † *Ibid*, Vol. 1., pp. 331-2.

The point here raised is in fact the chief point at issue.
Mr. Spencer alleges that the ultimate cause is inscrutable;
and here the issue is joined. We do not admit the right of
any man to refer phenomena to a cause which is inscrutable;
for the very obvious reason, that before the reference is
thought of, he must observe something in the phenomena
warranting and suggesting the reference. No such reference
is ever made by any intelligent being, except on the observance of qualities or actions in the phenomena which can,
in his estimation, be accounted for only on the assumption
that a cause possessing certain attributes has produced
them. This is, of course, all one with saying that before
he makes the reference he has some conception of the cause
to which he makes it. Mr. Spencer regards the unthink-
ableness of the creation hypothesis a sufficient reason for
rejecting it. This hypothesis, he remarks, "implies the
establishment of a relation in thought between nothing
and something—a relation of which one term is absent
—an impossible relation."* Now if it be impossible to establish a relation in thought between nothing and something, or to establish a relation where one term of the
relation is wanting, how are we to establish a relation
between the phenomena of the universe and an alleged
inscrutable cause? An inscrutable cause is an unknown
cause, and with an unknown thing no relation can be
imagined. The term of the relation represented by the
unknown cause, is a term which cannot be present to
thought, and must, therefore, be regarded as not furnishing
the additional element of the relation, which, according to
Mr. Spencer, is indispensable "to the framing of coherent
thought." Judged, therefore, by his own crucial test of all
truth, and his own postulated condition of all thinking, this
position is indefensible. It is not only unphilosophical to
ascribe phenomena to an inscrutable cause, but the ascription is absolutely unthinkable. Let any man make the
experiment, and he will soon be convinced that the thing
adventured is impossible even in imagination. Of an inscrut-

* "Principles of Biology," Vol. I., p. 336.

able thing, nothing can be affirmed save that it is inscrutable, and to it nothing implying knowledge of it can be ascribed or referred ; and of all the imaginable predicates, the predicate proposed by the evolutionists is at the farthest remove from admissibility. The predicate embraces the entire phenomena of the entire universe, including the evolutionist himself; whilst the something of which all these are predicated is, in his own view of it (if view of the inscrutable be possible), absolutely unknowable and unknown!

It is well that the laws of thought will not permit even the ablest philosopher to conduct with impunity a process of thinking involving an absolute absurdity. Of the truth of this maxim, Mr. Spencer's writings furnish abundant illustrations ; and of these, one of the most notable is his account of the manifestation of this same inscrutable cause. In his " First Principles,"* he informs us that "matter and motion, as we know them, are differently conditioned manifestations of force ;" and, in the very same breath, he affirms that this same force, of which matter and motion are the manifestations, "must for ever remain unknown"! It would seem impossible to write down two sentences more palpably at variance than these. First, we are told that force manifests itself under the conditions furnished by matter and motion ; and then we are told that these "differently conditioned manifestations" of it give us no information whatever of what force is! That is, force manifests itself, and yet does not make itself manifest! When a man can believe that a thing can be, and at the same time not be, he may be able to believe that a thing can manifest itself, and yet impart no information respecting itself.

On the relation of matter to force, Mr. Spencer is exceedingly unphilosophical. He regards matter as simply a condition of the manifestation of force. This is exactly the reverse of the actual relation, and involves the subordination of a substance to its own qualities. Matter sustains

* " First Principles," p. 169.

to force no such relationship. Of the force referred to, matter is the source; and were there no matter in existence, there would not only be no manifestation of this force, but there would be no such force to be manifested. The force in question is not an entity existing outside and independent of matter, availing itself of matter as a medium of manifestation; it is itself the offspring of the qualities of matter, and through it matter reveals itself. The fact is, Mr. Spencer's notion of the relation in question would reduce matter to the rank of an occasional cause, and, stripping it of all claim to causal efficiency, would make the elements of which it consists a source of perpetual delusion. It is not only the common conviction of mankind, but it is the conviction of those who have investigated most thoroughly the domain of molecular physics, that matter is the possessor, and not the mere revealer of force.

It is unnecessary formally to establish this position. The physical sciences are founded upon it. The astronomer, and the molecular physicist, alike proceed upon the assumption that the forces with which they are dealing, are not extra-material entities, but qualities or attributes inherent in matter itself. This fact is fatal to the claims put forth in behalf of Mr. Spencer's "ultimate of ultimates," as it reduces it to the category of a mere quality of matter. A mere quality can never take the rank of an ultimate cause. An ultimate cause, and especially the ultimate of ultimates, must exist prior to, and independent of, all things except itself, and must account for their existence. This a mere quality cannot do. As it implies, from its very nature, the existence of a substance in which it inheres, and without which it can have no being, it is manifest that it cannot be regarded as antecedent to that substance, or independent of it. As all this is true of force in its relations to matter, it follows, of necessity, that force cannot be regarded as the ultimate cause from which this stupendous universe, with its fauna and flora, has come forth.

But even though it were conceded that there is outside and independent of matter, a distinct entity called force,

it is difficult to see how this concession would aid the
cause of the Spencerian evolutionist; for either this
entity is possessed of intelligence, or it is not. If it be
intelligent, and display that intelligence in the determination of ends to be wrought out, and the adaptation
of means for working out the ends determined, it must be
possessed of all the essential attributes of personality—
must be capable of purpose and contrivance—must, in fact,
possess reason and will, as well as power. In a word, it
must be the very entity for whose existence theologians
contend—it must be God. If, however, it do not possess
intelligence and will, it is, *ipso facto*, disqualified for the
exercise of the imperial prerogatives assigned to it by the
evolutionists. Stripped of all ambiguity, what is this entity?
As described by men of science, its functions are expressed
by the two terms, attraction and repulsion, or, to use the
popular language of Dr. Tyndall, by the terms "push" and
"pull." Will any man, who has any regard for his reputa-
tion, venture to say that all the phenomena of the universe
are the offspring of "push" and "pull"? Does anyone
imagine that any amount of pushing and pulling would
ever originate matter? Does any evolutionist believe that,
by pushing and pulling, matter absolutely neutral, if there
could be such a substance, could be invested with diverse
attributes; or that one kind of matter could be differentiated
into the distinct elements which actually exist? Or, to go
farther back, can any intelligent being believe that, prior to
the existence of any substance, whether material or spiritual,
there could be any such actions as are expressed by "push"
and "pull"? He who speaks of "push" and "pull" as
ultimate, simply uses language without import. The idea
attempted defies thought. Let Mr. Spencer test it by his
own crucial test of all truth—let him try a mental presentation of "push" and "pull" where there is nothing to push
or pull, and nothing to be pushed or pulled, and he will
find that the elements necessary to coherent thought are
wanting.

Common sense repudiates the Spencerian ultimate as

absolutely unthinkable. If, as all admit, out of nothing nothing comes, there can be no "push" or "pull" apart from an antecedent pusher or puller. Nor is this all; for this same principle of causality demands the existence of *suitable materials* to be pushed and pulled. To take an example from magnetic pushing and pulling; "push" and "pull," intelligently regulated, will account for the systematic grouping of iron filings around the poles of a magnet; but if one substitute for the magnet, a piece of lead, or for the iron filings, a number of marbles, he will find that there will be neither pushing nor pulling, and that the systematic grouping which elicited his admiration in the former case is altogether wanting in the latter. And as it is with proximate, so it is with more remote effects. The "push" and "pull" incident to gravitation will account for the movement of our earth around the sun, and for the modifications of its orbit, which extend over cycles embracing, perhaps, more than a million of years; but let there be a globe of iron, or even of carbon, or of any other single element of matter, hung in the place of our wondrously constituted orb, and "push" and "pull" may put forth upon it all their might through all the æons of the coming eternity, without originating a single form of animal or vegetable life, much less an organism possessing conscious intellect and will.

In a word, the evolution hypothesis advocated by Mr. Spencer breaks down at the very outset. It is only by veiling itself in a haze of so-called first principles, which seem plausible in the abstract, that it can for a moment impose upon any intelligent being. Its ultimate cause, which it dignifies with the superb title of "the ultimate of ultimates," on which it hangs the mighty burden of the entire universe, is absolutely unthinkable, except as a quality or attribute of those substances for whose existence and phenomena it undertakes to account. In other words, the only conditions under which force is thinkable as having existence at all, are such as to render it simply preposterous to assign to it the position of the ultimate cause.   If there can be no force apart from a substance, material or immaterial ; and if the qualities or attributes of a substance cannot be the cause of the substance in which they inhere, it must follow that force, which is itself but a quality, cannot be the ultimate cause of all substances and of all phenomena.   However limited our knowledge of the ultimate cause may be, we know of a certainty that it cannot be the mere quality of something else.   That which is subordinate and dependent cannot be ultimate.

Wrong in his conception of the ultimate cause, Mr. Spencer is also in error as to the ultimate question at issue respecting its operation.   The question is not, as stated by him, " how has it worked ?" but the far easier one, " has it worked with design ?"   These are very different questions, presenting widely different problems.   It is one thing to enquire *how* the operations of nature are carried on, and another to enquire whether they are so carried on as to indicate a design.   So diverse are these enquiries, that the one may be successfully prosecuted where the other transcends finite capacity.   A passage which I take the liberty of quoting from a sermon by Professor Huxley, on " The Origin of Species," will enable us to judge of the warrantableness of the distinction referred to, and of the comparative feasibility of the two lines of investigation.   " The student of nature," says this eminent physiologist, " wonders the more, and is astonished the less, the more conversant he becomes with her operations ; but of all the perennial miracles she offers to his inspection, perhaps the most worthy of admiration is the development of a plant or of an animal from its embryo. Examine the recently-laid egg of some common animal, such as a salamander or a newt.   It is a minute spheroid, in which the best microscope will reveal nothing but a structureless sac, enclosing a glairy fluid, holding granules in suspension.   But strange possibilities lie dormant in that semi-fluid globule.   Let a moderate supply of warmth reach its watery cradle, and the plastic matter undergoes changes so rapid, and yet so steady and purpose-like in their succession, that one can only compare them to those operated by a skilled modeller upon a formless lump of clay. As with an invisible trowel, the mass is divided and sub-divided into smaller and smaller portions, until it is reduced to an aggregation of granules not too large to build withal the finest fabrics of the nascent organism. And then, it is as if a delicate finger traced out the line to be occupied by the spinal column, and moulded the contour of the body ; pinching up the head at the one end and the tail at the other, and fashioning flank and limb into due salamandrine proportions in so artistic a way, that, after watching the process hour by hour, one is almost involuntarily possessed by the notion that some more subtle aid to vision than an achromatic would show the hidden artist, with his plan before him, striving with skilful manipulation to perfect his work." *

Now if we are to trust the testimony of Professor Huxley, who has watched with an achromatic the very process about which the enquiry is raised, our verdict must be given against Mr. Spencer's statement of the question at issue in this controversy. According to Professor Huxley, the question raised by Mr. Spencer cannot be answered. The *how* of the operation by which that semi-fluid globule is transformed into the resultant organism, is the very point on which physiological research has thus far shed no light.

But whilst science cannot answer Mr. Spencer's question, it can answer the one raised by creationists. While it cannot detect the artist in the act of moulding the plastic material into the nascent organism, it declares that the changes which take place are " so steady and purpose-like in their succession," that " one is involuntarily possessed by the notion" that if he had keener vision he would see the artist at work. In a word, the facts of embryology, as testified to by Professor Huxley, on whose testimony Mr. Spencer acknowledges he has to depend, reveal a process of modelling in harmony with a plan. The *how* of the process is not revealed—the trowel, and the hand that wields it so

* " Lay Sermons," &c., pp. 260, 261.

dexterously, elude all scrutiny—but voluntarily, or involuntarily, the observer becomes possessed of the notion or the conviction that the mystic process is carried forward under the guidance of a designing mind.

Whether, then, we enquire into Mr. Spencer's doctrine of the unknowableness of the ultimate cause, or into his position in regard to the question respecting its operation, we find his views to be indefensible. In the one case he is at war with philosophy, and in the other, with the inevitable convictions generated by a careful observation of the chief phenomena in question. Science proves that, behind matter and its qualities, there is a cause which works with design.

Reserving for a future lecture the specific arguments by which Mr. Spencer endeavours to sustain his hypothesis, it is proposed, at present, simply to examine his reasons for rejecting the doctrine of special creation.

His first reason is that there is a presumption against it because of its association with primitive beliefs. " The primitive beliefs of the race respecting the structure of the heavens were wrong ; and the notions which replaced them were successively less wrong. The original belief respecting the form of the earth was wrong ; and this wrong belief survived the first civilisations. The earliest ideas that have come down to us concerning the natures of the elements were wrong ; and only in quite recent times has the composition of matter in its various forms been better understood. The interpretations of mechanical facts, of meteorological facts, of physiological facts, were at first wrong. In all these cases men set out with beliefs which, if not absolutely false, contained but small amounts of truth disguised by immense amounts of error. Hence," Mr. Spencer concludes, " the hypothesis that living beings resulted from special creations, being a primitive hypothesis, is probably an untrue hypothesis. If the interpretations of nature given by aboriginal men were erroneous in other directions, they were most likely erroneous in this direction. It would be strange if, while these aboriginal men failed to reach the truth in so many cases where it is comparatively conspicuous, they yet reached it where it is comparatively hidden."

Mr. Spencer tries to strengthen this *argumentum ad invidiam* by classing this primitive belief with the abandoned conceptions of fetichism and polytheism, and the various anthropomorphic conceptions of the unknown cause, which he alleges are " everywhere fading away." If all the other parts of the story put into our minds in childhood have long since been rejected, this remaining part of it, he expects, will ere long be relinquished also.*

On this argument, or rather attempt to create prejudice against the doctrine attacked, it may be remarked—

1. The principle on which this objection to the doctrine of creation is founded, is strangely out of harmony with the position assumed by Mr. Spencer, in his " First Principles," in regard to ancient and widely-prevalent beliefs. In his " Principles of Biology," he assumes that the probability is against the truth of a primitive hypothesis, whilst in his " First Principles" he takes the ground, that the probabilities are always in favour of " beliefs which have long existed and are widely diffused."† Now, if there be, in the wide range of human beliefs, one of which it can be said that it has existed long, and is widely diffused, it is that belief against which Mr. Spencer here urges the invidious argument of an *a priori* improbability. The belief in question is as old, and as widely spread, as the human race. There is no well-authenticated instance of any section or tribe of our species, which has not possessed the conviction that the universe, together with its living organisms, is the workmanship of an Almighty Creator. If this be an unquestionable fact, does it not follow, on Mr. Spencer's own showing, in his " First Principles," that there exists a very strong probability in favour of the truth of the new belief which he here antagonises on the assumption that the probabilities are against it? If his own principles are to be carried out in estimating this ancient, universal belief, there will be found, as the residuum, the primary, ineffaceable

* " Principles of Biology," Vol. I., pp. 333-6.   † " First Principles," pp. 3, 4.

truth, *that whatever exhibits marks of design must have had an intelligent author.* When all the superstitions and crude notions wherewith the belief in creation has been associated, have been dissipated, this conviction abides. Constituted as the human mind is, it cannot ignore the evidence of the operation of mind presented in the universe, and must reject, as unphilosophical, any system of biology which dispenses with intelligence in the structure of earth's fauna and flora.

2. That it assumes that man's primitive estate was that of a savage. As this assumption is contrary to historical facts, and has nothing to rest upon save a few remains of pre-historic man, which admit of interpretations differing widely from that put upon them by scientists of the school of Mr. Spencer, he need not be surprised if this, his primary assumption, be rejected as a mere begging of the question.

3. That it assumes that all the tribes of the human race, existing throughout the earth at the time the remains in question were deposited, were in the estate indicated by the remains. Granting that the remains prove the savage estate of the individual and of the tribe to which he belonged, does it follow that other tribes, inhabiting other and more congenial regions of the earth, were in the same estate? Men of science have need to be reminded of what the doctrine of Scripture on this point is. Scripture does not teach that the human race retained its moral integrity, or that each of the families into which it was divided retained the knowledge possessed by the common ancestor. On the contrary, it tells a sad story of apostasy, dispersion, and degradation —a degradation retarded by special Divine interposition in the case of some, but allowed to go on in the case of others. If the morally degraded wandered away from the primitive seat of the race, and descended lower and lower in the scale the farther they receded from the parent stock and penetrated into uncongenial environments, might it not be expected that their remains would testify, as the remains in question do, to a low estate of civilisation? But what is there in all this to warrant the sweeping generalisation

B

assumed by Mr. Spencer as a premiss from which to argue ?
Do these instances, exhumed from European caves, warrant
the conclusion, that the tribes resident in the Asiatic fontal
centre, were, at the time indicated, in the same estate of
social degradation ?   Never was there a more unwarrantable inference ; and yet it is assumed by some of the most
eminent scientists of the day as absolutely unchallengeable !

4. In the next place it may be remarked, that the belief
in the doctrine of a special creation can be proved, and has
been proved historically, as well as by internal evidence, to
have been handed down to us, not by savages, but by men
whose writings demonstrate that they have no mental or
moral superiors in the school of Mr. Spencer. On the score
of its credibility, as well as of its harmony with scientific
facts, we can afford to compare the cosmogony of Moses, or
David, or Isaiah, or Paul, or Peter, with the biology of
Herbert Spencer any day, notwithstanding all the advantage he has derived from the writings of Tyndall and
Huxley, or the prelections of Professor Owen.

5. However little store Mr. Spencer may set by primitive
beliefs, if primitive man had not been possessed of some, he
would never have ascribed the phenomena of his environment to any cause whatever. And if we are to speak of the
necessity of some of these beliefs as compared with others,
we would specify one which is subversive of that form of
the evolution hypothesis which he has set forth in his
biology.   The belief referred to is the intuitive, innate conviction, that a phenomenon implies the existence and
operation of a cause.   This primary belief is universal, and
involves the principle that the phenomenon reveals the
attributes of the cause concerned in its production.   It is,
therefore, irreconcilable with the position, which is really
the ultimate one of Mr. Spencer's biology—viz., that the
ultimate cause is inscrutable. Either the principle which
ascribes inscrutability to a cause is universal, or it is not.
If it be universal, it must apply to immediate and proximate
causes as well as to ultimate ; and if so, the immediate
cause, to which we instinctively refer the phenomenon, is to

us, at the time of the reference, inscrutable and therefore
unknown ; in which case the reference is as unintelligent as
it is unwarrantable. If it be alleged that it is not universal,
but true only of the ultimate cause, the question arises, on
what authority·is this limitation of the dark attribute of
inscrutability to the case of the ultimate cause made ? As
already shown, there can be no reason for regarding the
thing pronounced inscrutable a cause at all, which is not
equally valid for denying its inscrutability. This belief is
as old as humanity, and as wide as the human race; and it
is fatal, not only to the specific argument which Mr.
Spencer has tried to draw from the other alleged primitive
beliefs with which the belief in the doctrine of a special
creation is found to be associated, but fatal to the fundamental principle of his whole system, which postulates the
inscrutability of the ultimate cause.

6. Moreover, it were very easy for the advocates of the
doctrine of special creation to retort this *argumentum ad
invidiam*. Evolutionists should be the last to reproach
their opponents with holding opinions " belonging to an
almost extinct family of beliefs." It is not so long ago
since we were told, on the high authority of the president
of the British Association, that the evolution hypothesis
was as old as the Greek philosophy. Now, however, if we
are to credit Mr. Spencer, " it is a conception born in times
of comparative enlightenment." We are quite ready to
compare the enlightenment of the age of Moses with that
of the age of Democritus, or to compare the prophets of
Israel with the sages of Greece. And if we were to pass in
review the various evolution hypotheses from the time of
the Greek evolutionists to Mr. Spencer, we might be able
to show that the one advocated by him belongs to a very
large family of not only almost, but altogether, extinct
hypotheses. Where now is the hypothesis of Thales, who
held that water is the original of all things, and that God
is the intelligence who from water formed all beings ? or
the hypothesis of Anaximander, who substituted an absolutely indeterminate thing called infinity for the elementary

water of Thales? or the hypothesis of Anaximines, who traced all things to air? or that of Anaxagoras, who referred all things to a number of primitive elements called by him homœomeriæ? Where now is the hypothesis of Pythagoras, who deduced all things from a monad, embracing in its constitution both matter and spirit fused together into an absolute unity of substance? or the same hypothesis as more fully developed into hylozoism · by his followers? What scientist would now accept, unmodified, the atomic theory of Democritus, who represented all things as proceeding from eternal atoms possessing the same qualities and specific gravity, and differing only in size; and that their general compounds, such as lead and iron, differ from each other merely in the arrangement of their atoms? It is questionable whether even Professor Tyndall or Mr. Spencer would embark in the business of world-building with a stock of such atoms, however diverse in size, or however unlimited in number. With atoms whose qualities are generated by their own movements, and whose movements are not the offspring of their previously existing qualities, it is more than probable that even our modern atomic chiefs might fail to construct even our inorganic world. And as to their entering upon the task with such material as water, or air, or the primitive elements of Anaximines, or the monad of Pythagoras, of course this were out of the question altogether.

This brief review of some of the evolutionary hypotheses is sufficient to prove that, however it may be with others, evolutionists should be the last to speak of the presumption which exists against an opinion found associated with " an almost extinct family of beliefs." If Mr. Spencer's hypothesis is to be judged upon this principle, it must be condemned; for it is associated with a class of speculations which no scientist, except for the purpose of producing a temporary sensation, would entertain or endorse for a moment.

Equally liable to retort is our author's next reason for rejecting the doctrine of a special creation. He alleges that it is not countenanced by a single fact. "No one," he says, "ever saw a special creation." "No one," he adds, "ever found proof, of an indirect kind, that a special creation had taken place." Quoting a remark of Dr. Hooker's, he continues, "Naturalists who suppose new species to be miraculously originated, habitually suppose the origination to occur in some region remote from human observation. Wherever the order of organic nature is exposed to the view of zoologists and botanists, it expels this conception ; and the conception survives only in connection with imagined places, where the order of organic phenomena is unknown."*

Here is an appeal to facts, and we accept the authority invoked. It is a fact that no one ever saw a new species of organism created ; but it is also a fact that no one ever saw one brought into existence by a process of evolution ; and it is a fact that no one ever found proof, of an indirect kind, that such an evolution of new species had taken place. Wherever the order of organic nature is exposed to the view of zoologists and botanists, as in the case already quoted from Professor Huxley's sermon on the origin of species, it expels the Spencerian conception of evolution without the intervention of intelligence, and supplants it by the irresistible conviction that the process of organisation is under the guidance of a skilful artist ; and the conception for which the authority of facts is claimed by Mr. Spencer survives only in connection with flights of the so-called scientific imagination, by which the vision is prolonged backwards beyond the boundary of experimental evidence. There is not a single fact presented in these two volumes which gives the slightest countenance to the hypothesis which its author advocates; nor is there one which, when fully analysed, does not add strength to the argument in support of a presiding intelligence and a special creation.

After the author had reached the 351st page of his first volume, he felt constrained to make the following confes-

* "Principles of Biology," Vol. I., p. 336.

sion :—"Though the facts at present assignable in *direct* proof that, by progressive modifications, races of organisms that are apparently distinct may result from antecedent races are not sufficient, yet there are numerous facts of the order required." Is this not a distinct and explicit acknowledgment that no one has ever seen the evolution of a new species? If he regards this fact as furnishing an argument against special creation, how can he refuse to admit its force as against his own evolution hypothesis?

But if he has not direct proof sufficient for the establishing of this hypothesis, he has, he informs us, "numerous facts of the order required." What are these facts? Here they are :— "It has been shown beyond all question, that unlikenesses of structure gradually arise among descendants from the same stock. We find that there is going on a modifying process of the kind alleged as the source of specific differences—a process which, though slow in its action, does, in time, produce conspicuous changes—a process which, to all appearance, would produce in millions of years, and under the great varieties of conditions which geological records imply, any amount of change."* And yet he confesses that the palæontology of these records cannot be held to prove evolution, and that only some few of them yield it support! †

Such, then, are the facts ; what is their value in this argument? It will be observed that while Mr. Spencer speaks of the gradual rise of unlikenesses of structure among descendants from the same stock, he has not ventured to say that these have, in any instance, amounted to the origination of a new species, and that he confesses that palæontology does not furnish a single instance. All he says is, that this fact is of the order required! His hypothesis requires structural change, and here is a fact of this class. It is true the change to which it testifies is not great enough for his purpose ; but it "bears as great a ratio to the brief period in which it has been produced," as the whole change required "bears to

* "Principles of Biology," Vol I., p. 351.   † *Ibid*, p. 399.

that vast period during which living forms have existed on the earth." This is very like a confession which Mr. Darwin makes at the close of his remarks on the effects of increased or decreased use of parts. "Although man," he concludes, "may not have been much modified during the latter stages of his existence through the increased or decreased use of parts, the facts now given show that his liability in this respect has not been lost ; and we positively know that the same law holds good with the lower animals." Such is his confession ; what is his conclusion? With an inferential boldness that brooks no barrier, he adds :— "Consequently (!) we may infer, that when, at a remote epoch, the progenitors of man were in a transitional state, and were changing from quadrupeds into bipeds, natural selection would probably have been greatly aided by the inherited effects of the increased or diminished use of the different parts of the body"!* It is truly painful to observe in the writings of these really able men, so persistent an endeavour to establish their favourite hypotheses by facts which they are compelled to admit do not furnish the evidence required. Frustrated by the facts, not only of historic and prehistoric times, but of palæontology also, they overleap the boundary of experimental evidence, and assume transitions and structural changes which they have failed to prove. When the facts adduced, even as estimated by themselves, do not give the slightest indication of a specific change, they comfort themselves with the reflection that changes of the class observed must, if continued long enough, effect the change required! Of course, a change of the right kind, however small in amount, if increased by however small an increment, must, if unchecked, at some future epoch of duration, amount to the *quantum* required ; but only if unchecked. Ay, there's the rub—only on the assumption that the change shall be unchecked! What warrant is there for this assumption? Certainly there is none in the phenomena of the observed changes of the cosmos.

* " Descent of Man," Vol. I., p. 121.

Speaking of the external factors of evolution, Mr. Spencer refers to the fact, that our earth, in its annual motion round the sun, does not move constantly along a rigid, unvarying curve, but along a curve constant in its inconstancy—now approaching a circle, and anon an ellipse. This change is a very slow one, and the cycle which embraces its extremes has the astounding range of one or two millions of years. Now suppose that an astronomer, who was not aware of the demonstrations of La Place, were watching the movements of our globe referred to, and observed that, in a given period, the divergence towards a more eccentric curve amounted to several miles, might he not, if he reasoned with Mr. Spencer and the evolutionists, begin to apprehend an elongation of the major axis of its orbit, and a shortening of the minor, which must eventually evolve extremes of heat and cold absolutely destructive of organic life in our world? As an evolutionist, he might thus reason; but the scientific astronomer would inform him that his fears were groundless, and had their origin in a too narrow induction. He would allay his alarm by assuring him that this variation in the orbit of the earth has its limits, and that when these were reached, the apparently errant orb would swing gradually back to the less hazardous curve.

Now we charge upon the evolutionists the perpetration of a like error, in their argument from the observed structural changes which have been induced, or developed, in vegetable and animal organisms. The organic variation has been shown, again and again, to have bounds set to it which it cannot pass. Even Mr. Darwin, as quoted by Mr. Spencer, remarks that "'sports' are extremely rare under nature, but far from rare under cultivation." And Mr. Spencer himself admits* that competent judges do not doubt that our extremely variable domestic animals have become variable under the changed conditions implied in domestication, and holds that these animals were constant prior to their subjection to man. Is this not a palpable surrender of the very citadel of evolution? It

* "Principles of Biology," Vol. I., p. 262.

is neither more nor less than an acknowledgment that constancy is the rule, whilst variation is the exception ; or, as Mr. Spencer puts it, "the wild race maintains its type with great persistence," whilst "the domestic race *frequently* produces *individuals* more unlike the *average* type than the parents are." *   "The life of a species, like that of an individual," he says, "is maintained by the unequal and ever-varying actions of incident forces on its different parts."†

This is conclusive, but it is conclusive against the evolution hypothesis.   If, as Mr. Spencer has shown, variation is essential to specific life, what becomes of the notion, that by the operation of this same law of variation, new species can be originated ?   Can the causes which are held to be capable of transmuting one species into another, be held capable of rendering such transmutation impossible ? If uniformity, as "inter-breeding" demonstrates, produces specific deterioration, whilst variation, as those skilled in cattle-breeding inform us, promotes the well-being, and tends to the perfection of the species, surely it is most unwarrantable to infer, that variation may eventually result in specific destruction by improving one species into another.   It is no wonder, then, that these two classes of related facts led Mr. Spencer to enunciate the foregoing remarkable law of specific life. The law, as we have seen, is universal, extending to the very orbs of heaven.   The stability of the universe, as well as the stability of the species of earth's fauna and flora, is maintained by variations which are limited and bounded by an unseen power which ever acts in reference to the original type, and maintains its image, substantially, in every individual movement or organism, through the instrumentality of the very forces which evolutionists regard as all-potent to effect its destruction.

The case of a particular family, in which digital variation occurred, adduced in support of the evolution hypothesis,‡ will serve to illustrate this point. The case is

* " Principles of Biology," Vol. I., p. 261.   † *Ibid*, p. 286.
‡ *Ibid*, pp. 258-60.

cited from an essay by Dr. Struthers, and the conclusion
drawn is quoted with approval by Mr. Spencer. After
stating the history of the variation through four generations, Dr. Struthers, referring to a daughter who was born
with six fingers on each hand and six toes on each foot,
says, "In this, the most interesting sub-branch of the
descent, we see digital increase, which appeared in the first
generation on one limb, appearing in the second on two
limbs, the hands ; in the third on three limbs, the hands and
one foot ; in the fourth on all the four limbs. There is as
yet no fifth generation in uninterrupted transmission of the
variety. The variety does not yet occur in any number of
the fifth generation of Esther's descendants" (the female
ancestor to whom the variety is traced back), "which consists as yet only of three boys and one girl, whose parents
were normal, and of two boys and two girls, whose grand-
parents were normal. It is not known whether, in the
case of the great-grandmother, Esther P——, the variety
was original or inherited."

Such is the case ; what conclusion does it warrant? Does
it prove that variation may go on indefinitely? or does
it prove that it is held in check by a specific law restraining
it, like the motions of the planets, within unalterable limits ?
The case proves that the normal type rules; for in the
generations specified, only six instances of variation occur,
whilst there are one hundred and two of the normal type ?
If Mr. Spencer can adduce nothing in favour of his hypothesis better than a woman who has acquired, through the
mystic process of evolution, three digits more than her
great-grandmother, he had better be a little more modest in
his averments about the absence of evidence in support of
the doctrine of a special creation. It would, indeed, seem
as if he felt the weakness and unprofitableness of this argument ; for he immediately tries to buttress it with an *a priori*
borrowed from his " First Principles," to the effect, that
an idea which cannot be presented to the mind in a definite
shape or form, is a false idea, and is to be rejected. In
addition to what has been said on the point here raised,

when speaking of the impossibility of regarding an inscrutable thing as a cause, it may be sufficient to cite a passage from Mr. Spencer's " Principles of Psychology," from which it appears that he does not always regard the unimaginableness of a thing as a sufficient reason for rejecting it. Avowing " the belief that mind and nervous action are the subjective and objective faces of the same thing," he confesses that " we remain utterly incapable of seeing, and even of imagining, how the two are related.   Mind," he adds, " still continues to us a something without any kinship to the other things ; and from the science which discovers by introspection the laws of this something, there is no passage by transitional steps to the sciences which discover the laws of these other things." *

Here, then, is a belief which cannot abide the crucial test of one of Mr. Spencer's first principles, and yet he holds it ! If he can hold this belief despite its inconceivableness, with what show of consistency can he reject, on the ground of its inconceivableness, the belief in the doctrine of a special creation?   To quote his own words, at the close of this argument against the Scripture doctrine, if " belief, properly so-called, implies a mental representation of the thing believed ; and," as he confesses, " no such mental representation is here possible." how can he believe that there is any relation between " those thoughts and feelings which constitute consciousness," and the action of the nervous system?   In a word, then, even though the doctrine objected to were that of the creation of an organism, *ex nihilo*, Mr. Spencer could not consistently reject it on the ground specified.   As the common and Scriptural doctrine, so far as organisms is concerned, is not that of a direct creation *ex nihilo*, but a *mediate* creation out of previously existing matter, Mr. Spencer is constrained to frame his objection so as to meet this aspect of the question.   This hypothesis, he alleges, involves, ultimately, " the creation of force ; and the creation of force is just as inconceivable as the creation of matter."   He asks, " The myriad atoms

* " Principles of Psychology," Vol. I., pp. 140–56.

going to the composition of the new organism, all of them previously dispersed through the neighbouring air and earth, does each, suddenly disengaging itself from its combinations, rush to meet the rest, unite with them into the appropriate chemical compounds, and then fall with certain others into its appointed place in the aggregate of complex tissues and organs ?" This, he says, is " to assume a myriad of supernatural impulses, differing in their directions and amounts, given to as many different atoms," and is, therefore, " a multiplication of mysteries rather than a solution of a mystery. Every one of these impulses, not being the result of a force locally existing in some other form, implies the creation of force ; and the creation of force is just as inconceivable as the creation of matter."

Now, it will be observed that Mr. Spencer has some difficulty in bringing his mental-representation principle into conflict with the doctrine of the creation of organisms out of existing matter. Not only is the doctrine, on his own showing, capable of mental presentation, but he has himself given us a sketch of the process. He has figured the atoms disengaging themselves and entering into new combinations, and taking, as if by magic, their places in the aggregate of complex tissues and organs. He has put before us a process not unlike the process of crystallisation, so beautifully described by Professor Tyndall in his " Fragments of Science," and in his late Manchester lecture on " Crystalline and Molecular Forces," and one which is actually realised in the evolution of the animal from the embryo, as described by Professor Huxley. In the following passage, Dr. Tyndall gives a very graphic sketch of the process by which, materialists allege, the thing pronounced by Mr. Spencer to be inconceivable, may be done.

" And now let us pass from what we are accustomed to regard as a dead mineral to a living grain of corn. When *it* is examined by polarised light, chromatic phenomena similar to those noticed in crystals are observed. And why ? Because the architecture of the grain resembles the architecture of the crystal. In the grain also the molecules are set in definite positions, and in accordance with their arrangement they act upon the light. But what has built together the molecules of the corn? I have already said, regarding crystalline architecture, that you may, if you please, consider the atoms and molecules to be placed in position by a power external to themselves. The same hypothesis is open to you now. But if in the case of crystals you have rejected this notion of an external architect, I think you are bound to reject it now, and to conclude that the molecules of the corn are self-posited by the forces with which they act upon each other. It would be poor philosophy to invoke an external agent in the one case, and to reject it in the other.

"Instead of cutting our grain of corn into slices, and subjecting it to the action of polarised light, let us place it in the earth, and subject it to a certain degree of warmth. In other words, let the molecules, both of the corn and of the surrounding earth, be kept in that state of agitation which we call warmth. Under these circumstances, the grain, and the substances which surround it, interact, and a definite molecular architecture is the result. A bud is formed; this bud reaches the surface, where it is exposed to the sun's rays, which are also to be regarded as a kind of vibratory motion. And as the motion of common heat with which the grain and the substances surrounding it were first endowed, enabled the grain and these substances to exercise their attractions and repulsions, and thus to coalesce in definite forms, so the specific motion of the sun's rays now enables the green bud to feed upon the carbonic acid and the aqueous vapour of the air. The bud appropriates those constituents of both for which it has an elective attraction, and permits the other constituent to resume its place in the air. Thus the architecture is carried on. Forces are active at the root, forces are active in the blade, the matter of the earth and the matter of the atmosphere are drawn towards the root and blade, and the plant augments in size. We have in succession the bud, the stalk, the ear, the full corn in the ear; the cycle of molecular action being completed by the production of grains similar to that with which the process began.

"Now there is nothing in this process which necessarily eludes the conceptive or imagining power of the purely human mind. An intellect the same in kind as our own would, if only sufficiently expanded, be able to follow the whole process from beginning to end. It would see every molecule placed in its position by the specific attractions and repulsions exerted between it and other molecules, the whole process and its consummation being an instance of the play of molecular force. Given the grain and its environment, the purely human intellect might, if sufficiently expanded, trace out *à priori* every step of the process of growth, and by the application of purely mechanical principles demonstrate that the cycle must end, as it is seen to end, in the production of forms like that with which it began. A similar necessity rules here to that which rules the planets in their circuits round the sun.

"You will notice that I am stating my truth strongly, as at the beginning we agreed it should be stated. But I must go still further, and affirm that in the eye of science *the animal body* is just as much the product of molecular force as the stalk and ear of corn, or as the crystal of salt or sugar. Many of the parts of the body are obviously mechanical. Take the human heart, for example, with its system of valves, or take the exquisite mechanism of the eye or hand. Animal heat, moreover, is the same in kind as the heat of a fire, being produced by the same chemical process. Animal motion, too, is as directly derived from the food of the animal, as the motion of Trevethyck's walking-engine from the fuel in its furnace. As regards matter, the animal body creates nothing; as regards force, it creates nothing. 'Which of you by taking thought can add one cubit to his stature?' All that has been said, then, regarding the plant may be re-stated with regard to the animal. Every particle that enters into the composition of a muscle, a nerve, or a bone, has been placed in its position by molecular force. And unless the existence of law in these matters be denied, and the element of caprice introduced, we must conclude that, given the relation of any molecule of the body to its environment, its position in the body might be determined mathematically. Our difficulty is not with the *quality* of the problem, but with its *complexity;* and this difficulty might be met by the simple expansion of the faculties which we now possess. Given this expansion, with the necessary molecular data, and the chick might be deduced as rigorously and as logically from the egg as the existence of Neptune from the disturbances of Uranus, or as conical refraction from the undulatory theory of light."*

So far, therefore, as Mr. Spencer's own crucial test is concerned, Dr. Tyndall has shown that the doctrine of creation out of existing matter can abide the ordeal. It may be said, and is said, that the hypothesis postulates "the necessary molecular data," or, as Mr. Spencer says, organic matter, to begin with; but if vital, and chemical, and mechanical forces be, as the school of Mr. Spencer would have us believe, both quantitative and qualitative equivalents, surely one who is master of the laws of chemical and mechanical forces ought to be able to construct living organisms, without creating a new force. If *vital forces* be the same both in *quality* and quantity with chemical and mechanical forces, there can be no difficulty about producing vegetable or animal embryos.

It was doubtless this fact which led him to fall back, by way of supplement, on the creation *ex nihilo* hypothesis, which he had, in his own opinion, already demolished. The doctrine of a creation out of existing matter, involves, ultimately, the doctrine of "the creation of force ; and the creation of force is just as inconceivable as the creation of matter." This is the fable of the wolf and the lamb over again. If you did not do it, your father or grandfather did, and you must pay the forfeit.

* " Fragments of Science," pp. 116–119.

Here, then, is a plain issue raised by Mr. Spencer, and we accept it. The question at issue is simply this—Does the disintegration and reintegration of matter imply the creation of force? The mere statement of the question is sufficient for any man competent to form an opinion on the subject in dispute. If the process referred to involves the creation of a force not "locally existing in some other form," how is it that processes of disintegration and integration can be carried on by chemists, who have confessedly no power of creating new forces? The disengagement of atoms, and the recombination of them into new compounds, pronounced impossible except on the assumption of the creation of a new force not locally existing in some other form, take place in every instance of chemical analysis and synthesis, without any such adventitious aid. All that is needed in either case is an operator possessing the requisite knowledge of the elements concerned. If the chemist can perform such wonders in his laboratory without the help of a new force, is it incredible that the author of the elements should be able to employ them in the construction of living organisms? There is no escape here possible to an evolutionist of the school of Spencer. If vital force be the correlate of chemical and mechanical, the origination of life cannot, as Mr. Spencer alleges, imply the creation of a force not previously existing. It is, therefore, only on the assumption that vital force is not the correlate of mere material forces, that Mr Spencer's objection can have any meaning. The thing assumed, however, is fatal to his biological hypothesis, which rests, ultimately, on the convertibility of material forces into vital.

Assuming that those who hold the doctrine of special creation regard the demonstration of divine power made in the origination of species as designed solely for the benefit of mankind, Mr. Spencer asks, to whom was the demonstration made? As "the great majority of these supposed special creations took place before mankind existed, to what purpose," he asks, "were the millions of these demonstrations which took place on the earth when there were no intelligent beings to contemplate them? Did the Unknowable thus demonstrate His own power to Himself? Few," he remarks, "will have the hardihood to say that any such demonstration was needful. There is no choice but to regard them either as superfluous exercises of power, which is a derogatory supposition ; or as exercises of power that were necessary because species could not be otherwise produced, which is also a derogatory supposition." *

Now, in the first place, no person properly instructed in the Scriptures would, for a moment, think of representing the entire series of creative acts as having for their *sole* end the demonstration of the power of God to man. Other ends by no means derogatory to the Creator may be assumed, such as delight in the exercise of His wisdom, and power, and bounty, and sovereignty. Mr. Spencer assumes that if His acts had not reference to man alone, they must have been designed to demonstrate His power to Himself, or were necessary because species could not be otherwise produced—both of which suppositions, he alleges, are derogatory. As we have seen, the alternative assumed is not the only one open to the advocates of special creations. Besides the one mentioned above, the student of the Bible can specify many others. It were not a derogatory supposition that God, in those remote creations, was demonstrating His attributes to other orders of intelligences of which the Scriptures speak, and against whose existence science has no facts to urge. Or it might be said in reply, that as the Author of the earth, with its successive orders of vegetable and animal organisms, knew that in the latter days scoffers would arise, who would call in question His existence, and endeavour to prove that all organic forms were evolved from uncreated matter, by an impersonal power resident in matter itself, or conditioned by it, He so ordered the manifestations of life on our globe, as to show that the links of the great biological chain have been separately created, and not consecutively evolved.

* " Principles of Biology," Vol. I., p. 339.

C

And lastly, it may be observed, that if this earth were to furnish a text-book for geologists, it was necessary that it should be printed before it was published or read. If our earth was to instruct men, and serve as a school for their mental and moral discipline, it was essential that, prior to their matriculation, it should be properly furnished. That admirable scholastic arrangements have been made, is attested by the earnest competition and enthusiasm displayed by the ever-increasing band of scientists who crowd its halls; and few who have thoroughly investigated the problems prepared for them, have ever imagined that they were propounded by a blind, unintelligent, unconscious force.

Mr. Spencer regards it as an objection to the doctrine of special creation, that beings endowed with capacities for wide thought and high feeling did not exist on our globe millions of years before man appeared. The answer has been given already, and is obvious. It is simply this—Our globe was not fit at an earlier stage to receive such beings. Special creation does not set aside order and adaptation; and is perfectly consistent with an original incandescent state of our globe watched over by the Creator, who, at the proper stages in its history, introduced such organisms as were suited to its condition, and fitted to prepare it as a dwelling-place for man.

Equally unhappy is the argument against design drawn from the structure of animals of prey, exhibiting, as such structures do, countless pain-inflicting appliances—appliances which have been doing their deadly work all through the geological eras. "How happens it," our author asks, "that animals were so designed as to render this bloodshed necessary?"* For the advocate of design, he alleges, there is but the one alternative—viz., that the Creator was either unable or unwilling to make animals so as to avoid the infliction of such misery. Still greater, he thinks, is the difficulty when we consider that branch of the arrangement in which provision is made for the support of the inferior by the sacrifice of the superior, as in the case of parasites.

* "Principles of Biology," Vol. I., p. 341.

To these objections we reply, that they assume several things which are not conceded.   1. They assume that the design of creation, as held by teleologists, is the production of the greatest possible amount of happiness throughout the entire orders of organic, sentient life.   For this assumption, there is no warrant to be found either in teleology, or in nature.   There is a manifest subordination running throughout the whole chain of sentient existence, from the mollusk to the man.   No inferior order lives for itself or simply for its own enjoyment.   It is a link in a series constituting one great whole, from which no member can be removed without causing universal detriment, and the final link of which lives, not for himself, but for Him to whom he owes his being.   The theology of the whole may be expressed in one sentence: each inferior order not for itself, but for a higher ; all the inferior for man, and man for God.   Such is the testimony of the organic worlds, and such is the doctrine of man's moral nature and of the Word of God.   In this system there is suffering, but it is none the less in harmony with the facts.

2. Mr. Spencer's objections assume that if we cannot point out a beneficent design, there is no proof of design at all.   Such an objection may possibly have force with one under the fascination of an hypothesis which he would fondly sustain against all comers ; but no man, whose mind is not warped by prejudice, can for a moment believe that benevolence is a necessary element in design.   Any arrangement embracing means for the attainment of a definite end carries with it evidence of design, and is so regarded by all men as soon as the arrangement and the end are apprehended.   It matters not whether the end be benevolent or malign, whether the arrangement be ingenious or clumsy, the moment the connexion between the means employed and the end aimed at, is discovered, the mind instinctively infers a design and a designer.   The horn of the sword-fish, the teeth of the lion, the talons of the eagle, are regarded by all men, whether evolutionists or creationists, as instruments of design ; and the philosopher who challenges the

evidence does but proclaim his folly, and reveal his prejudice.

3. It is obvious that Mr. Spencer's objections to the
doctrine of design are drawn, not from the facts under
investigation, but from certain inferences in regard to the
effects of this doctrine upon our views of the character of
the Creator.   He finds organisms not constructed so as to
prevent suffering, and immediately concludes that organisms
have not been designed.   Why ?   Because the designer
must have either been unable or unwilling to design them
so as to prevent suffering.   This alternative he thinks fatal
to the doctrine of design, as it either casts an imputation on
the Divine character or involves a limitation of the Divine
power.*

Now, as we have already seen, our recognition of the
marks of design does not depend upon the character of the
end aimed at in the contrivance, but simply upon the adaptation of the means to the attainment of the end, whatever
the end may be.   Constituted as we are, it is absolutely
impossible to discover such adaptation without immediately
inferring a design and a designer.   This is a first principle,
which the human mind cannot relinquish without doing
violence to its own constitution.   It is, in fact, but another
form of the principle, that every effect must have a cause.
In view of this fact, it is manifest that the only course open
to the impugner of the doctrine of design, is to meet the
teleologist on the question of fact, and to prove that animal
and vegetable organisms bear in their structure no traces
of design.   If he cannot do this (and Mr. Spencer's work
on Biology, by leaving it not only undone but unattempted,
is sufficient proof that he cannot), he must surrender at
discretion.   Instead of facing the facts and divesting them
of those marks of design which the human mind instinctively recognises, our author carefully evades the real
question at issue, and raises an entirely distinct one respecting the effect of the doctrine of design upon our views of
the Divine character.   This procedure is as unmanly as it

* "Principles of Biology." Vol. I., p. 341.

is unphilosophical and unscientific. It is unmanly not to face the facts presented in the structures of the fauna and flora of our world ; and it is unphilosophical and unscientific not to follow out, to their legitimate conclusions, irrespective of imaginary ulterior consequences, the principles revealed by a fair analysis of the phenomena they present. With a philosopher, the question is not, " What effect will a fair interpretation of these facts have upon some other doctrine ?" but simply, " What do the facts, fairly interpreted, teach ?"   To borrow a manly and truly philosophical sentiment, uttered by Professor Huxley in his address before the late meeting of the British Association, " Logical consequences are the scarecrows of fools and the beacons of wise men."*   Theologians are not afraid of the logical consequences of the doctrine of design upon their views of the Divine character ; nor will Mr. Spencer be able to turn them aside from the question at issue, by hanging up, for the thousandth time, the old weather-beaten scarecrow of optimism, fashioned, to suit his own purpose, out of the straw of a false speculative theology.

Of course, if the God of the Bible be the God assumed in Mr. Spencer's critique on His works, and the end aimed at by Him be the end ascribed to Him by His reviewer, it might be difficult to reconcile the actual phenomena of the organic world with the character of such a Being.   If the Creator possess but two attributes—benevolence and power —and if His design in creation be the production of the greatest possible amount of happiness, it might puzzle the ablest of optimists to reconcile those pain-inflicting contrivances which abound in the actual organic arrangement, with the character, and aim, and capacities of this optimistic Deity.   But as the God of the Bible possesses more attributes than the two specified, and sets before Him higher ends than the mere happiness of His creatures—as He is holy and just, as well as almighty and benevolent, and regards the interests of His moral creatures as superior to those of the mere sentient orders of animal organisms, and considers

* " Fortnightly Review," Nov., 1874, p. 577.

their moral culture a higher end than their happiness, yea, has linked their happiness to their moral and spiritual character, and set His own glory before them as their highest end, and the source of their highest enjoyment—as this is the character, and these the aims, of the God of the Bible, Mr. Spencer's objections are as irrelevant as the premises on which they are based are false. As our critic cannot take in the whole issues of the mighty cycle embraced in that plan of which these phenomena strewn on the shores of time are but the initial movements, it is nothing short of arrogance to pronounce, as he has ventured to do, upon the moral character of the Author of the system.

4. Mr. Spencer's objections proceed upon the assumption, that a theory which does not account for every class of phenomena, however remotely connected with the subject under investigation, is, *ipso facto*, discredited. For example, as in the present instance, if the advocate of design cannot solve the problem of the ultimate design of the various orders of animal and vegetable organisms, he is not to be permitted to speak of the immediate and proximate design of these closely correlated kingdoms of nature. If he cannot tell why, or for what ultimate end, God made great whales, and then constructed sword-fish equipped with a weapon for their destruction, he must be told that he has failed to prove that either whales or sword-fish are the offspring of design! If a teleologist cannot tell why God created *acari* to burrow in the skin and torture man, he has failed to prove that either man or his tormentors exhibit marks of intelligent purpose! If he cannot take in the vast range of organic relations (embracing, as multitudinous orders do, organisms which nothing but the most powerful microscope can reveal), and grasp the scheme of creation in its entirety, he is not entitled to speak of any class of relations as evincing contrivance!

In a word, so long as anything remains unexplained, nothing is explained. Will any scientist accept this principle? Will any astronomer venture to affirm that Kepler had explained nothing, when he enunciated the law that "planets revolve in elliptic orbits about the sun, which occupies the common focus of all these orbits," because he had not then discovered the second great law, that "if a line be drawn from the centre of the sun to any planet, this line, as it is carried forward by the planet, will sweep over equal areas in equal portions of time"?   Or, is it to be held that the foregoing laws explain nothing, because Kepler had yet to ponder the relations of the members of the solar system for seventeen years before he discovered the third law, that the squares of the periodic times of the planets are to each other as the cubes of their mean distances from the sun ?   Are all these laws to be repudiated, because their discoverer was not able to tell why the orbits of the planets and satellites should be ellipses rather than any other curve, or to tell, as Newton has done, what power holds these mighty masses "steady in their swift career, producing the most exquisite harmony of motion, and a uniformity of result as steady as the march of time."*   Will Mr. Spencer abandon the evolution hypothesis, because, as confessed by himself, it does not explain the connexion of consciousness with nervous action ?   Will he give up his hypothesis because of its failure to explain this mysterious relationship?   Teleologists are entitled to press this question with all the confidence of an *a fortiori*, for they are asking evolutionists to give up a hypothesis for which there is no positive proof, and which fails, absolutely and confessedly, at the most important point in the evolutionary sequence ; whilst, on the other hand, the doctrine of design is engraven on every organism within the realm of organic nature, and engraven so manifestly, that the ablest advocate of the evolution hypothesis—the philosopher of the school— has nothing to advance against it, save certain consequences which he alleges flow from it—consequences which, as we have already seen, lie only against a speculative, theological optimism, which has no basis in the word of God.

In a word, then, it is only by petty criticisms, based on the assumption that the theology of the Bible is optimistic,

* Mitchell's "Orbs of Heaven," p. 71.

that this prince of evolutionists can make even a show of argument against the doctrine of design in creation. His assumption is false, and his critique pointless and worthless. To use his own language in his estimate of the doctrine he assails, his hypothesis must be pronounced worthless— "worthless by its derivation," from Democritus and Lucretius; "worthless in its intrinsic incoherence," as demanding continuity, and yet admitting the existence of impassable gulfs between the most important elements in the series; "worthless as absolutely without evidence," no evolutionist having as yet been able to point to the evolution of a single new fertile species from any other; "worthless as not supplying an intellectual need," failing, as it does, to conform to the primary belief that evidence of design implies the existence of a designer; "worthless as not satisfying a moral want," repudiating, as it does, the very idea of the existence of a personal, moral intelligence, who sustains to us the relations of Creator, Governor, and Judge. "We must, therefore, consider it as counting for nothing, in opposition to" that Scripture doctrine of Creation which fulfils all these conditions, and meets all the intellectual and moral requirements of our nature. Constituted as man is, he cannot rest in any theory of this wondrous universe, which does not place an omnipotent moral Intelligence first in the absolute order of existence, as the efficient cause of all forces, whether chemical, mechanical, vital, or mental.

The Doctrine of an Impersonal God.

REV. W. TODD MARTIN, M.A.

LIFE AND CHARACTER OF CHRIST.

THE evidences of the truth of Christianity are manifold and varied, addressing themselves not only to different types of mind, but also to different parts of our mental and moral nature. One of the strongest and most convincing of these is to be found in the life and character of Christ as portrayed in the gospels. To set forth the nature and value of this evidence is the object of the present lecture. In the time at our disposal it will not be possible to do more than give an outline of the argument derivable from this source.

We have in our hands four writings or compositions, generally known as "The Gospels;" and according to the present results of criticism, the first of these was in existence before A.D. 70, the second and third some few years later, and the fourth about the close of the first century.* We do not assume the truth of these writings, for that would be to take for granted the matter in dispute, but simply that they now exist, and that they can be traced back to the dates that have been mentioned.

When we examine these compositions, we find that they are memoirs or biographies of a remarkable person called Jesus Christ, and that they represent him as possessing a character transcendently excellent and beautiful, faultlessly pure and perfect, unique and unparalleled in history. They do this, not by any formal description or delineation of his character—nothing of that kind is attempted—but by the simple record of what he said and did. Our limits forbid anything but a mere sketch of the character thus set before us ; and no such sketch can do it anything like justice. Indeed, no delineation or description can—nothing but the gospel narratives themselves.

These memoirs introduce us to this remarkable person

* Christlieb's " Modern Doubt and Christian Belief," p. 395.

in his infancy.   After intimation, by an angel, to his
mother of his birth and of the name by which he should
be called, he is miraculously conceived through the power
of the Holy Ghost (such is the representation), and is born
a " Holy Thing."   He is born in a stable and laid in a manger, yet an angel from heaven announces his birth to men,
and a multitude of the heavenly host praise God for his
appearance in our world.   And thus we meet at the very
commencement of his earthly life that combination of greatness and lowliness, dignity and abasement, which marks it
throughout and distinguishes it from every other life.

The child Jesus is not a prodigy, displaying superhuman
wisdom and doing wonderful things from his very infancy.
He is a perfectly natural and truly human child, but pure
and holy, without any taint of evil or any stain of sin.   He
grows like other children, both physically and mentally, in
stature and in intelligence.   He attracts the affection of all
who come in contact with him, and has favour with God,
whose grace is upon him.

This is the picture given us of his infancy.   Of his boyhood we have but a glimpse—one recorded incident, but
it is in harmony with the childhood that has preceded.
When twelve years of age, he goes up to Jerusalem with
his parents, and is left behind there at their departure.
When they return to seek him, they find him " in the
temple, sitting in the midst of the doctors, both hearing
them and asking them questions "—the impression made
upon all who hear him being one of amazement " at
his understanding and answers."   There is nothing in his
conduct or bearing to offend—no pertness nor forwardness,
no want of modesty or humility ; yet he shows a measure of
intelligence and an interest in Divine things so far beyond
those of an ordinary and merely human youth, that those who
hear him are " astonished."   His mother gently reproaches
him for having remained behind his father and herself without their knowledge, and thereby caused them anxiety on
his account : and then we have that first recorded word of
his—"Wist ye not that I must be about my Father's busi-

ness?"—the "solitary floweret plucked out of the enclosed garden of the thirty years," which shows us that he had come to know himself and his relation to the Father—a knowledge which surprised his mother, and which, not understanding, she carried away to meditate on and ponder.

Now it has been well shown by Bushnell that, whether fact or fiction, we have here the sketch of a perfect and sacred childhood—that, in this respect, the early character of Jesus is a picture that stands by itself—that in no other case has a biographer, in drawing a character, represented it as beginning with a spotless childhood. He adds—" If any writer, of almost any age, will undertake to describe not merely a spotless but a superhuman or celestial childhood, not having the reality before him, he must be somewhat more than human himself, if he does not pile together a mass of clumsy exaggerations, and draw and overdraw, till neither heaven nor earth can find any verisimilitude in the picture."* This is strikingly exhibited by the apocryphal gospels in their portraiture of Christ's childhood. While the writers of the gospels we are considering say so little of the infancy and youth of Jesus, and expressly tell us that he did his first miracle at Cana of Galilee when entering upon his public ministry, the apocryphal gospels fill his childhood and youth with all manner of grotesque and absurd miracles and prodigies, showing us what it was in the power of that age to invent, and in what a contrast it stands to the naturalness and reserve of the canonical gospels.

When we pass from Christ's childhood to his manhood, and consider his character as it is then presented to us, we find that it is just the development of his pure and spotless youth, to which it stands in the same relation as the flower does to the bud from which it has expanded.

As we survey this character, the first thing that strikes us is its perfect innocence and sinlessness. According to the representation given of him in the gospels, Jesus Christ is a perfectly innocent and sinless being. During his whole life, he neither does wrong, nor gives just cause of offence to

* " Nature and the Supernatural," p. 280.

any one. He never injures any one, by word or deed. Many, no doubt, are offended with him, but it is with what is good in him that they are offended—with his faithfulness and truth, his purity and holiness, his compassion and benevolence. The Scribes and Pharisees are offended with his humility because it rebukes their pride, with his benevolence because it reproves their selfishness, with his holiness because it contrasts so strongly with their moral turpitude and vileness. But this is their blame; he is blameless. The idea of Christ, in this respect, conveyed by the gospel narrative, is that of a perfectly innocent and harmless being, one whose life is altogether inoffensive, and to whose heart every feeling of hatred and unkindness is a stranger. And, while thus innocent and harmless, he is so without sustaining any loss of dignity—without giving any idea of feebleness or weakness, such as we often associate with mere innocence—nay, while conveying the strongest impression of greatness and power.

Nor is Christ innocent and harmless merely; he is sinless. This, we are aware, is denied by some; but we contend that it is the representation of the gospel narrative. There is no act attributed to him that can, with any show of justice, be regarded as a sinful act. His driving of the traffickers out of the temple, especially when taken in connection with his claim as Son to rule in his Father's house, is an act not only compatible with sinlessness, but positively holy and even godlike in its character. And the fact that so many retire without resistance before a single man, implies a consciousness of wrong-doing upon their part, and shows the majesty of reproving holiness. As to the charge of injustice and unreasonable resentment, founded on his smiting a fig-tree with barrenness, it is almost unworthy of serious refutation. There was no injustice and no resentment in the case. It was a warning expressed in symbol, an admonition given by an act. It was Christ's taking an inanimate object—and, therefore, one that was incapable of suffering—and using it to reprove the people of Israel for their unfruitfulness, and warn them of impending doom.

Then we have most important testimony on this point
borne by Christ's enemies.   Pilate washes his hands before
the multitude, in token of his freedom from all participation
in the crime of putting an innocent man to death ; and says,
"I am innocent of the blood of this just person."   Judas,
who knew what Christ was, not only in public but in private,
so far from having anything to allege against him that
might have excused him to himself and others for what he
had done, testifies to his innocence, and says, "I have sinned
in that I have betrayed the innocent blood."

And what shall we say of Christ's own declarations
respecting himself?   That he claims to be a perfectly sinless being is undeniable.   His challenge to his enemies is,
"Which of you convinceth me of sin?"   Of his invulnerability to the assaults of Satan, he declares, "The prince of
this world cometh and hath nothing in me ;" and of his
obedience to the Father, he says, "I do always the things
that please him."   And not only does he make this claim ;
he carries it through without faltering in its assertion, or
abating it for a single moment.   During his whole life
he never makes a confession of sin, drops a tear of penitence, nor offers a prayer for forgiveness.   He has no
remorse, no regrets, no sense of having failed in any duty—
no feeling that he should have done anything different, or
in a different manner, from what he has done.   "It is clear,"
as Dorner says, "in the most decided moments of his life,
that he is conscious of no sin.   That his self-consciousness
was really of such a sort that his conscience never accused
him of any fault or error, is the firmest and most indisputable historical fact, explain it as we may.   That he
imposed upon himself as his life-task the salvation and
reconciliation of the world ; that he was conscious, too, of
being occupied with the solution of this problem, in suffering even to the cross ; and that he died in the full
consciousness of having solved the problem, as well as of
unbroken communion with God, is just as undeniable as
that it would have been an insane and absurd thought to
wish to redeem and reconcile others, if he had been con-

scious of needing redemption himself. How, then, can the phenomenon be explained, that he, to whom even sceptics do not deny the rarest measure of purity and clearness of mind, stands before us without being conscious of a single sin, or of the necessity of conversion and amendment, which he requires of all others; if not in this way, that he was *conscious* of no sin because he *was* not a sinner." This is the only adequate explanation of it: for as Bushnell has well said, "If Jesus was a sinner, he was conscious of sin, as all sinners are, and therefore was a hypocrite in the whole fabric of his character; realising so much of Divine beauty in it, maintaining the show of such unfaltering harmony and celestial grace, and doing all this with a mind confused and fouled by the *affectations* acted for true virtues! Such an example of successful hypocrisy would be itself the greatest miracle ever heard of in the world."

No; Christ lived in a world where he was exposed and tempted to evil, but the purity of his nature constantly repelled it. As he touched the leper, and no uncleanness followed, so he mingled with sinners and received no contamination from them. He had evil suggested to his mind by Satan, but his holy soul did not admit it. "He did no sin, neither was guile found in his mouth." He was "holy, harmless, undefiled, and separate from sinners." And in this sinlessness of Jesus, in the midst of a sinful world, we have something that separates him from all other men, in which he stands solitary and alone, the one sublime exception to a universal sinfulness.

But not only is Christ free from all stain of sin; he is distinguished by the highest positive moral excellence, even perfect love to God, and pure, disinterested, self-sacrificing love to man. This love is the groundwork of his character, its grand distinguishing peculiarity. He shows his love to God by a regard to His will in all things—a constant, cheerful, devoted obedience. At twelve years of age, as a matter not more of duty than of delight, he must be about his Father's business. As he fulfils his ministry, it is his meat, the joy and invigoration of his soul, to do the will of Him

that sent him, and to finish His work. And when his earthly
life is closing, he contemplates it with satisfaction, because he
can say to the Father—"I have glorified Thee on the earth ;
I have finished the work which Thou gavest me to do."

And what shall we say of his love to man, but that the
world has never witnessed anything like it before or since.
His whole life on earth was just the expression of that love
—the shedding of its light on the world's darkness, the
pouring of its life-giving and healing waters on the world's
barrenness and drought.   This love showed itself in his
tender sympathy with all human woe—with the deprivations
of the blind, the heart-sorrows of the bereaved, the infatuation
of the erring.   How he pitied the widowed mother of Nain
in her bereavement, the sisters of Bethany in their grief,
his disciples when they sorrowed in the prospect of his
departure, the inhabitants of Jerusalem in their sinful and
infatuated rejection of himself!

Nor was his an empty and barren sympathy, but one
accompanied and made efficacious by an active benevolence.
"He went about continually doing good, healing all manner of sickness and all manner of disease among the people."
He declared that he "came not to be ministered unto, but
to minister, and to give his life a ransom for many."   And
he fulfilled this, his own high ideal, at once of his mission
and of true greatness. His whole life was one constant ministry of self-sacrificing love. He ministered to man in his physical and earthly wants, healing the sick, cleansing the lepers,
opening the eyes of the blind, comforting the sorrowing,
restoring the dead to life.   And he ministered to man in
spiritual wants. He did so by the gracious words that proceeded out of his mouth, his words of compassion and
tenderness and absolving love.   He ministered thus to the
paralytic, when he said, "Son, be of good cheer, thy sins are
forgiven thee ;" to the woman who was a sinner, when he said,
"Thy faith hath saved thee, go in peace ;" and to the woman
of Samaria, when he revealed himself to her as the Messiah, and gave her the true water of life.   And the crowning
act, the climax of this ministry of love, was when he

ascended to Calvary, and there, by a voluntary death of agony and shame, gave his life a ransom for many. " Herein, indeed, was love"—greater than ever man has shown.

To the highest active benevolence Christ united the passive virtues. It has been justly remarked that, by his life and teaching, Christ has revolutionised the world's estimate of these as an element of greatness. Before his time, men associated greatness almost entirely with the heroic virtues, and regarded meekness under injury, patient endurance of wrong, forgiveness of enemies, as little more than weaknesses. But Christ, by his example, has taught the world not merely that true greatness is compatible with the passive virtues, but that they form an important element of it. He exhibited these not only in the greater trials of life, but also in what are said to be their severest test, its commoner and minor trials. During his life he was a man of sorrows and acquainted with grief. He was so poor that he had no dwelling he could call his own. He knew what it was to hunger, to thirst, and to be weary. He was misunderstood by his friends, and misrepresented and maligned by his enemies. His good was evil spoken of, and his works attributed to Satan. His disciples clung tenaciously to their mistaken views of the Messiah, and were slow to believe all that the prophets had spoken, and all that he taught respecting his sufferings and death. His words were often watched for ground of accusation against him, and plots were formed against his life. But amid all this privation, misconception, and opposition, so fitted to discourage and provoke, he is never ruffled or chafed in spirit, never manifests fretfulness or impatience, displeasure or discontent, never complains or murmurs, but holds on his way with an unclouded serenity and a sublime and undisturbed composure. He is not insensible either to physical or mental ills. Exquisitely sensitive both in soul and body, he feels these acutely; but in virtue of his perfect unselfishness, his devotion to the Father, and his love to man, he rises above them and possesses his soul in a celestial patience.

When we view him in the closing scenes of his earthly life, in what is specially called his passion, he presents a spectacle of meek endurance of wrong, and of undeserved, yet patient and uncomplaining suffering, such as the world has never seen. None ever suffered as he did ; but, although innocent, he is an uncomplaining sufferer. He is silent in the hall of judgment when the mockery of a trial is conducted for his condemnation—silent when he is blindfolded and buffeted, spit on and scourged, ridiculed and crowned with thorns—silent when he toils with his cross along the road to Calvary, the only word that he utters being one not of self-lamentation, but of pitying regard for others, " Daughters of Jerusalem, weep not for me, but weep for yourselves, and for your children." Well might it be said of him, " He is brought as a lamb to the slaughter, and as a sheep before her shearers is dumb, so he openeth not his mouth." If, therefore, to suffer even to death uncomplainingly, being innocent, manifest greatness of soul, none ever exhibited such greatness as Jesus of Nazareth.

Then think of his forgiveness of injury ! When Peter came to him on one occasion, and asked, " Lord, how oft shall my brother sin against me, and I forgive him ? till seven times ? " his reply was—" I say not unto thee until seven times, but until seventy times seven." And what he thus preached he practised. He forgave Peter for denying him, Thomas for doubting him, all the disciples for forsaking him at his apprehension. Nay, he forgave those who crucified him. As they drive the nails into his hands, he raises his meek eyes to heaven and prays, " Father, forgive them ; for they know not what they do." No wonder that even Rousseau felt constrained to say that if Socrates suffered and died like a sage, Christ suffered and died like a god.

And not only did Christ combine the different *classes* of virtues in his character ; he united in himself *all* the virtues. Unlike any other great man of whom we read—of whom the most that could be said was that he possessed one or more virtues in a high degree—Christ possessed every virtue in its perfection, so that it is not possible to name any moral excellence that did not belong to him. He possessed these virtues, moreover, in such just proportion, that his character was not only complete and full, but in perfect equipoise and balance, exquisitely symmetrical and harmonious. His love to God was in beautiful accord with his love to man. The one of these virtues did not outrun the other, or develop itself at its expense, but wrought harmoniously with it. And what was true of these fundamental elements of character was true of the various virtues into which they resolved themselves. In him, love for the race co-existed with love for the individual. Shepherd of the whole family of man, he could leave the ninety-and-nine in the wilderness, and go after the one that was lost. With a world upon his hands, he could stand and call one blind man to him for healing, converse with and lead to faith and repentance one erring woman by the well of Jacob, receive one anxious inquirer who comes to him by night, and make known to him the way of eternal life.

The heroic and the gentle virtues met in him. To the highest manly virtue, the courage that could stand undauntedly against an opposing world, he joined "the highest characteristics of womanly virtue—infinite devotion and singleness of purpose, the unruffled serenity of a calm and gentle spirit, pure and modest feeling in the maintenance of the finest moral distinctions, and the power peculiar to women of passive obedience—power to bear, to suffer, to forego in unspeakable loyalty." *

Never were contrasts so blended, and apparent contradictions so reconciled, as in him. He is grave without being gloomy, unworldly without being unsociable, self-denied without being austere, spiritual without being ascetic, intolerant of sin, while gentle and tenderly compassionate to the sinner. His dignity is wedded to humility, his zeal guided by wisdom, his enthusiasm joined with calmness and self-possession. He is in harmony with himself, with nature, with duty, with everything but sin ; and he is so because he is in harmony with God—because the law of God is

* Martensen's "Christian Ethics," p. 252.

within his heart, and he is filled and pervaded by love to
him.   And in virtue of this inner harmony he does all
things well.   He is never taken by surprise, nor at a loss
what to do.   He is never unprepared for the occasion, or
unequal to the emergency, but always does the right thing,
at the right time, and in the right manner.

He is truly a perfect character, "fairer than the children
of men." Whatever he may have been in bodily person, he is
altogether matchless in the beauty of his character. His life
is a picture, not only without a blot, but without a defective
line.   It is a majestic anthem, running through the whole
scale of love and service, sounding every chord of thought
and feeling, and rising to heaven without a discordant note.

If we view Christ as a teacher, all admit that none ever
taught as he does.   He has not learned in the schools of the
Rabbis, and yet he speaks with a wisdom which amazes those
who hear him, and leads them to ask in wonder, " Whence
knoweth this man letters, having never learned ?   Whence
hath this man this wisdom and these mighty works ?" He
has had no training as an orator, and yet from the first
moment he opens his lips to teach, he shews himself to
be a perfect master of human speech.

His teaching is not after human methods, but after a
manner of his own.   He does not speculate, nor make
guesses at truth.   He does not reason and infer, build up
and prove by elaborate process of argumentation or induction.   He announces rather, and reveals.   He speaks that
which he knows, and testifies that which he has seen.   The
truth lies before him—is within his mind and heart—and
he simply utters it ; and it is seen and felt to be the truth
by those who hear.

His instructions are not imparted in an artificial and
formal system, but in precepts and statements of truth,
each of which has often a kind of completeness in itself, and
which, as they fall from his lips, might be likened to the
stars as they drop one after another into the evening sky
and light up the heaven with glory.   He teaches, moreover,
not in the language of the schools, but in that of the com-

mon people, so that all can understand ; and often in para-
bles which are pictures of Divine truth, drawn from nature
and every-day life, and which come home to all hearts, and
live in the memory for ever.

When we consider the matter of his teaching—confining
ourselves at present to his ethical system—we find it to be
the highest and purest morality—a morality which even
sceptics and unbelievers acknowledge to be the noblest and
most perfect that has ever been propounded, and before
which the world has bowed down for the last eighteen
hundred years.   It is to this effect—" Whatsoever ye would
that men should do to you, do ye even so to them ;" "Love
your enemies, bless them that curse you, do good to them
that hate you, and pray for them which despitefully use you
and persecute you ; that ye may be the children of your
Father which is in heaven : for he maketh His sun to rise on
the evil and on the good, and sendeth rain on the just and on
the unjust.   .   .   .   Be ye therefore perfect, even as your
Father which is in heaven is perfect."

And this teaching is with authority.   He speaks not as
if there was any doubt of the truth of what he says, but
with the manner of one who is assured and certain, who
speaks what he knows, and who has a right to declare the
laws of the kingdom.   His teaching is after this manner—
" Blessed are the poor in spirit, for their's is the kingdom of
heaven;" "Ye have heard that it hath been said, An eye for
an eye, and a tooth for a tooth : but *I say* unto you, That ye
resist not evil ;" " Heaven and earth shall pass away, but
my word shall not pass away;" " The word that I have
spoken, the same shall judge him in the last day."   Well
might it be said, " Never man spake like this man."   And
well might we ask, and leave the sceptic to reply—" Whence
hath this man this wisdom ?"

Closely connected with Christ's teaching are his claims.
When we examine these, we find them to be such as have
never been advanced by any human being before or since.
Time will permit us to do little more than mention some
of these.

First of all, then, he declares his humanity, and again and again calls himself "the Son of man." But by this designation, as applied to himself, he intimates not merely that he is a possessor of our nature, a member of the human family; but that he is something more than this—that he stands in a peculiar relation to the race—that he is the Son of man as no other is—the ideal, the representative man—the second man, the head of a new humanity—the "Son of man" spoken of by Daniel, the destined possessor of universal kingdom and dominion.

But while thus calling Himself the Son of man, he claims no less emphatically to be the Son of God. He calls God his Father. "All things are delivered unto me of my Father." "My Father worketh hitherto, and I work." When the High Priest adjures him, by the living God, to tell whether he be "the Christ, the Son of God," his unhesitating and unequivocal reply is, "Thou hast said." And when he claims to be the Son of God, he claims to be so in a high and peculiar sense, a sense in which no mere creature can aspire to the title, and which implies the possession of the same nature with God. This is clear from the distinction which he always makes, in speaking to the disciples, between *their* relation to God and *his*. He never places Himself on a level with them in this respect—never says of God *our* Father, but *my* Father and *your* Father. The opening words of the Lord's prayer are no exception to this; for he is there teaching the disciples to pray, and does not include himself. His language is, "After this manner pray *ye*."

In accordance with this lofty claim he speaks of himself as being "from above," having "come from God," having "come out from the Father." He places himself on a level with the Father, as when he says of the Jews, "They have both seen and hated both me and my Father," when he commissions the disciples to baptize in the name of the Father and of the Son and of the Holy Ghost; and when speaking of the Father and himself, he says, "We will come unto him and make our abode with him." He claims co-ordi-

nate authority with the Father—"My Father worketh
hitherto, and I work." And when the Jews take up stones
to stone him because he called God his Father, and
thereby, in their view, made himself equal with God, he
says nothing to intimate that they were wrong in the inference they had drawn from the claim which he advanced.
He declares himself "Lord of the Sabbath;" asserts his
power to forgive sins and to enact the laws of the kingdom ;
claims to be honoured equally with the Father; declares
that the dead shall hear his voice and come forth to life—
that, as the appointed judge of all, he will come in glory
and judge all nations—and that men will be accepted or
rejected according as they have shown love and attachment
to him as represented by his people, or have disregarded
and neglected him. He proclaims himself to be "the light
of the world," "the way, the truth, and the life," by whom
alone any one can come to the Father—the only one who
knows the Father, and can make him known to men. He
invites all who labour and are heavy-laden to come to him
that he may give them rest—bids all men follow him, and
forsake everything that they may do so—declares that he
will draw all men to him. He demands the highest affection of the human heart, and avers that whosoever loveth
father or mother more than him is not worthy of him, and
cannot be his disciple.

Such are some of the claims of Christ. Every one will
admit that they are the most wonderful ever made by any
being. If any man, any merely human teacher, even though
he were a prophet or an apostle, were to make such claims,
would he not cover himself with ridicule, and excite either
the world's pity of his fanaticism, or its indignant scorn of his
unfounded and arrogant imposture? Imagine any man, even
one "charged with a special, express, and unique commission from God to lead mankind to faith and virtue,"* standing forth, and saying, "All power is given unto me in heaven
and in earth," "I and the Father are one," "He that hath
seen me hath seen the Father"—holding out hands to a

* J. S. Mill's "Essays on Religion," p. 255.

unprofitable members ; and they therefore concluded that the painless destruction of infant life, and especially of those infants who were so deformed or diseased that their lives, if prolonged, would probably have been a burden to them-selves, was on the whole a benefit. . . Minute and scrupulous care for human life and human virtue in the humblest forms, in the slave, the gladiator, the savage, or the infant, was, indeed, wholly foreign to the genius of Paganism. It was produced by the Christian doctrine of the inestimable value of each immortal soul. It is the distinguishing characteristic of every society into which the spirit of Christianity has passed."*

Suicide cannot on the ethical principles of sensationalism be condemned as a crime. When life becomes a weariness, when it is felt that the pain outweighs the pleasure of living, shall we condemn the act of the man who seeks quietude in death ? The teaching of the elder Mill was sadly carried to its legitimate conclusion by one of his sons, who, learning from his physician that his disease was mortal, shot himself to avoid a lingering death.†

The doctrine of the dependence of sociology on biology,‡ in other words, the dependence of a right theory of social life on correct knowledge of the laws of organic life, affords ample field for conjecture as to the ways in which utilit-arianism might apply Darwin's law of the " indefinite modi-fiability"§ of the human species by natural selection. A State free from the " theological bias," and in the hands of philosophic legislators, would offer a tempting field for experiment in the direction of a higher development of organism and intelligence, by careful scientific oversight of the question of population. Utilitarian ethics would facilitate this great enterprise by abolishing the Christian sentiment which protects the purity of the family and

* " History of European Morals," Vol. II., p. 27.
† M'Cosh's "Scottish Philosophy," p. 378 ; cf. also Lecky's "European Morals," pp. 40–63.
‡ Spencer's " Sociology," chap. xiv.
§ Spencer's " Sociology," p. 329.

B

guards the sanctity of home. Plato, the most elevated of all non-Christian thinkers, gives in his "Republic" a curious example of speculation on this subject.* James Mill suggests, rather than avows, very peculiar views in his "Political Economy."† John Stuart Mill, who has done more than any other man of this century to lead educated young men into senationalism in philosophy and utilitarianism in morals, has with great candour professed opinions which cannot be other than shocking to every Christian. In referring to this matter, I must crave the indulgence of my audience, if it be such as I should rather bury in oblivion than expose to your scorn; but an illustration of the sort indicates to Christian parents better than argument the direction in which atheistic morals would guide their sons and daughters. Mill tells us that for twenty years he was the devoted friend of a talented lady, whose affections he won, though her husband, whom he describes as "a most upright, brave, and honourable man," was still living. He was in the habit of visiting her and travelling with her in the absence of her husband. He takes care to inform us, however, that they gave not the slightest ground for any other supposition than the true one, that their relation to each other at that time was one of "strong affection and confidential intimacy only." For, he adds, "though *we did not consider the ordinances of society binding on a subject so entirely personal*, we did feel bound that our conduct should be such as in no degree to bring discredit on her husband, nor, therefore, on herself."‡ The words of Jesus Christ plainly and emphatically exhibit the character of such a relationship. I would have you note, especially, the tone of morality suggested in Mill's quietly avowed belief in the lawfulness of conduct which the rudest and least informed member of a Christian community will instinctively condemn. Yet the leader of the school of so-called progress in morals was carrying out consistently the

---

* See Grote's "Plato," Vol. III., p. 202.
† "Political Economy," chap. i., § 2.
‡ "Autobiography," p. 229.

principles of his ethical creed.   It was not his moral code, but the healthy instincts of Christian society, that saved him from abominable crime.

6. If society should cast off belief in God, and remove from contemplation the example of Jesus Christ, it would be impossible to discover any moral type towards which life might be ever approximating, by which the conflicting motives and emotions might be justly regulated, and after which the whole man might be formed in " the beauty of holiness."   The golden, the heroic age has ever been placed in a far distant past ; while philosophic dreams of perfection have been localised in cloud-land.

It may indeed be argued, as Mill has argued, that the " benefit, whatever it amounts to," of the precepts of Christ " has been gained.   Mankind have entered into the possession of it.   It has become the property of humanity, and cannot now be lost by anything short of a return to primeval barbarism."*   The doctrine of Christ may be rejected, His Divine mission denied, His obedience of the Father accounted a delusion, His sacrifice denounced as a theological fiction, His resurrection derided as a fanatical dream ; but the " benefit, whatever it amounts to," of His morality, remains a part of the inheritance of mankind. Let us suppose the Gospels read by one who is fully convinced that Jesus Christ was not a Divine Saviour, but a self-deceived enthusiast, at first simple-minded and sincere, then gradually deteriorating into a fanatic, deceiving as well as deceived—how much of influence, think you, would His precepts, however beautiful, retain ?   Take away from the life of the Son of man the power that is derived from our belief in him as the Son of God, let there be removed from our thoughts all sense of the world unseen, from which He came and to which He returned, and the Perfect Man will have little power to fix our hearts upon His example, and mould us into His likeness.   The Christ of the atheist cannot be the Healer and Guide of mankind.

The example of Jesus Christ would be wholly out of

* " Essays on Religion," p. 98.

place in the morality of evolution. The evolutionist must reject Him as but ill-suited to illustrate a wise adaptation of the sensitive organism to its environment. His life does not furnish a good type of skilful adjustment of " constitution to conditions." " He was a man of sorrows, and acquainted with grief ;" by no means the pattern of a morality whose foundation-principle is pleasure.

Utilitarianism of the older sensational school is equally at fault, when it passes outside the Church of Christ, and searches among men uninfluenced by religious motives for a life which youth might regard with admiration and follow with enthusiasm. It searches in vain.* It is thrown back from example to doctrine, and its doctrine, mechanical and not vital, is without reforming and renovating power. The scorpions of legislative enactment, following the whips of an education resolutely directed to the formation in each person's mind of " an indissoluble association between his own happiness and the good of the whole,"† might do much to make members of the community submit to the utilitarian yoke, in so far as concerns property and the administration of justice ; but Benthamism has no power to subdue the anarchic passions of the soul, to eradicate vice out of the heart, to clothe society " with the garments of salvation," and cover it with the " robe of righteousness."

Mill himself acknowledges that, " although educated intellect enlightening the selfish feelings is prodigiously important as a means of improvement in the hands of those who are themselves impelled by nobler principles of action," not one of the " survivors of the Benthamites or utilitarians of that day now relies mainly upon it for the general amendment of conduct." ‡ In old age he reached on this point a well-founded mistrust of the favourite opinions of his youth. For a morality framed out of materials derived

* *Cf.* on "Our Lord's Character," "Some Elements of Religion," by Canon Liddon. The testimony quoted by him from Goldwin Smith is especially worthy of attention.

† Mill's " Utilitarianism," p. 25.

‡ " Autobiography," p. 111.

wholly from the senses—which has no reward but this life's
pleasure, and no dread but earthly pain—which is enclosed
wholly within the organism and its affections (whether the
individual organism or the collective organism, called
society), can have no power to regenerate or elevate mankind.   It cannot, even when supported by the powerful aid
of education, renovate the heart within. Clough, who drifted
from his early faith into cheerless naturalism, gives us the
sum of this new revelation when he says :—

> " It seems His newer will
> We should not think of Him at all, but turn,
> And of that world which He hath given us, make
> What best we may."

But we can make nothing of it if we cease to "think of
Him at all," if we turn from the True Light, and with
the shadow on our faces look only towards this, in the
judgment of Mill, immoral and cruel world.*   Know
God is the first maxim in moral progress ; Know thyself, the
second.   But neither is possible, save in that mediation in
which God is revealed to man, and man is made known to
himself.   In the life and death of Jesus Christ the complete
ethical ideal is realised.   Here is perfectly exemplified
righteousness without defect, holiness without taint ; mercy
clasping the hand of vileness, yet receiving no stain ; love,
which is the fulfilling of the whole law ; calm assertion of
authority in the face of power, the supremacy of the eternal
life, the marvellous spiritual alchemy by which the very
pangs of the earthly lot are transmuted into pleasures of
the soul.   Nor, truly, has this holy Redeemer lived and died
in vain.   His Gospel has been gradually revealing its power,
awaking humanity from the bestial sleep of sin to a sense
of the nobler aim of goodness.   This work of healing will,
by God's grace, go on till the ethical idea shall be a second
time realised in " the new man, which after God is created
in righteousness and true holiness." †

7. The negation of a personal God, the Creator and

* Essay on Nature, in " Essays on Religion."
† Ephesians iv. 24.

Ruler of all things, annuls the doctrine of sin, and breaks
down all distinction between moral good and evil.

Pantheism identifies the soul with the One as a pheno-
menal manifestation of it; the pantheist cannot, then,
condemn any act as essentially evil. The One is as truly
revealed in the murderer as in the philanthropist. There
can be no wrong in wrong-doing, if right and wrong are
alike the unfolding of the same existence, if they rise out of
and sink again into that One Mysterious Life.

Nor is our argument on this point less effective when it is
directed against the evolution hypothesis. For if the whole
man be a product of evolution, the evil in him is as really a
product as the good. His temper and disposition are the
necessary outgrowth of his inheritance and his surroundings.
Sin is no longer sin. Immorality is an essential factor in the
evolution of humanity, and is no more worthy to be condemned as involving guilt or responsibility than is the formation of the lips or the colour of the hair. Nature evolves
the serpent as well as the dove. That the serpent has a
poisonous fang is not a fault, but a virtue. Its destructive
venom has aided the cobra in the struggle for existence.
The brutal Nero and the benevolent Howard have been
alike evolved by the necessary laws of nature. It is unreasonable, then, to praise or blame. No man can be called
a sinner. Each person is what he is as a part of the
irresistible movement of the cosmos. The molecular
activities which constitute thought and emotion and conscience and will are the physically certain outgrowth of the
primeval nebula.*

* Professor Huxley, in his address at the recent meeting of the
British Association, cited the great masters in Calvinistic theology as
witnesses on behalf of his doctrine that sensation and intellection are
automatic. But the certainty which is involved in Calvinism is *toto
cœlo* different from the necessity of physical development. Calvinism
deals with the acts of rational moral beings having the causes of their
voluntary acts *in se*, in their own intellectual and moral nature; evolution makes all voluntary action to be the necessary result of physical
causes operating as a part of the material cosmos. How far the
exercises of reason and conscience may be fore-ordained is a question

The scepticism of John Stuart Mill on the question of religion will not provide a door of escape out of this difficulty. In his posthumous "Essays," we have a most repulsive picture of the cosmos. He finds in its constitution and operations all manner of vice and crime ; to follow nature, he maintains, would be to arrive at the consummation of villany. But if there be no God, or, what is the same thing, if there be no proof which makes it reasonable to believe that there is a God, and if there be no hereafter, whence comes the light to show us that crime is crime, and to commit crime is criminal ? The murderer or the thief may defend himself on the ground that nature, his only guide, sets him a wicked example, if his deeds be wicked, and encourages him in his evil course, if it be evil. Nature as it is constituted, he may, on the authority of Mill, allege, lies and cheats, violates every principle of honest dealing, subjects its victims to torture, commits wholesale murder, prompts to every manner of wickedness by internal motives and external enticements.* Above nature, he may add, there is no God, and beyond the present, no immortality ; what right, then, has the moralist to set up an artificial rule of conduct, and enforce what nature has not enjoined ? It may be easy for a philosopher, who has been under intellectual drill from infancy, and who has found his world not in real life, but in thought, to control himself and conform to a non-natural standard of morals ; but the great majority of people are not philosophers. They are certain that they have bodies, and are furnished with many reasons to make them look upon it as very doubtful whether they have souls. Morality is, then, altogether a question of taste ; and the classical canon has never been repealed: *de gustibus non disputandum.* As nature has distributed to every man, so let

insoluble by philosophy, and belonging properly to revelation. Such fore-ordination, however, stands related only by way of contrast to the fatalistic predestination of physical necessity. The necessity of materialism renders moral action impossible. If all volition be the necessary result of physical causes, then clearly whatever is is right. Stains on the character are no more blameworthy than spots on the sun.

* Mill's " Essays on Religion," pp. 28–36.

him enjoy its bounties. He presumes too far who demands a pretence of virtue beyond the rule of nature. The individual may well rest self-satisfied if his morals reach the standard of the universe.

8. To remove from human thought belief in a personal God, and to fix before consciousness a kingdom of natural law in His stead, tends to weaken and impair our moral faculty. The effect of this—which I may call the distinctively scientific—habit of mind is to repress the higher individual energies—the energies dependent on the will, and to produce a quietism favourable to the supremacy of the passions in the individual, and to the domination of evil in society. The ceaseless consciousness of law, and that not as the ordinance of a higher intelligence addressed to man for his direction, but as the fatalistic order of a universe without a God, must weaken our sense of power, making us less inclined to "envisage circumstance," and assert the supremacy of mind. Now one of the most valuable elements in a high moral nature is that consciousness of inner strength. It may sometimes run into stoic pride, or be soured into cynic contempt, or be perverted into impudent self-assertion, but without it there is no high and noble spirit. Christianity on this point, as on many others, mediates between two contraries : it at once bows the soul to the lowest depths in self-abasement, and lifts it to the highest pitch of conscious strength. Such sense of power has always shown itself in what we might call the heroic periods of Christian struggle. We have a notable instance in English Puritanism, whose masculine faith crushed with strong hand and resolute will the proud nobility of England.

9. A godless morality can supply no motive power within the breast adequate to sustain man's ardour in the pursuit of goodness.

" No heart is pure that is not passionate ; no virtue safe that is not enthusiastic."* But how can utility or pleasure-seeking kindle this purifying flame of holy ardour, or feed

* " Ecce Homo," p. 8.

this glowing enthusiasm ? It can furnish no such "impulse
to virtue." It may theorise about devotion to humanity ;
it cannot create such an emotion, much less nourish it with
life-long sustenance. It has, indeed, been argued* that, as
among the Greeks and Romans a passionate love of country
inspired the most heroic deeds, so the love of mankind
might become the source of ennobling inspiration. But it
is forgotten that patriotism has only produced one kind of
virtue—the virtue of soldierly fidelity and fortitude. The
Spartan died for Sparta, the Roman died for Rome ; for to
each his country was a camp, and the citizen a soldier.
But love of country did not impart to Spartan or to Roman
the power needful to wrestle against sin and conquer the
enemy within himself. Expand the idea of citizenship so
as to embrace mankind, and what hope is there that this
dim generality will enkindle warmth enough to maintain
the motive force needed to carry the soul through all the
impediments it must encounter in an incessant effort after
goodness ? How different is the persuasive power of
Christ ! How far-reaching and penetrating are His words,
how effectual His ethical lessons ! His Gospel addresses
itself to every right motive principle by which man is animated, and fills each with Divine vigour. It appeals to our
filial affection, " Be ye followers of God as dear children ;"
it wields over us the mighty power of love, " As Christ also
hath loved us ;" it binds us by the strong cords of gratitude,
"And hath given Himself for us ;" it inspires by the example
of self-sacrifice, " An offering and a sacrifice to God for a
sweet-smelling savour." By such powerful influences it
removes out of the heart the two cardinal lusts—impurity and greed. " But fornication, and all uncleanness, or
covetousness, let it not be once named among you, as be-
cometh saints."† That these springs of moral vigour may
flow perennially, it identifies our life with the sacrificial
death of the Redeemer in every exercise of the faith in
which we find salvation ; " I am crucified with Christ :

* Mill's " Essays on Religion," p. 107.
† Ephesians v. 1-3.

nevertheless I live ; yet not I, but Christ liveth in me : and
the life which I now live in the flesh, I live by the faith of
the Son of God, who loved me, and gave Himself for me."*

Here is the inexhaustible source of passionate personal
devotedness, which can do and bear all things.

10. The philosophy of evolution is equally impotent to
set before the mind an end or final motive adequate to sustain an elevated moral purpose.   Indeed, one of the fundamental principles of this philosophy is to discard altogether
the doctrine of final causes.   But let us for the moment
suppose it to be sufficiently inconsequent to cast about
among the conceptions proper to it for a final end in life,
what aim will it set before us ? the individual perfection ?
The growth of knowledge makes this end more and more
evidently unattainable ; and even though it were, we
have the dismal prospect that when the mind shall have
perfected itself in knowledge and in skill, the cunning
instrument must be broken, the wondrous rythmic corre-
lations of molecular change must be resolved, and the brain,
with its priceless treasures, perish.   Shall we aim at the
perfection of the race ? What part can any of us have in
that far-off future ?   Why toil in pain after results which
may or may not be achieved, and which, if such blessedness
be in store for man, cannot be enjoyed by him for ages after
we shall have become part of the earth's dust ?

Evolution throws no gleam of sunshine on the future ;
the sweet rose of hope will not bloom when budded on that
stock.   Atheistic philosophy has had always gnawing at its
heart the secret consciousness that the world can never on
its principles be made the home of a blessed race.   If
atheism ever enjoyed an hour of hopefulness, it was that
brief day of its triumph in France at the outbreak of the
Revolution—a day which had scarce dawned when it was
overcast with blood-tinted clouds and closed in fearful
darkness.

Pessimism, half-muttered or openly avowed, has ever
been the creed of scepticism and infidelity.   David Hume

* Gal. ii. 20.

has left on record a curious picture of his mental unrest, in which one may trace how the new wine of his youthful enthusiasm became acidified into scepticism.* John Stuart Mill has given an elaborate account of a very similar experience. " It occurred to me," he writes, " to put the question directly to myself : ' Suppose that all your objects in life were realised ; that all the changes in institutions and opinions which you are looking forward to could be completely effected at this very instant : would this be a great joy and happiness to you ?' And an irrepressible self-consciousness distinctly answered, ' No.' At this my heart sank within me : the whole foundation on which my life was constructed fell down. All my happiness was to have been found in the continual pursuit of this end. The end had ceased to charm, and how could there ever again be any interest in the means ? I seemed to have nothing left to live for."† The state of feeling in which he continued for a considerable time, he afterwards saw exactly pourtrayed in the lines of Coleridge—

> " A grief without a pang, void, dark, and drear—
> A drowsy, stifled, unimpassioned grief,
> Which finds no natural outlet or relief
> In word, or sigh, or tear."

In his posthumous " Essay on Nature," he gives a dismal picture of this world as it left the hands of its Creator—if, indeed, it had a Creator. Herbert Spencer argues out the conclusion that the sidereal system—including, of course, all life and thought—must in time be reduced again to the nebulous form out of which it has been evolved ; and he predicts for it successive integrations and disintegrations running on through an endless series.‡ Germany, formerly the nurse of transcendental idealism, has adopted pessimism as her favourite philosophy. The cynic Schopenhauer has become the master of German speculative thought through the popular exposition of his gloomy creed by his disciple

* Dr. M'Cosh's " Scottish Philosophy," p. 115.
† " Autobiography," pp. 132-149.
‡ " First Principles," p. 480.

Hartmann. M. Albert Reville, a competent authority, affirms pessimism to be the only philosophy now accepted by German opinion. To exhibit the depressing gloom of this final word of atheistic speculation, I shall quote a few sentences from M. Reville's article.*

"There is nothing real and constant but pain. All pleasure is negative, a diminution or temporary cessation of pain, but never a positive condition of happiness. All life is essentially suffering ; and as human life exhibits the most intense degree of willingness to live, it is natural that it should be the richest in sufferings. Our world is of necessity the worst of possible worlds."

"The world is bad ; life is an evil ; the only salvation is to be found in nothingness."

Hartmann treats with not unmerited scorn the shallow hope that humanity may be made more blessed through the progress of science, and the application of its discoveries to convenience and comfort.

"The world moves on, in spite of—or rather by virtue of —its progress in knowledge and in power, towards a future sadder than its past. The working classes are better educated, better housed, better fed, and more unhappy than before. Immorality may become more refined ; it is always the same, and bears the same poisonous fruits. Genius in science, as in art, will become more rare. A dead-level will become fixed in this domain, as in others ; and the toil will exceed the pleasure of knowledge. Earth is already in the afternoon of its planetary day ; it moves sorrowfully towards the twilight of the evening. Aged humanity will have no successors ; it will finally relinquish the vain pursuit of happiness, and will only sigh for insensibility, nothingness, the *nirvâna*. If the reader find this result distressing, he must learn that he has been mistaken if he has believed that he could find in philosophy consolations and hopes. There is but one hope that is not forbidden him—if, at least, he arrive at making the aim of the unconscious a

---

* "Un Nouveau Système de Philosophie Allemande ;" "Revue des Deux Mondes," 1er Octobre, 1874.

conscious aim for himself—that is to say, if he abandon
fully his personality to the logical development of the world.
He will rejoice himself by anticipation in the vision of that
end which will be the suppression of all individual and
collective life, and which will accomplish, by the return to
not-being, the grand redemption, the universal and final
emancipation into the bosom of the eternal silence."

The materialist may say, This is a disordered dream ; it is
not our teaching ; we repudiate such conclusions.   But, I
reply, it is demonstrable that if you eliminate from your
creed the doctrine of a personal God, the just and good
Governor of all things, this pessimism is a more consistent
conclusion than your talk of progress and improvement.
Your great master himself, Herbert Spencer, carries evolution, as we have seen, to its necessary issue in the annihilation
of all collective and individual life.   Hartmann, whatever
the historical succession of his philosophy, is undoubtedly
a materialist.   He holds firmly by the doctrine of philosophic unitarianism, or *monisme;* he resolves matter into
force ; he builds up his physical system on the atomic
theory ; he makes the brain the *sine qua non* of thought.
The materialist school has no right to disown him.   He
holds the fundamental principles of their creed ; but, with
the profound and fearless logic of Germany, he drives the
materialistic doctrine to its necessary ethical conclusions.
Having rid the universe of God, he finds it to be, instead of
a paradise, a hell ; and he can discover no hope of happiness
or rest but in the annihilation of conscious being.

Need I remind you who have been preserved in the faith
of Jesus Christ, how different is the light which Christianity
sheds around us on this world ?   Earth is not, indeed, a
paradise ; deep are the shadows resting on it ; dark the
stains on the conscience of man ; keen the pangs which
pierce his heart in the necessary discipline of suffering ;
" the whole creation groaneth and travaileth in pain together
until now ;"* but enclosing, embracing all are the heavens
filled with divine glory, ever bright with the clear light of

* Romans viii. 22.

righteousness, and shedding in upon our cold hearts the kindly warmth of a Father's love. The Gospel is a message of hope to man—of hope to the individual and to the race. It is not for finite intelligence to unravel the mystery of God's giving or withholding ; but we have abundant proof that the redemption of Christ is powerful to regenerate the most degraded, and quicken into moral health the vilest life. We are

> " Emboldened to prefer
> Vocal thanksgivings to the eternal King,
> Whose love, whose counsel, whose commands have made
> Your very poorest rich in peace of thought
> And in good works ; and him who is endowed
> With scantiest knowledge, master of all truth,
> Which the salvation of his soul requires."

No dungeon of despair can imprison the soul that hearkens to the Redeemer's voice. It is a fact of human experience, authenticated by an induction based on countless instances, that the Great High Priest is "able to save them to the uttermost that come unto God by Him ;"* and that in a salvation which waits not to bear fruit in the eternal world, but is evidenced to be a real and vital healing by the most convincing proofs in this. The disciples of Jesus Christ are warranted in preaching the Gospel of the kingdom, and in offering up the petition, " Thy kingdom come," with unfaltering faith.

But even though the future of humanity should prove darker than we believe ; though the mysterious hand that governs all the ages should permit the sin of human souls to rise like a thick cloud and cast a shadow over the last days ; still, for each Christian there is a final aim, on which if he fix his heart, he will find it lift him into a constant hopefulness, and sustain him under all the burdens he may have to bear. The *summum bonum* of the believer is God Himself ; it is, as we have been taught in childhood, " to glorify God, and to enjoy Him for ever." In this " chief end" the lines of faith and of philosophy converge and are lost in the light ineffable : for here is the supreme of self-

* Hebrews vii. 25.

annihilation, and therefore, the annihilation of all pain ; here at the same time is the perfecting of individual and self-conscious being, and, therefore, the perfection of enjoyment.

Materialism, wearied with its doubts, its toils, its sufferings, its despair, turns sadly away from this world's wretchedness, and wrapping itself in the cerements of the grave, sighs for death : Christianity, her face wet with tears shed over the sin and misery of man, yet trustful, ardent, enthusiastic, stretches in hope towards an unbounded future, with the exultant exclamation on her lips—Life, life, eternal life !

The effects on religion of the doctrine against which my argument has been directed, need not long detain us. To remove from our minds the idea of a Divine Personality is to destroy religion. For if God be an impersonal Something, separated from us by the vast æons of evolution, faith is impossible. We might believe that Infinite Power exists ; we could not in any real sense trust in it. Love is extinguished ; we have no capacity for loving an inscrutable and unknowable It. Hope must die ; we have nothing either to expect or dread, since the decay of the cerebrum brings everlasting unconsciousness. Prayer is an absurdity ; to address petitions to an unknown Something would be ridiculous : can this Something hear ? and if it can, the law of evolution sweeping on in pitiless night would render it impotent to aid us. The voice of praise is silenced : our psalms are but silly rhapsody—the music of foolish words, such as a moon-struck poet might address to the unheeding stars. Bereft of faith, and love, and hope, and prayer, and praise, what is left of religion ? Who would care to keep the earthen vessel from which the precious ointment has been poured out, and which has been so effectually cleansed by the acids of philosophy, that there clings to it not a trace of the old perfume to recall the ineffable sweetness that has perished ?

No. 5.

MIRACLES AND PROPHECY:

Direct Proofs that the Bible is a Revelation from God.

REV. A. C. MURPHY, M.A.

17/1063

MIRACLES AND PROPHECY.

THE Bible is a grand fact, and a prime factor in the moulding of the modern world. It claims to be a revelation from God, and an account of the way of man's salvation. It contains a record of miracles performed and prophecies accomplished in attestation of that claim. The historical structure of the book permits of the easy authentication of these two forms of evidence. Our object is to show that the performance of miracle and the accomplishment of prophecy afford a full and sufficient vindication of the claim of the Bible to be the Word of God and the Gospel of salvation.

I.—THE MIRACLE.

What, let us first inquire, is a miracle? There is an orderly course of nature going on around us, resulting from the action of countless forces which work according to their own established laws. Let an event occur, then, which cannot be accounted for by the forthputting of any force or group of forces in the existing system of things, and which requires for itself the supposition of some power superior to every force or group of forces in the existing system, and we call that event a miracle. And as God alone can put forth a power superior to every force in the existing system, so every miracle is the immediate work of God.

So much for the nature of the miracle; but what about the fact? Is there any such thing as a miracle at all? Is it not, after all, but the phantom of an inflamed imagination? Must it not be held that nothing can happen which is not in accordance with the established laws of nature? There are those who strenuously maintain this doctrine, and who appeal to the universal experience of men in evidence of its truth. Where is the man, they ask, who has ever seen a miracle? They make bold to say that no amount of evidence in favour of a miracle could counterbalance the antecedent unlikelihood of the thing itself—that it is easier to believe in the untrustworthiness of the most intelligent, honest, and unanimous testimony, than in the actual occurrence of that supernatural event on behalf of which the testimony is brought forward.

Now, in opposition to this doctrine, let me lay down the three following propositions :—(1.) That the existence of God implies the possibility of the miracle ; (2.) That God's moral government of the world implies the probability of the miracle ; (3.) That God's redemptive interference on behalf of the world implies the necessity of the miracle.

I.—*The existence of a personal God implies the possibility of the miracle.* God can do according to His will with the world which He has made. If the countless forces which are at work in the world have been forged upon the anvil of the Divine purpose, and if, by their manifold play and counterplay, they produce the existing constitution of nature, it is obvious that the Creator of these forces can supplement them or arrest them in whatever way may be pleasing in His sight.

Let me seek to illustrate the point before us by a sort of sliding scale of instances.

Suppose a world in which *gravitation* is the only force at work—a world the separate particles of which exert no more complex influence upon each other than the heavenly bodies do in their widely-divided revolutions through the sky—a world for which a rough resemblance may be found in the aspect of some desolate sea .beach, or some huge heap of débris lying at the mouth of a mine. Introduce now into this world of atoms, loosely thrown together, the force of *chemical attraction.* A remarkable agitation immediately ensues. The old places and relations of things are thoroughly disturbed by the play of the new powers.

Whatever is peculiar to chemical force stamps its distinctive character on the whole system. The old solitude and desolation is broken up into wild insurrection and revolt. A great natural leaven works within the mighty mass, and the dark and formless void cakes into solid land and cleaves into seas, ferments into mountains and steams into atmosphere, breaks into light and bursts into thunder.

Introduce, again, into the world we are supposing, the fresh element of *vital force*. Let the organific principle lay hold upon the gravitating and chemically-propertied elements, and dissolve and blend and compact them according to its own distinctive forms. The world forthwith receives a new character and aspect. Forests clothe the hills ; grasses grow along the brooks ; ferns creep out into the air in moist and shady places ; mosses wrap themselves round the stones ; seaweeds flap to and fro with the swaying waves against the bases of the headlands ; not the coming and going of the white snow only, but the coming and going of the green foliage also, serves now for a distinction between the wintry and the summery world. And these organific forces tell mechanically, as well as chemically, upon earth and water and atmosphere. They act in the capacity of natural ploughshares and aqueducts and ventilators. Results follow, therefore, in the realm of organic life, which could not have been possible under the reign of naked chemistry, just as results followed in the chemical sphere which could not have been possible under the reign of naked gravitation.

Introduce, in the next place, into the world we are imagining the element of *animal instinct*. Let beings endowed with sense and impulse, and the power of movement from place to place in response to some instigation from within, be set at large upon its surface. Thereupon nature is invested with a new character and aspect. As gravitating force was grappled with and moulded to ends outside of itself by chemical force, and as these two forces in turn were grappled with and moulded to ends outside of themselves by organic force, so all these successive forms of force are grappled with and moulded to fresh ends by the force of sentient and self-impelling life.

Introduce once more into the world before our thought the element of *human reason.* Let beings endowed with intelligence and conscience and freewill make a place for themselves in the pre-existing system of things. Straight-way the world assumes a new character and aspect, in correspondence with the new infusion of force. Perception, foresight, self-restraint, calculation of the use and value of existing forces, employment of these for the production of fresh effects, the pictorial power and constructive power of the imagination, the faculty of distinguishing between true and false, right and wrong, beautiful and ugly, bene-ficial and harmful, transient and permanent—a group of powers such as these, placed under the control of a single will, must necessarily effect a marvellous transformation upon the face of nature. The existing life, whether sentient or non-sentient, becomes but the handmaid of this higher life that has broken into the midst of it. Forests are cleared ; mountains are mapped off into sheep-walks or shooting-grounds; valleys are cultivated; oceans are navigated; rivers are spanned with bridges, swept with dredging-machines, strained through fishing-nets; lands are honeycombed with mines and tunnels, and scored with roads and railways and telegraphic systems. The new force of free intellectual and moral life, playing in among the pre-existing system of forces, checks or extends, neutralises or amplifies the action of these in ways that were otherwise unprovided for and impossible.

Let me then make one more supposition. Introduce into the world under view the play of some superior power, pro-ducing results which transcend the operation of the whole catalogue of forces already enumerated, from that of gravi-tation up to that of the human will, and those results are what we call *miraculous.* He who called into existence, whether successively or in one grand moment of originating power, the gravitating force, the chemical force, the vital force of the vegetable, the sentient and instinctive force of

the animal, the intellect, conscience, and will of the man,
can carry on His interfering agency to any extent, either
by the introduction of still higher intelligences and energies,
or by the forthputting of His own undelegated might among
the complicated system of existing things. There is no
region within the range of the universe at which it could
be reasonably said to the advancing tide of the Divine
omnipotence, " Hitherto shalt thou come, but no further ;
and here shall thy proud waves be stayed." There can be
no partition wall between the power of God and any
imaginable amount of Divine intervention, except the saving
clause of some Divine promise of non-intervention. But
who can quote any such saving clause ? Who can point to
any charter in which the King of kings renounces His prerogative of playing in among the powers of nature in
whatever ways and for whatever purposes may please Him ?
The very existence of a personal God implies the possibility of the miracle.

The dogma of the absolute immutability of the laws of
nature, with its two corollaries of the correlation of forces
and the conservation of energy, is the favourite watchword
of the physical science of the day. It is true that the laws
of nature, when left to their characteristic play, as they
virtually are, by Him who has established them, are immutable. And it is true that the men of science have
shown the validity of the doctrines of the correlation of
forces and the conservation of energy in certain important
spheres of physical research. But the allegation that the
laws of nature are not subject to the government of God,
or that their action cannot be to any extent interrupted
or added to by Him, is an unscientific assumption. What
God begins He can equally augment, or interrupt, or end.
What God establishes He can disestablish, whether with
or without compensation for the loss sustained by the
surviving system of things. To affirm the absolute immutability of any laws except those moral and spiritual
laws which are the very transcript and exposition of the
character of God, and for the unchangeableness of which

we have at once His own pledged word and the deepest
intuitions of our nature, is to rob Him of His royal prerogative, and depose Him from the throne of the universe.
God has not made the laws of nature independent of Himself.   He does not abrogate His eternal power and Godhead
on their behalf.   Only on the ground that God is nature
and nature God—that is, on the ground that there is no
God at all—can we affirm the absolute immutability of the
laws of nature, and deny the possibility of a miracle.

II.—*God's moral government of the world implies the
probability of the miracle.*   It may be urged that, though a
miracle is not beyond the sweep of the Divine omnipotence,
it is inconsistent with the idea of the Divine wisdom.
While the possibility of it is not challenged, its propriety,
its conformity to any good purpose, its compatibility with
a system of things emanating from a Being of perfect
prescience and perfect might, is called in question.   The
laws of nature, if not absolutely immutable, it is urged,
must be morally immutable, as being the expression of the
will of Him who is without variableness or shadow of
turning.

This criticism may be most effectually dealt with by
being counter-criticised.

1. In the first place, then, there is a fallacy involved in
the statement that the laws of nature are the expression
of the will of God.   The laws of nature, as we employ the
phrase, are not the expression of the will of God ; they are
only our own account of the way in which the will of God
expresses itself.   They are, in the last resort, but human
generalisations.   They are the *ex cathedrâ* utterances of a
mind that at its best is not infallible.   They are the ultimate
deliverances of a never-exhaustive analysis of natural phenomena.   There is a chasm, which can never be crossed from
the human side, between the counsel of the Creator and the
works and workings of His hands.

2. In the next place, it is illegitimate to argue from the
unchangeableness of the Divine mind to the unchangeableness of the attitude and action of that mind.   Unchange-

ableness of mind is one thing; unchangeableness of
attitude and action is altogether another thing. It may be
the very unchangeableness of a man's mind which is the
cause of the incessant variation of the modes in which he
gives expression to his mind. A general enters the field of
battle with the unchangeable purpose of gaining the victory.
Yet on that very ground he changes his tactics with every
new vicissitude in the events of the day; and it is by the
promptitude, variety, and soundness of his successive evolu-
tions that he drives back the enemy, and bears away the
palm of triumph. A shipmaster puts to sea with the
unchangeable purpose of weathering the storm and gaining
the haven. Yet on the very ground of the fixity of his
purpose he flings forth orders, hot and frequent, to the
mariners with every fresh change in the relations of ship
and atmosphere and ocean; and it is by the variety and
promptitude and timeliness of these particular forthflashings
of his will that he snatches his craft out of the white teeth
of the tumbling billows, and carves for himself an avenue
through the tangled wilderness of wind and wave, and
reaches the port in peace.

Now what holds good of man holds good of God, if we
superadd these three considerations—(1.) That God foresees
and pre-arranges from the beginning every change of
attitude and action to which He may see good to resort in
the course of the world's history; (2.) That whenever the
power of God is put forth afresh among the forces of nature,
it is not to supplement the imperfection, but to secure the
perfection of His work; and (3.) That God infallibly accomplishes everything at which He aims.

And the combined force of these three considerations is
amply sufficient to establish the probability of the miracle
as an engine in the moral government of the world. For
consider the motive of the miracle. The miracle is for
man, and for man alone. There must be a man to
behold, as well as a God to do, in order that there may
be a miracle. Now it is obvious that moral impressions
could be produced upon the mind of man by direct inter-

ventions of Divine power, which could not be produced by
an everlastingly unbroken routine of natural laws and
processes.   These interventions, for one thing, would tend
to withdraw man from the danger of offering that homage
to nature which is due to God.   A world so constructed
that the example and expectation of supernatural power
were totally excluded could scarcely escape becoming
hopelessly godless and immoral.   The miracle, rightly
interpreted, is like the tender tone of the voice and touch
of the finger by which friend endears himself to friend.   It
tells us God is near.   It teaches us, by rare and transient
glimpses of His glory, that His glory is always hovering
around.   It is the flash of His eye bent full upon us for one
brief moment to bespeak the perpetual remembrance of His
presence and His sympathy.

We conclude, therefore, that the moral government of
the world by God establishes the antecedent likelihood of
the miracle.   Granted that God retains any connection with
and superintendence over the world He has created—
granted that God has left Himself as free to deal with the
forces of nature as He has left man free to deal with these
—granted that God is disposed in any measure to control
and educate the intellectual and moral nature of the
crowning work of His hands—granted that He is in anywise
sympathetic with the need and responsive to the faith of
His creature—granted that man is to have any assurance
or aspiration beyond the barrier lines of time and sense—
granted that there is an unseen and eternal world casting
its great shadow athwart the world that is seen and
temporal, and that across the chasm dividing those two
worlds there is to be any interchange whatever of thought
or influence, and the probability of miraculous intervention
is established.

III.—*God's redemptive interference on behalf of a fallen
world implies the necessity of the miracle.*   The circumstance that the human family has involved itself in the coils
of sin beyond all power of self-extrication opens up the
solemn question—Will God interfere or not to provide for

man that way of escape from ruin and doom which the laws of his own being and the laws of surrounding nature alike refuse to provide? To answer that question in the affirmative is to assert the necessity of the miracle. For any such interference must be, by the very nature of the case, miraculous. It must include superhuman appeals to the human understanding, and superhuman appliances to the human heart. For salvation, according to the only religious system that declares the necessity and unfolds the method of a redemptive interference—I mean that expounded in the Bible—involves two principal results, a change of state and a change of nature—a change of state, consisting in the forgiveness of sin and reconciliation with God; and a change of nature, consisting in the sanctification of the soul, and its assimilation to the image of God. God therefore must manifest Himself in some supernatural way to the soul which He would save by a plan of forgiveness and reconciliation, and by a method of sanctification and moral ennoblement. Jesus Christ is this supernatural manifestation of God. We pass over the long series of Divine manifestations by which God maintained faith and hope and piety in the family of man in the interval between the fall and the Advent; and we fix our eyes upon the Birth, Life, Death, and Resurrection of the Son of God as the grand miraculous epoch in the spiritual history of the world. To this all that went before points forward, and to this all that came after points back. Mark what takes place. A man miraculously born appears upon the scene. He is immaculate by the miracle of His birth. In Him is Divine everlasting life, derived from the Divine everlasting Fountainhead. He invites all who will to join and follow Him, and promises them deliverance. Those who accept His invitation are by their faith made mystically one with Him. As it fares with Him, therefore, so shall it fare with them. And how, then, does it fare with Him and them? This man of God's right hand, though "holy, harmless, undefiled, and separate from sinners," lays down His life, as if He were a sinner, paying the penalty of his sin; and all who

are mystically one with Him lay down their lives along with
Him.   This man of God's right hand takes up his life again,
because it is Divine everlasting life; and all who are
mystically one with Him take up their lives along with
Him.   The Divine expedient, then, is briefly this—that the
transgressor pays his penalty in the death of the Divine
man, and in the resurrection of the Divine man receives
everlasting life.

The Advent of the Son of God in the form and nature of
man is, therefore, the grand miracle of all time.   And in the
Advent in turn there are two miraculous occurrences which
infold in themselves all that go before or follow after—
His Incarnation, or the act by which He entered into our
earthly life; and His Resurrection, or the act by which He
passed away from it.   I do not say that the supernatural
does not run along the whole course of His life, from the
cradle to the cross.   I do not say that the mysterious
moment in which each penitent and contrite heart is joined
to Jesus Christ, by faith in His person and work, is not the
occasion of a direct interposition of Divine power.   What I
do say is that the two conspicuous forthputtings of Divine
power, round which the whole supernatural system involved
in redemption circulates, are the Incarnation and Resurrection of the Redeemer.

As to the chain of minor miracles which signalised the
life of Christ and His apostles, all that has been already
said as to the bearing of the miracles upon the moral
government of the world comes into play.   No one was
witness of the Incarnation.   No one was witness of the
Resurrection.   Only a few hundreds were permitted to
behold the form of the risen Lord.   But it was necessary
that a whole world should sooner or later become convinced that Jesus of Nazareth was the Christ, the Son of
the living God.   Herein we find an ample justification of
the chain of minor miracles recorded in the Gospels and
the Acts of the Apostles.   The evidential force of a con-
secutive series of supernatural works, countless in number,
infinitely varied in character, situation, and surrounding

circumstance, performed not only by the Master in His own person, but also in His name by those to whom He had entrusted the splendid prerogative, was irresistible in the minds of the first followers of the cross, and sufficient to inspire them with an enthusiasm of personal conviction and missionary zeal, such as should render the employment of the miracle largely, if not entirely, unnecessary in all the subsequent campaigns of the Christian Church.

As to the character of the minor miracles, they are in strict accordance with the remedial system of which they are the proofs. Otherwise, indeed, they would be disproofs instead of proofs. They are all, virtually without exception, in the form of rescues, reliefs, restorations. They furnish a standing symbol and exposition in the material sphere of what the Saviour was prepared to do in the spiritual sphere. Their office was subsidiary, not principal. They were but physical means pointing towards spiritual ends. They were thrown down into the field of sense as the humble, though wonderful, endorsement of that Divine truth by which the world was to be redeemed. They were the grand Amen of the God of nature to the glorious proposals of the God of grace. They pointed with patient and undeviating finger to the doctrine of the cross. They were flashing chains flung round the neck of the new truth, compelling men to examine and admire the figure that bore so fair an ornament ; but let the new truth once take its proper place, and make its proper mark, in the mind of the world, and all that brilliant jewellery may be laid aside as needless and embarrassing.

Let me endeavour to illustrate the principles laid down in a somewhat abstract form in the course of the preceding discussion, by a brief analysis of two memorable incidents in the life of Christ—the miracle of the marriage feast, and the three water miracles on the lake of Gennesaret.

Of the miracle of the *marriage feast* it is recorded by the Evangelist :—" This beginning of miracles did Jesus in Cana of Galilee, and manifested forth His glory ; and His disciples believed on Him." We learn from this signifi-

cant statement that there is a twofold effect of the miracle
in the Christian system, a *personal* and a *propagandist:*
it shows forth the glory of the worker, and it calls forth
the faith of the beholder.

The first effect is to show forth the glory of the worker.
And the worker is always God. He who does a miracle in
His own name proves that He is Divine. He who does a
miracle in the name of Christ proves that Christ is Divine.
He who does a miracle in the name of God proves that he is
a messenger and representative of God. The disciples did
every deed of superhuman might in the name of the Lord
Jesus Christ. If, again, the Lord Jesus Christ did deeds of
superhuman might indifferently in His own or in His
Father's name, it was because He and His Father were
one. A miracle is always a work of God; it is a fresh
forthputting of Divine power, through whatever agency it
may be wrought; it is therefore a manifestation of the
glory of the Most High. The statement that Christ, by
the miracle of Cana, manifested forth His glory, implies
that the Divine might which already resided in Him now
for the first time burst into view. His glory He had with
the Father before the world was; but from this point
forward, coruscations of the glory were to be flashed forth
incessantly in the Divine deeds He was about to perform in
the field of sense in attestation of His mission.   Before
this "beginning of miracles" the assembled guests regarded
Him as no more than an ordinary man.   There was nothing
in His conversation or deportment that materially distinguished Him from the vast miscellaneous human family
to which He belonged. He spoke wise words, no doubt,
with soft and winning voice; and the kindly deeds which
it was His custom to do found a faithful reflex in His
benignant countenance. But any other man might have
been all that He appeared to be, so far as the bridal company could judge. The glory was for so far hidden from
their view. It had found as yet no exit in speech or deed,
in glance of the eye or gesture of the body. But now His
hour is come. He bids the firkins be filled with water.

That done, He bids the fluid be drawn forth and borne to the governor of the feast. And lo! the fluid that went in water—colourless, odourless, tasteless water—comes out wine. How the transformation was effected, it is bootless to inquire. Numberless incursions may be made into the outskirts of the mystery; but the heart of the mystery, like the heart of the mystery of matter, or the heart of the mystery of life, or the heart of the mystery of the human spirit, remains a sacred shrine, unviolated by footfall or voice of man, possessed by the lone and awful glory of God. How the transubstantiation was brought about, the wedding guests could not imagine; of one thing only they were assured that a Divine power had been put forth to effect the astonishing result, and put forth by Him who bade the waterpots be filled. Through the tones and gestures of that wonderful man, as through windows in the walls of an illuminated temple, streamed forth upon every eye the unspeakable glory of God.

Accordingly, the second effect of the miracle is to call forth the faith of the beholder. "His disciples believed on Him." He was invested with an entirely new character in their eyes. Although the moment after the miracle He was the same in appearance and speech as the moment before, yet by that intervening event a dividing line has been withdrawn, enabling them to gaze into inexhaustible depths of excellency in the person of the Man of Nazareth. He that has done this single supernatural thing, they reflect, must be equally able to do a thousand supernatural things. Supreme wisdom and power and goodness must be His native prerogative. In a word, He must be Divine.

Thus the miracle has performed its twofold function: it has opened the eyes of the pious-minded to the personal glory of Emmanuel; it has demonstrated His Divineness by a momentary work of wonder, that His disciples might evermore remember Him to be Divine, although in the prosecution of His vicarious work He should need to submit to all the wearinesses of our frail flesh, wound up by the crowning ignominy of death. "He must be one," they will

ever afterwards be able to say, "who has entered the world
by some grand portal of His own—one who, in some mysterious region of His nature, is a stranger to human gene-
alogies and inheritances—one who is allied by some ineffable
bond to the eternal King—one who, in all that is deepest in
His being, is to be classified with God, and not with man."
Such must have been the spontaneous testimony of any spec-
tator of the miracles which Christ did, whose intelligence and
conscience had not been hopelessly distorted by the power
of sin-born prejudice.   The exclamation of Nicodemus puts
in the most moderate and cautious form the conviction
which all proper apprehension of Christ's mighty works was
fitted to create :—"Rabbi, we know that Thou art a teacher
come from God : for no man can do these miracles that
Thou doest, except God be with him."

The other incident in the life of our Lord to which I
desire to allude is the triple water miracle on the sea of
Galilee.   I choose this illustration as suggesting an analysis
of the *physics* as well as the *ethics* of the miracle.   "In the
fourth watch of the night," when the disciples had battled
long with wind and wave, "Jesus went unto them, walking
on the sea."   To Peter He gave power, in proportion to his
faith, to use the waves in the same lordly way as He Himself was doing.   As to the crew in general, He made the
moment of His entrance into the ship the moment also of
the stilling of the storm.

A word or two on each of these miraculous results.

Christ works the first miracle upon His own person.   The
swift-running waves are framed into a firm causeway
beneath His feet; and he stands erect upon the tide as upon
an undulating pavement.   There are only two other analogous miracles wrought by Christ upon His own person—
the Transfiguration, and the Ascension, including that chain
of mysterious visits and vanishings which led up to the final
act of the Ascension.   The miracle before us may be said
to be a stepping-stone to that of the Transfiguration, as that
of the Transfiguration is to that of the Ascension.   In the
first case His body treads the water, in the next the air, and

in the last the infinitely attenuated ether that fills all space.

Was the miraculous result then due, in the present instance, to an etherealisation of the body of our Lord, by means of which it pressed upon the water with no more weight than a column of superincumbent air? Or was it due to a consolidation of the water underneath, by which the pavemented wave presented a firm resistance to His feet? It is not necessary to suppose any change in the substance or in the properties either of the body above or of the water beneath. The force of gravitation acts as resolutely as ever. The inherent tendency of that material frame to sink through the bruised billows is as strong as ever. And why then does not the sinking follow? Is it not enough to suppose that a force, sufficient to neutralise the downward force of gravitation in the body of our Lord, was exerted in the upward and opposite direction by the immediate power of God? Whether nature was paid back in some other quarter for the fresh infusion of force in this quarter, is a question which is most wisely left in the hands of the Most Wise. Scientists, in the dreadful picture they are prone to draw of the consequences of a single hitch in the machinery, or lurch in the movement, of the physical system of things, make no proper allowance for the elasticity and self-adjusting power of nature. It is not likely that God's will, playing in among the physical forces of the world, will work more mischief or confusion than man's will would. Yet nature is not put out of countenance by man's ingenuity and energy, even when these are directed to the most perverse ends. There is nothing difficult, then, in the idea that a drawing up by invisible hands above, or a holding up by invisible hands below, whether attended or unattended by some equivalent compensation to nature for the local and temporary check upon her processes, may sufficiently account for the miracle of walking on the waves.

Pass now to the next miracle. Our Lord put forth on Peter's body in the second instance the power which in the first instance He had put forth upon His own. But here a

B

new element comes into play. The power put forth upon
His own person infallibly secured the end in view, but that
put forth on Peter's was expressly made contingent on the
faith of Peter.   Peter had said, "Lord, if it be Thou, bid
me come unto Thee on the water."   And He said, "Come."
That "come" carried with it the necessary support, on
condition of the necessary faith.   Let Peter but believe
that this is the very Lord Himself, and that He is prepared
to sustain him upon the sapphire pavement of the wave,
and the disciple will walk as well as his Master on the sea.
But let Peter lose faith in that mysterious Being that stands
upon the lake in his near neighbourhood, and the nexus
between his spirit and the spirit of Christ is so far sundered,
and the sustaining strength withdrawn, and the unem-
barrassed powers of nature return to their inexorable work.
Christ could have kept the man from sinking, apart from
his own will, if He had chosen.   But He did not choose to
do so.   He meant that the hazardous experiment should
be a trial of his faith.   Jesus never idly played with the
laws of nature.   He never interfered with the action of any
physical force except for some spiritual end.   He meant
that Peter and all the crew should gain a lesson in faith
which they should never lose.   Peter then adventured into
the deep, relying on the word of the Lord ; but, distracted
by the terror of the storm, he lost sight of his Refuge and
Strength ; and, losing sight of his Refuge and Strength, he
began to sink, and sinking, he was forced violently backward into his fast-vanishing faith in Christ, and cried,
"Lord, save me ; I perish ;" and so crying, he was caught
up by that watchful hand, and lifted into the ship.

Let us glance next at the third miracle in the group.
"When they were come into the ship, the wind ceased."
There is no violation of the laws of nature in this, any more
than in the other instances.   Every force acts in its accustomed way.   When a storm rages, certain natural causes
are at work producing the result.   When those causes are
withdrawn from the field, nature returns to its more
tranquil and equable course, and the storm becomes a calm.

The causes do not cease to be causes ; they do not cease to be operating causes ; they have only disappeared from the field. They may have resolved themselves into other forms of force, or they may have been transferred in their original form to some new geographical area. But is there not a third event that might befall them, besides being resolved into other forms, or transferred to other regions ? May they not be more or less suddenly met in mid-career by other forces equal and opposite to them, freshly launched from the hand of God ? In that case, the very same effect will be produced in the world of sense as if they were transformed in quality or transferred in situation. The Divine Hand does not by such a course infringe in the least degree upon the laws of nature, but only substitutes a supernatural counteractive force, at the time required, for the natural counteractive force that would otherwise follow at some later time. Determine the point at which, and the manner in which, and the extent to which one force works upon another ; and, I ask, cannot the Divine finger, by a sublime substitution, be applied at the point in question in the very same manner and degree ? A group of forces are at work in the atmosphere above Gennesaret, producing the boisterous wind. God meets those forces with counter-forces that interrupt their action, and there is a calm in the atmosphere. But the sea still rocks and surges underneath. God meets the forces that are at work in the water with counter-forces that arrest their action, and there is calm upon the deep.

But mark here also the spiritual end which our Saviour had in view. It is unfolded in the conduct of the crew. They that were in the ship came and worshipped Him, saying, " Of a truth, Thou art the Son of God." They had seen Christ walking on the wave, and that had so powerfully affected them that they exclaimed in terror, " It is a spirit." They had seen Peter stumblingly imitating Christ, and that must have added to their wonder and awe. But when the roaring hurricane is hushed, and summer wavelets gently lap the sides of the weather-beaten craft, and the smooth pebbles and brown bands of seaweed are seen through the crystal waters of the lake, they are filled with conviction, and say enthusiastically, " Of a truth, Thou art the Son of God ! " In order to draw that acknowledgment forth—in order to burn the belief that lay behind it deep into the hearts of the disciples—Christ completed the splendid chain of miracles of that night upon the waters, by the lulling of wind and wave to rest.

The miracles of the Gospels, then, viewed in the light of incidents such as these, are seen to be at once benefits, symbols, and evidences. First, and most simply, they are *benefits*, or fruits of the Divine compassion. In the next place, they are *symbols*, accomplishing in the material sphere, and on the mortal bodies of men, what Christ was prepared to accomplish in the spiritual sphere, and on their immortal souls. Finally, they are *evidences*, proving, by irresistible inference, first, the claim of the miracle-worker to be "a teacher come from God ;" and second, the truth of what He teaches. To those who complain that the miracle is not continued still in the Christian Church for the fixing and strengthening of human faith, it is enough to answer that we have all that made the miracle valuable and efficacious. We have the Bible, the miraculous heir-loom of the old inspiration. We have the Sabbath-day, the standing record of the miracle of the Resurrection. We have Baptism and the Lord's Supper, sacred projections along the centuries of the Christian era of two grand epochs in the miraculous life of Christ. But, above all, we have Jesus Christ Himself. Christ, in His person and character, is indeed the great world-miracle, about which all the minor miracles play like scintillations round a central fire, associated with which their reasonableness is morally demonstrated, divorced from which they melt into unmeaningness. With Jesus Christ, born and risen, they stand and fall, even as with Him stand and fall also all human faith and hope and piety and peace.

II.—THE PROPHECY.

"The Lord thy God will raise up unto thee a Prophet from the midst of thee, of thy brethren, like unto me ; unto Him ye shall hearken." Such are the words with which Moses, in the midst of his great farewell discourse, encourages the children of Israel. And the children of Israel, all along the line of their subsequent history, regarded these words as an authoritative promise of Messiah ; and to the hope which that promise inspired they clung with a terrible tenacity through their darkest days of corruption and captivity. It was a sort of spiritual star, leading them on by many winding ways to the manger of Bethlehem. In the light of that high hope the mother-love of Israel went forth in deep, mysterious yearnings towards the cradle of Emmanuel.

Long before Moses had given a characteristic shape to the great world-hope, indeed, it had exercised its fascinating sway over the minds of men. Adam himself had caught hold of it in the form of the "seed of the woman," bruised, but victorious. Noah had caught hold of it when God made with him and with his seed "an everlasting covenant." Abraham had caught hold of it, when God guaranteed to the childless old man that in him and in his seed, nevertheless, should "all families of the earth be blessed." And Abraham passed on the hope to Isaac, and Isaac to Jacob, and Jacob to the fathers of the twelve tribes. And now, in turn, Moses comes forward to record that hope ; and with all the mingled authority and pathos with which last words are invested, he speaks of a Prophet, like unto himself, unto whom the people should be constrained to hearken.

And when Christ came at last, we find all classes of His contemporaries coming forward to endorse the truth of that interpretation which the piety and hope of so many centuries had put upon the words of Moses. "Philip findeth Nathanael," in the exciting days of our Lord's first public introduction to the world, "and saith unto him, We

have found Him, of whom Moses in the law, and the prophets,
did write." On the occasion of the banquetting of the five
thousand on the green-sward of Gennesaret, the people
cried out, under the stimulus of that stupendous miracle,
" This is of a truth that Prophet that should come into the
world." After the Master had passed away, Peter stood
forth in Solomon's porch, and preached of Jesus Christ,
" Moses truly said unto the fathers, A prophet shall the
Lord your God raise up unto you of your brethren, like
unto me ; Him shall ye hear in all things whatsoever He
shall say unto you." Stephen, uplifting upon his murderers
a face like the face of an angel, made application of Moses'
words to the man of Nazareth, " This is that Moses, which
said unto the children of Israel, A prophet shall the Lord
your God raise up unto you of your brethren, like unto
me ; Him shall ye hear." Nay, before either of these
had learned the language of the cross, Moses himself
had come mysteriously forward in company with Elias,
in that Transfiguration scene for the account of which
we are probably indebted to Peter himself, and spoken
of His "decease, which He should accomplish at Jerusalem."

It is unquestionable, then, that the Prophet, whose advent
was announced by Moses, was understood to be none other
than Messiah Himself. It will be of importance, therefore,
to show that the words, "a prophet like unto me," were appropriate in the mouth of Moses in a way in which they could
not have been appropriate in the mouth of any other man.
It is recorded in the concluding chapter of the book of
Deuteronomy, by way of epitaph upon the mighty dead, that
'' there arose not a prophet since in Israel like unto Moses,
whom the Lord knew face to face." Moses, in his standing
in the kingdom of God, and most probably in his personal
character too, is the sublimest figure on the stage of human
history, He alone being excepted whose shoe-latchet the
great lawgiver, in common with the humblest child of God,
was unworthy to unloose. Let me proceed briefly to show
that he was not only a prophet, but the prophet of prophets;

that there was no prophet like him among men ; and that, in a deep and real sense, he alone among men was like that greater Prophet who was to come.

What, then, is a prophet ? A prophet is one who bears a message from God to man. It matters not whether the message refers to the past, the present, or the future; if it be a burden brought down from the Most High, the bearer of the burden is a prophet. It is not the nature of the announcement, but the source of the announcement, that brackets it under the head of prophecy.

All revelation then, it appears, is of the nature of prophecy; and all men who have taken part in revelation belong to the class of prophets. We cannot attempt to enumerate the men whom God has raised up from the beginning of time, to be the depositarians and expounders of His messages to men. If the "goodly fellowship of the prophets" could be gathered together out of all lands and ages, many a strange figure would rise up by the side of Moses and Isaiah and John the Baptist ; many a new name would become familiar in men's mouths ; many a fresh character would be furnished for the reverent or ruthless analysis of our modern criticism. God has doubtless spoken to the fathers, by the prophets, "at sundry times and in divers manners," of which no record has come down to these lower generations. Only those members of the august fraternity, whose messages marked some epoch in the history of the Church or of the world, still live in the memories and mouths of men. The rest have been swept into the circle of some subsequent revelation, and vanished from our view. How many of these old fragments of prophecy may have fallen under the eye of Moses, as he penned the book of Genesis, we cannot surmise. God could, no doubt, have given him the whole story fresh from His own lips, if He had chosen ; but the mode in which the story is told irresistibly suggests the conclusion that the writer has embodied and embalmed in his narrative old messages from the antediluvian and patriarchal ages, and has worked them up, under fresh breathings of the Spirit, into that wonderful

book of the beginnings of things, which stands as vestibule
to the entire temple of revelation.

But however the first book of the Bible may have risen
into form in the mind of Moses, the narrative from the
beginning of Exodus to the end of Deuteronomy, with the
exception of a chapter or so at either extremity, is the
record of the personal exploits and experiences of the great
deliverer himself. The Pentateuch, therefore, is virtually
the prophecy of Moses. And what a message from the
Most High do these five books contain! It is true that
history, psalmody, proverbial philosophy, prediction, are to
follow, filling up the interval between Moses and Christ ;
but the total mass of revelation embodied in these is little
more than the elucidation and enforcement of the ordinances
of the Pentateuch. In that intermediate chasm no pinnacle
springs up into the air to the level of the summit either of
Sinai or of Calvary. Take your station in the gorge
between these two mystic mountain heights, and you will
find many secondary ranges, running parallel, or thrown
down athwart ; but take your station on the top of Sinai,
and towering over all you see the top of Calvary ; or take
your station on the top of Calvary, and towering over all
you see the top of Sinai.

Let me seek to substantiate these statements. What
then, in brief, is the burden of the revelation made to man
through Moses? It is based upon three great facts, each
one of which is stationed in the very forefront of the prophecy—the fact that man was originally upright ; the fact
that he is now fallen ; and the fact that he is still salvable.
The garden of Eden, the flaming sword of the angel, the
promise that the seed of the woman should bruise the serpent's head—these are the three foundation-stones on which
the whole structure of revelation rests. Thus on the very
first cloud that stained the horizon of human history is
planted the rainbow of promise and hope.

The salvation thus shadowed forth, however, is still in the
far future. And what, meanwhile, is man to do? Is he to
dream away the long millennial day between the promise

and accomplishment in wistful wonderings and longings?
Or is he to defile it with foul continuations of the original
offence?   No : he has a work to do, and to do as diligently
as though upon the doing of that work depended his entire
salvation.   That work consisted of two departments—
*obedience to the moral law, and the offering up of sacrifice
for sin.*   Both these departments of the work of God
date from the very spring of human history.   The first-born
son of Adam, neglecting the one part, and thereby vitiating
the other part, rose up in a fit of ungovernable spleen, and
slew the second-born, who, though performing both parts
rightly, had brought upon himself the blessing of God.
Noah obeyed and offered sacrifice in his own earnest yet
imperfect way, amidst an utterly demoralised society—a
society which, even after it had been swept away by the
flood, left the traces of its baleful influence in the old patri-
arch's deed of intemperance, and in the mockery of Ham
and curse of Canaan.   Abraham was called out of the
freshly accumulating gloom to begin anew the work of God ;
and he obeyed and offered sacrifice with a trust so simple
and unswerving, that he was dignified with the title of the
" friend of God."   And so the double work of obedience and
oblation was handed down as an heirloom from father to
son, till the day when Moses asked leave from Pharaoh to
take Israel out a three days' journey into the wilderness, to
sacrifice to the Lord their God.

     But now that Moses appears upon the scene the work is
to be put upon a more definite and settled basis than before.
The law regulating conduct is given in the form of the ten
commandments, and the law regulating sacrifice is given
in the form of the tabernacle service.   The moral code and
the propitiatory system of Moses lift up into themselves all
the rules of conduct and sacrificial customs that had hitherto
found place among the people of God, and fill them with
fresh significance.   And these remained precisely as Moses
left them, till they were gathered up in turn into that greater
dispensation, to which, like finger-posts, they pointed forward
along the labouring centuries.

For through these very two things of which I have been
speaking, obedience and oblation, the salvation of man was
to be achieved. A perfect obedience was the Divine event
to which all these isolated acts of imperfect obedience were
tending. An efficacious sacrifice was the Divine event of
which all these ineffectual slaughterings of bulls and goats
were the foreshadowings. Although the obedience which
men were able to render, and the oblation which they were
able to make, could not bring salvation, they were in the
providential line of that which was to bring salvation. After
the innumerable failures there was to be a grand success,
both of obedience rendered, and of propitiation made.
Jesus Christ was to do perfectly that double work of God
which all men of God had been more or less successfully
striving to do from the beginning of time. He was to render
the great obedience, and make the great oblation, that
should bring salvation into the world.

Now Moses had already sketched the scheme of salvation,
in all its leading elements, in the ordinances which he brought
down with him from Sinai. The tabernacle—its various com-
partments and articles of furniture—the ark of the covenant,
containing the tables of stone, and covered by the mercy-
seat with its shadowing cherubim—the table of shew-bread,
and the branching candlestick—the brazen altar, smoking
with slaughtered victims ; and the golden altar, sending up
columns of white incense towards heaven—the unapproach-
able glory, and the dividing veil—the series of feasts, and
the series of offerings—the lustrations, the unctions, the
consecrations by sprinkling of sacrificial blood—all these
told forth more and more of their mystic meaning as the
ages passed, till at last they flashed out into full realisation
in the substitutionary life and death of our Lord, and found
their exegesis for all coming time in the graphic and beautiful epistle to the Hebrews.

It appears, therefore, that the plan of salvation which
God devised from the beginning was fully formulated by
Moses, and fully accomplished fifteen hundred years after-
wards by Christ. Enough has been said to substantiate the

twofold affirmation that none of all the prophets was like
Moses, and that Moses alone of all the prophets was like
Messiah. Moses wrought out a national emancipation,
which was itself a striking type of the spiritual deliverance
wrought out by Emmanuel. Moses founded a dispensation
in the kingdom of God, which was the preparation for the
dispensation founded by Emmanuel. Moses uttered the
most stupendous and adventurous prophecy of Christ the
world has ever listened to—that involved in the ceremonial
system of the wilderness. Moses brought down from
heaven in the form of perfect precept that which Christ
sent up to heaven in the form of perfect obedience. Moses
beheld "the similitude of God." God spoke with him,
"mouth to mouth, even apparently, and not in dark
speeches." He was the standing representative of God
from the day when he met with Him at the burning bush
to the day when he passed back to Him from the peak of
Nebo. His prophecy formed the text of which all other
prophecies were but so many fragmentary expositions.
Not only Micah and Malachi, but Isaiah and Jeremiah, were
minor prophets in this grand comparison. They did little
more than catch up the detached parts of his great prophecy,
and give them forth in novel forms to the new generations.
They succeeded at the best in scattering somewhat of the
haze that hung about the figure of the Prophet towards
whom the sin-laden centuries were hastening, and in
clothing Him beforehand in some of His most significant
attributes and fortunes. Isaiah's imagination of the man
who was "wounded for our transgressions, and bruised for
our iniquities," or Daniel's divination of the day when Messiah
should be "cut off, but not for Himself," and should "cause
the sacrifice and the oblation to cease," and "finish the transgression, and "make an end of sins," and "make reconciliation for iniquity," and "bring in everlasting righteousness,"
and "seal up the vision and prophecy"—what were these, or
whatever other delineations like these may be gathered
out of the songs of the prophets, but the piecing together
of the various parts of the sacrificial system instituted

under the shadow of Mount Sinai, and their application to the person of that Prophet whom God was to "raise up like unto" Moses.

At the same time, there was a more or less continuous chain of prophets connecting the testimony of Moses with the Advent of Messiah. It was the business of these to explain the spirit of the ceremonial system, to show the subordination of all ritual observance to spirituality of mind and morality of life, and to bring out into more and more vivid relief the lineaments of that all-glorious Person, in whom a perfect obedience was rendered, and a perfect propitiation made.

Before individualising the prophets, however, it may be well to refer to some of their common characteristics.

1. *The first characteristic of the Old Testament prophecy is, that it points away onward to a larger and happier day than any that had yet dawned upon the world.* This pathos of prophecy can perhaps nowhere be more fittingly illustrated than by the language of Moses himself, "Unto Him shall ye hearken." "Against me ye have been murmuring my whole life through : but in that kindlier time when the Prophet like unto me shall arise, ye shall be moved to awe and to obedience." But passing Moses, all the prophetic messages, however dark and terrible in their import, are illuminated by glorious plays of light flung down upon them from some distant dawn, to which, with unfaltering finger, they point forward through the gloom.

2. *Another characteristic of the Old Testament prophecy is, that it continually clashes with the spirit of the age in which it is uttered.* The catholicity of the prophets contrasts with the narrow-mindedness of the nation. The Israelites believed themselves not only to have a first charge upon the grace of heaven and covenant promises of God, but to be also the residuary legatees of these. The prophets, on the other hand, uniformly spoke of a world-wide Gospel of salvation, and a universal gathering of the nations within the bonds of the everlasting covenant. Again, the spirituality of the prophets contrasts with the carnal-mindedness of the nation.

Israel was evermore going forth after fresh idolatries and immoralities. Doubtless, there was always among them a residue of godly-minded and right-living men. We are aware, however, that even the best specimens of any given generation of men will not rise strikingly high above the general level of religion and morality. Men mount up into pinnacles of good, or sink back into abysses of evil, in masses, and not by isolated efforts of the individual. Yet even in the darkest days of Israel's apostasy arose the prophets, sometimes in sublime solitariness, sometimes in groups of two or three, addressing the degenerate mass of men in burning words of rebuke or admonition, and proving their sincerity by lives in the main in harmony with their message, and at all points at variance with the thought and feeling of the time.

3. *The prophets invariably approach their task with a deep sense of responsibility, amounting often to reluctance, or even to anguish of spirit.* The message they had to deliver sometimes crossed their own prejudices as much as those of the people they addressed. Moses shrinks from his mission, and can scarcely be persuaded to assume the leadership of the Israelitish host. Jonah writhes and strains like a dog upon the leash to escape from Nineveh. But even when the will of the prophet was entirely subdued to the will of God, the character of his message was such as to fill him with painful misgivings. It must have been trying in the highest degree to Nathan to announce to David, " Thou art the man !" and to Gad to give the king the ghastly choice between famine, war, and pestilence. Right well did Michaiah, the son of Imlah, know that bread of affliction, and water of affliction, would be the reward of his unwelcome disclosure to a monarch who had already said, " I hate him ; for he doth not prophecy good con-cerning me, but evil." Isaiah begins his great prophecy, " Hear, O heavens, and give ear, O earth : for the Lord hath spoken, I have nourished and brought up children, and they have rebelled against me." Jeremiah testifies, "As for me, I have not hastened from being a pastor to follow Thee ;

neither have I desired the woeful day, Thou knowest."
A roll of a book is spread out before Ezekiel; "and it was
written within and without ; and there was written therein
lamentations and mourning and woe."

4. *The treatment which the prophets received at the hands
of the people, besides, tended to intensify the gloom which
brooded over their spirits.* Not for nothing did they set
before Israel the story of her spiritual sorceries. Moses
himself was more than once on the brink of being mur-
dered. Elijah was hounded out of the land by the emis-
saries of Ahab. Jeremiah was flung into a miry pit, and
finally put to death. To sum up, "they were sawn asunder,
were tempted, were slain with the sword : they wandered
about in sheepskins and goatskins ; being destitute, afflicted,
tormented ; of whom the world was not worthy; they
wandered in deserts, and in mountains, and in dens and
caves of the earth."

5. But irrespective of the treatment which they received,
*it added to the embarrassment of the prophets, that the import
of the burden which they bore was to a large extent unknown
to themselves.* The accomplishment of prophecy is the only
real interpretation of prophecy ; and the accomplishment of
all that was greatest in prophecy did not take place till four
centuries after the last of the prophets had ceased to speak.
Yet who could be so absorbingly concerned in the import of
each particular prediction as the man who uttered it ?
Hence those wistful scrutinies of which the apostle Peter
speaks :—" Of which salvation the prophets have inquired
and searched diligently, who prophesied of the grace that
should come unto you, searching what or what manner of
time the Spirit of Christ which was in them did signify,
when it testified beforehand the sufferings of Christ and the
glory that should follow."

From the forward glance into futurity, then, which is the
common characteristic of the prophets; from the catholicity
and spirituality of the kingdom which they announced; from
the shock which these announcements gave to the popular
prejudice; from the gloom with which the prophetic function

was invested; from the reluctance with which it was assumed; from the painful consequences by which the testimonies of the prophets were attended ; and from the sore perplexities begotten within their own minds by the burdens which they bore, we are driven irresistibly to the conclusion that the Old Testament prophecy cannot be accounted for on natural grounds, and that those who uttered it must have been men who "spake as they were moved by the Holy Ghost."

But let me now proceed to particularise. There is a growth observable in the fulness and clearness of the prophetic revelations as we pass from the time of Moses to the time of Christ. I purposely pass over the great prophet-preachers, such as Samuel, and Elijah, and Elisha, because their influence was mainly personal, their mission was to deal with a present emergency rather than point forward to a future object of hope, and they have left no written record of their words behind them. Written prophecy is comprised within a period stretching from the middle of the ninth to the end of the fourth century before Christ.

The first author of written prophecy is *Jonah.* His mission was to Nineveh, and it was purely local and temporary in its nature. He brings out the great truth, however, that there is forgiveness with God where there is repentance with man ; that "God has no pleasure in the death of the wicked," whatever be his nationality ; "but that the wicked turn from his way and live"—a doctrine most unpalatable to the prophet himself, no less than to his fellow-countrymen.

Next follows *Joel.* Joel, coming less than half-a-century later, exhibits a very appreciable spiritual advance on Jonah. Jonah had said upbraidingly, "I know that Thou art a gracious God, and merciful, slow to anger, and of great kindness, and repentest Thee of the evil." Joel says approvingly, "Rend your heart and not your garments, and turn unto the Lord your God ; for He is gracious and merciful, slow to anger, and of great kindness, and repenteth Him of the evil." The phrase is the same in the two passages ; but the spirit is strongly contrasted. Moreover, Joel

shows that repentance is but the preparation for the pleni-
tude of spiritual life, a spiritual life which is imported into
the soul by the power of God—"It shall come to pass
afterward that I will pour out my Spirit upon all flesh."
And this promise, fulfilling itself at all times among the
people of God, meets with its grandest illustration on the
day of Pentecost.

Next follow *Hosea* and *Amos*. Widely diverse in style
as these two prophets are, they are filled with the same high
impulse. The lament of Hosea and the philippic of Amos
are alike called forth by the heartless formalities of the age.
(Compare Hosea vi. 6; and Amos v. 21-24.) Each, moreover, makes a remarkable statement regarding the future
state of Israel, in which its returning fortunes are mysteriously connected with the name of David (Hosea iii. 4.
5; Amos ix. 11). The sharp sword of a spiritual religion,
leaping out of the sheath of a ceremonial that serves but a
temporary end, and may soon be flung aside for ever, such is
the common thought which, under varied imagery, these
two prophets present to view.

Next follow *Micah* and *Isaiah*. Micah brings out more
eloquently than either Hosea or Amos the paramount
superiority of the moral over the ritual (Micah vi. 6-8).
He furnishes us with the most definite note yet given of the
Advent of Messiah, announcing in one sentence His earthly
birth-place, and the fact of His eternal pre-existence, "But
thou, Bethlehem-Ephratah," &c. (Micah v. 2.) In describing the diffusive and assimilative power of the kingdom
that is to come, he uses language which his greater contemporary, Isaiah, thinks it worth while to quote in the
beginning of his prophecy, "In the last days it shall come
to pass that the mountain of the house of the Lord," &c.
(Micah iv. 1, 2.)

It is Isaiah, however, that gives us the first vivid delineations of the Person and Work of Messiah. He tells how
"a virgin shall conceive, and bear a son, and shall call His
name Immanuel" (Isaiah vii. 14)—how "unto us a Child
is born, unto us a Son is given: and the government shall

be upon His shoulder: and His name shall be called
Father, The Prince of Peace" (Isaiah ix. 6, 7)—how "there
shall come forth a Rod out of the stem of Jesse, and a
Branch shall grow out of his roots: and the Spirit of the
Lord shall rest upon Him, the spirit of wisdom and understanding, the spirit of counsel and might, the spirit of
knowledge and of the fear of the Lord " (Isaiah xi. 1, 2)—
how " He is despised and rejected of men; a man of sorrows
and acquainted with grief. . . . But He was wounded for
our transgressions, He was bruised for our iniquities: the
chastisement of our peace was upon Him ; and with His
stripes we are healed" (Isaiah liii. 3, 5)—how "it shall come
to pass, that from one new moon to another, and from one
sabbath to another, shall all flesh come to worship before
me, saith the Lord " (Isaiah lxvi. 23).

Nahum's prophecy, like Jonah's, is exclusively concerned
about Nineveh. Yet it contains that evangelical echo of
Isaiah, "Behold upon the mountains the feet of him that
bringeth good tidings, that publisheth peace " (Nah. i. 15).

The prophecy of *Zephaniah* is a strain of denunciation
against the evil of the age, leaving room, however, for the
recuperative power of repentance—"Seek righteousness, seek
meekness : it may be ye shall be hid in the day of the Lord's
anger"—and wound up by an allusion to the happy time,
when "it shall be said to Jerusalem, fear not ; and to Zion,
let not thine hands be slack."

Next follows *Jeremiah*, the most hated of the prophets
while he lived ; the most highly honoured after his death.
He describes in one memorable passage the Davidic descent,
the Divine character, and the substitutionary work of Messiah :—"Behold, the days come, saith the Lord, that I will
raise unto David a righteous Branch, and a King shall reign
and prosper, and shall execute judgment and justice in the
earth. In His days Judah shall be saved, and Israel shall
dwell safely : and this is His name whereby He shall be
called, The Lord our Righteousness " (Jer. xxiii. 5, 6).

Contemporary with Zephaniah and Jeremiah is *Habakkuk*.
Habakkuk foretells the Chaldean invasion of Judah. His

C

prophecy forms a curious mosaic of holy psalms and musings, inlaid in broad margins of denunciation and derision. In the middle of it occurs that graphic forecast of the universal kingdom, copied from Isaiah, "The earth shall be filled with the knowledge of the glory of the Lord, as the waters cover the sea."

Next follow *Ezekiel* and *Daniel*, prophets of the captivity —Ezekiel, the prophet of obscure allusion ; Daniel, the prophet of categorical assertion. In his celebrated shepherd song, however, Ezekiel says as explicitly as any of the prophets, "I will set up one shepherd over them, and he shall feed them, even my servant David ; he shall feed them, and ·he shall be their shepherd. And I the Lord will be their God, and my servant David a prince among · them" (Ezek. xxxiv. 23, 24). In another place he catches up the thought of Joel concerning the work of the Holy Spirit, and puts it in a more emphatic form (Ezek. xxxvi. 25-28). His famous valley vision also contains a vivid description of the revival of spiritual life under the figure of a physical resurrection (Ezek. xxxvii. 1-14).

Daniel alone of all the prophets gives us a definite note of the time of the Advent—"After threescore and two weeks shall Messiah be cut off" (Dan. ix. 26). He sketches in bold pictorial strokes the successive rise of the great world-monarchies, and the introduction of the kingdom that shall never be destroyed. The temporary nature of the Mosaic economy, and the final and permanent nature of that dispensation in which it is to be absorbed—this grand prophetic truth, impregnating the teachings of all the prophets, and presented under various metaphors and analogies, is announced by Daniel with startling plainness of speech (Dan. ix. 24-27 ; xii. 11). Equally startling is the emphasis with which the prophet propounds the doctrine of the Resurrection (Dan. xii. 2, 3).

In *Obadiah's* brief prophecy against Edom occurs the evangelical forecast, "But upon Mount Zion shall be deliverance, and there shall be holiness" (i. 17).

Next follow *Haggai* and *Zechariah*, the prophets of the

second temple. With these sublime anticipations, Haggai encourages Zerubbabel and the builders, " I will shake all nations, and the desire of all nations shall come : and I will fill this house with glory, saith the Lord of hosts. The silver is mine, and the gold is mine, saith the Lord of hosts. The glory of this latter house shall be greater than of the former, saith the Lord of hosts : and in this place will I give peace, saith the Lord of hosts" (Hag. ii. 7-9).

Zechariah twice repeats Isaiah's and Jeremiah's promise of the Branch (iii. 8 ; vi. 12, 13). He foretells the Hosanna procession (ix. 9), the purchase of the potter's field with the thirty pieces of silver (xi. 12, 13), the outpouring of the spirit of grace and of supplications (xii. 10), the opening of the fountain for sin and for uncleanness (xiii. 1), the wounding and death of the man who is God's fellow (xiii. 6, 7).

Next, after a century's lapse, arises the last of the prophets, *Malachi*. Malachi announces with fresh impressiveness the catholicity of the coming kingdom of God (i. 11), and what was involved in that, the withdrawal of the prerogative from Israel. He tells of the Advent of the Forerunner, followed by the Advent of the Christ (iii. 1-3). Then at the very close of his prophecy occur these three significant announcements, " Unto you that fear my name shall the Sun of Righteousness arise with healing in His wings"—"Remember ye the law of Moses my servant, which I commanded unto him in Horeb"—"Behold, I will send you Elijah the prophet before the coming of the great and dreadful day of the Lord." Thus with Moses, Elias, and the Sun of Righteousness—the three great figures of the Transfiguration scene—the curtain falls for ever on the Old Testament prophecy.

Now the first thing that strikes us, from a review of the teachings of the prophets, is the essential concord of sentiment and testimony by which they are marked. A series of compositions, extending over several hundreds of years, and produced under every variety of circumstance, political, social, and moral, are found to sound in absolute unison with

one another; while at the same time they invariably clash
with the tone of the popular sentiment, and portray a
futurity which involves, among other things, the overthrow
of the national life, and the extension to all nations indis-
criminately of blessings which were supposed to be the
peculiar privilege of the Jew.   The prophets resemble a row
of lights, planted at intervals along a road leading through
a dark night towards a distant dayspring.   In one form or
other that line of illumination stretches from the time of
Moses down to the time of Malachi; whether as soldier-
prophets, like Joshua and Gideon; or as orator-prophets,
like Samuel and Elijah; or as those whose memorial remains
in what they have written.   Between the last of the series,
however, and the rising of the Sun of Righteousness, four
centuries must elapse without one murmur from a prophet's lip.   But in whatever form it appears, or through
whatever interval it disappears, the Old Testament prophecy speaks one uniform word of hope and promise.

And when in the fulness of time Christ came, and the
Christian system burst upon the world, the result abundantly
justified the promise.   Christianity more than accomplishes
all the conditions laid down in the sacrificial system, and the
continuous chain of prophetic testimony.   The unapproach-
able perfection of the person and work of our Lord was
brought out in living words and deeds as it could never have
been brought out in prophetic song or symbol.   The New
Testament contains a tremendous surprise.   Its introductory
angel-songs and salutations of holy men and women but
faintly shadow forth, indeed, the priceless benefit conferred
upon the world by the appearance of the Prince of Peace in
Bethlehem.   Society was not to know for some years yet
what a Plant of Renown had struck root in its unwholesome
soil.   Even to the end of His earthly days, none but Christ's
closest followers were furnished with a key to unlock the
mystery of that immaculate life, nor even they till the
Resurrection and the Outpouring of the Spirit had followed
the Death and Burial.   Christ's contemporaries could not be
judges, in the way in which their successors could be judges,

of the perfect correspondence which exists between the preparation and the accomplishment. Glimpses have been granted to us, such as were not granted even to Paul and Peter, into the character of the kingdom of Christ. They saw the machinery beginning its grand world-movement; we have seen something of the splendid spiritual effects of the movement. There is not a nation in the world where the glad sound has not been heard in its initial tones at least. Christianity came into the world, disappointing the hope alike of the godly and ungodly. While that disappointment deepened into hostility in the ungodly, it rose into an irresistible enthusiasm in the godly. Christianity has elevated and sweetened society, as a whole, beyond anything known in the preparatory dispensation; and in the precise proportion in which its precepts are carried out is man lifted up to the level of his own ideal of perfection in purity, charity, reverence, self-denial, and all that gives savour and dignity to life.

It is one of the paradoxes of prophecy that it announces almost in the same breath ruin and universal empire, doom and everlasting salvation. Israel is to be scattered and peeled; yet she is to gather all nations into her holy fold. The Christian Church is the only possible solution of the problem. The political Israel has passed away. The social Israel lives a life of painful and ignoble dismemberment—a life, nevertheless, that strikingly illustrates the forecastings of the prophets concerning her. The spiritual Israel, framed as she was in the beginning out of the materials of the social Israel, both in the founders and in the first professors of the Christian faith, is daily drawing the nations under her high influence.

It is another of the paradoxes of prophecy that the Messiah was to sink and perish, and yet to ascend an everlasting throne. So perplexing was the play of cross-lights here, that many students of prophecy resorted to the theory of two Messiahs, a suffering and a triumphing. It seemed incredible that the "Plant of Renown" should be "a Root out of a dry ground"—that the "Wonderful, the Counsellor, the mighty God" should be one who "was wounded for our transgressions, and bruised for our iniquities." We are aware how exactly the Divine and human nature of our Lord, taken in connection with His substitutionary work and mediatorial reign, has solved the problem.

The several books of the Old Testament prophecy then speak, as we have seen, in broken tones the same unbroken story. The story finds no adequate interpretation in the musings of a whole millennium of pious minds, ranging from the time of Moses till the time of Malachi. The story finds a full interpretation in the person and work of Christ. It would have been impossible that a series of separate treatises, spread over so many centuries, should have told the same story with an almost monotonous reiteration, amidst every variety of surrounding circumstance, and in the teeth of perpetual antagonisms, except upon the supposition that the impress of one mind was stamped upon them all. And whose mind could stretch over the intellectual vicissitudes of a thousand years, and preserve itself unchanged amidst the infinite flux of circumstance, save His, "with whom is no variableness, neither shadow of turning," and in whose sight "a thousand years are but as yesterday when it is past, and as a watch in the night"? Prophecy finds at length the full vindication of its claims, as, narrowing down through the advancing centuries, it peacefully alights, like a dove, upon the head of Christ.

Hence it is that the New Testament, or the account of the Advent, Sacrifice, and Triumph of Christ, based as it is upon the foundation of "Moses and the prophets," is the fortress of all truth and purity and hope to the end of time. The New Testament lies concealed in the Old: the Old stands revealed in the New. Each, therefore, at once proves and is proved by the other. The doctrine of the Cross can never be surmounted by anything higher than itself; for it teaches us to aspire after that which is highest both for ourselves and others; and the extent to which the ideals it holds forth are realised is precisely the measure of the extent to which either the man or the nation advances in whatsoever things are true, and honest, and just, and pure, and lovely, and of good report.

The Bible is grandly catholic too, alike in its spirit and applications. It speaks to all the lands and all the ages. The most widely-divided nations and centuries find a common home of pious thought and purpose in its pages. In whatever is merely scientific, or artistic, or industrial, it no more speaks to the nineteenth century before Christ in the language of the nineteenth century after, than it speaks to the nineteenth century after Christ in the language of the nineteenth century before. A phraseology in harmony with the scientific attainments of the present age would have been infinitely more embarrassing to the patriarchs and prophets than a phraseology in harmony with the opinions of those early ages could possibly be to us. But while using the popular speech of the time in things natural, in things spiritual the Scripture speaks like an everlasting oracle. Each age finds in it what suits its own distinctive needs, and thereby brings out by fresh experiment the prophetic power of the book. It is one wide-sweeping prophecy, responding evermore to the rising and falling cries of the coming and going generations of men. It is never obsolete, never out of place. There is a life in it that never dies, a light that never is eclipsed. It breathes. It moves. It has hands and feet. It has peering eyes and listening ears. It has a thrilling brain and a throbbing heart. It is "quick and powerful, sharper than any two-edged sword, piercing even to the dividing asunder of soul and spirit, and of the joints and marrow, and is a discerner of the thoughts and intents of the heart." The difference between the Bible and every other book is the difference between the coarse effects of a painting and the infinite finish of a piece of natural landscape. Apply the micro-scope to the most delicate and perfect work of art, and its comeliness is changed into ungainliness. Apply it to a blade of grass or the petal of a lily, and the grace of the fashion of flower or leaf is only enhanced by that narrower inspection. There are effects in art, but there are depths in nature ; there are effects in human literature, but there are depths in the Word of God.   There is wear and tear in art, but in nature there is a prerogative of perpetual youth. There is wear and tear in human literature, " but the Word of God abideth for ever." It discloses more and more of its meaning, moreover, alike to the advancing man and to the advancing race.   The youth sees what the child has failed to see ; the old man sees what the youth has failed to see. Augustine saw something which Ignatius had not seen ; Anselm saw something which Augustine had not seen; Luther saw something which Anselm had not seen; we are seeing something now which Luther did not see.   But all that all have seen, and much that may still remain invisible to us, is wrapped up in the living words of James and Peter, John and Paul.   Till the day of realisation comes, the words of the Book of books may be little different from other words ; for the minds of men are blinded by sin. But when the day of realisation comes, they clothe themselves with terrible power and glory ; they fall from men's mouths, carrying vital fragments of men's hearts along with them ; they form the core of all spiritual life, the spring of all missionary enterprise.

To such as sigh over the cessation of those supernatural signs that bound together, by physical links, the heaven and earth of an older age, let it suffice to say that it is not the outward prodigy, but the inward grace, that brings salvation to the soul ; and that, in the existence of the Word of God among us, in the perpetuation of its holy ordinances, in the immortality of its story of love, and in the victories it is hourly achieving in the world, we have a miracle perpetually performed, a prophecy perpetually accomplished.

Prayer in Relation to Natural Law.

REV. PROFESSOR WALLACE.

PRAYER in RELATION to NATURAL LAW.

CAN God answer prayer? One can fancy a simple-minded, true-hearted Christian, little acquainted with modern speculation, on hearing such a question, exclaiming with genuine dismay, "Did ever anybody doubt it? It is a profanation to ask it." Yet the question is by many in our day answered in the negative. We are obliged to deal with it as a debatable question, and to try to show that in the course and constitution of nature there is place for prayer, and for answer to prayer. The question of the efficacy of prayer is one of more than speculative interest. It is one which involves issues altogether vital to the Christian, vital to the human race. If prayer were displaced from the position of influence which it has occupied from the beginning in the religious life, who could estimate the change in nature and extent which religious thought and religious experience must undergo? Accustomed as we have been to regard prayer as a vital element in the Christian life, necessary to its strength, to its peace, to its confidence, to its practical activity, we cannot but feel that a cessation of its action would be the privation of life. Let any Christian remember, when at any time his prayer-faith has been low and languid, what the effect has been upon his experience, upon his peace, upon his joy, upon the spirit with which he fulfilled his usual round of duty, and it may help him to realise in some measure what the effect would be of losing all faith in its efficacy, and of abandoning it altogether. By the universal consent of all Christians, prayer is the exercise of all others in which the soul cultivates and maintains most intimately its intercourse with God, in which filial confidence and love find their sweetest and most earnest expression, and in which the sense of dependence glows into a fervour of joyful trust. There is not a living Christian who does not feel that if the conviction were forced upon him that prayer could not be answered, he would have no life left. And what would be his thought of God, and his feeling towards Him? He is told that God has bound Himself by laws of procedure so rigid and inflexible, that He has not left Himself at liberty to answer the petition of any suppliant, plead how he may. He sits apart, unmoved by his straits, his dangers, his sorrows, his cries for help. If this be true, trust is as unwarranted and vain as prayer. Faith has no resting-place for the sole of her foot, unless she takes fixed and immutable laws for her God; for upon such a theory, it is with law, and not with a living God, that man has to do. All filial feeling towards God must cease. If He has no power to help, why should we trust Him? If He manifests no care for us by answering our petitions, how can we believe Him to be a God of love? And how, then, can we love Him? We lose our trust. We lose our love. Religion cannot exist without faith and love. If prayer cannot be answered, there can be no religion. This is the inevitable, the appalling conclusion.

And with the loss of faith in the efficacy of prayer, faith in the truth of Revelation becomes impossible. The efficacy of prayer and the credibility of Revelation must stand or fall together. Revelation everywhere affirms the efficacy of prayer. It represents God as the hearer of prayer, commanding and encouraging men to pray to Him, promising to bestow every form of good, temporal and spiritual, in answer to prayer, and threatening to withhold good when prayer is restrained. He is represented as possessing such full and entire control over the laws and ordinances of nature, animate and inanimate, as ever to be free at His own will to bestow out of the fulness of nature's treasures whatsoever His suppliants may need and desire. In regard to everything which affects human interests for mind or body, over the elements and processes of nature, over all that ministers to the fertility of the earth—the rain, the dew, the sunshine—over health and disease, over all the laws of life, over death itself, there is ascribed to God a complete and sovereign control. No less there is ascribed to Him power over mind—to determine its judgments, to rule its experiences, to cause men to walk in His statutes, to keep His judgments and to do them. Kings' hearts, the life and interests of nations, peace and war, defeat and victory, the honour or disgrace of dynasties, their preservation or extinction—all are in His hands, at His free and sovereign disposal. Laws of matter, laws of life, laws of mind, laws of social order, are represented as His servants, serving, and not limiting, His freedom of will and of action —servants of His power, servants of His wisdom, servants of His free and generous beneficence to the children of men.

If this whole representation be false—if there be a proved impossibility in the nature of things, that God could answer prayer without deranging the order of nature and reducing it to chaos, with the effect of the destruction of all life— then the Bible is a fable, its whole internal evidence is discredited, and no other form of evidence could prove it divine. The efficacy of prayer, therefore, is just as decisive a battle-ground as any other for testing the claims and credibility of Revelation.

There are some who are willing to acknowledge that, although prayer can have no effect in changing the course of nature, yet that God in answer to prayer may influence the human mind for good. But the laws of mind are as fixed and steadfast as the laws of matter ; and it would be as much an interference with natural law to change the succession of thought as to dispel clouds or send a shower to water the earth.

Others say that although the answer to prayer is impossible, yet that men ought to pray, because the reflex influence is good—the mind is benefited by the exercise. This is altogether contrary to reason and common sense, and I think it very doubtful whether the experiment has ever been tried on any considerable scale, or with much perseverance. A reflex benefit implies a direct benefit as its proper antecedent—just as there must be a direct

incidence of a ray of light before there can be a reflection
of it.   Prayer would be universally abandoned as purpose-
less and vain if no answer were ever to be expected.   The
answer to prayer is necessary to prayer.   Could it be felt to
be a healthy and helpful exercise of mind to repair to some
great man's door, morning by morning, or as often as I felt
the pressure of want and the need of help, to present my
petition with a reverence due to his greatness, and with an
earnestness and importunity inspired by my need, while I
know that he has bound himself by inflexible rules never to
grant a petition?   God ever treats us as rational beings,
and never so outrages the gift of reason which He has
bestowed upon us as to require life-long prayer, knowing
beforehand that all our asking is vain.

I am restricted by the terms of the subject before me to
treat of prayer in its relation to natural law; and I shall
first seek for an answer to the question—

I.—WHAT IS PRAYER?

And here let us regard it strictly in its own proper nature,
with whatever diversity its proper nature admits, without at
present including such collateral ideas as may attach themselves to it, or be attendant upon it.   Thus regarding it, we
have a statement of the nature and end of prayer, which, even
apart from the source whence it springs, commends itself to
every mind by its truth, by its simplicity, and by its ex-
haustiveness—"Ask, and it shall be given you; seek, and
ye shall find; knock, and it shall be opened unto you."*
Observe that asking and receiving are correlative ideas; as
are also seeking and finding, knocking and opening.   The
aim of the first term in each of these pairs is to secure the
second.   In other words, the very nature of prayer consists
in its direct influence, and not in its reflex.   Its reflex
influence is not noticed, because not entering into its proper
nature.   Receiving proves the direct influence of asking,
finding of seeking, opening of knocking.   Our Lord gives

* Luke xi. 9.

two illustrative examples of prayer in the social relations of human life. One is the case of a man who wakes up his neighbour at night, to ask him to lend him three loaves to set before a friend who has come to him unexpectedly. By dint of importunity he overcomes the drowsy reluctance of his neighbour, and he receives what he asks. The other instance is stated thus—" If a son shall ask bread of any of you that is a father, will he give him a stone ? or if he ask a fish, will he for a fish give him a serpent ? or if he shall ask an egg, will he offer him a scorpion ?" In each case an answer is expected ; and hence our reason teaches us that the desire and expectation of an answer enters into the very nature of prayer. When a man asks bread, it is bread he desires to receive, and not a change of the state of his mind. If prayer were only beneficial in its reflex effect, then, whether a son gets bread or a stone or nothing for his asking, the reflex benefit ought to be experienced all the same. The answering must correspond to the asking ; and then the reflex benefit may often be more precious than the direct. When you have received the gift you ask, there may be a very welcome feeling of relief from some strait or embarrassment—there is peace, there is a grateful sense of the kindly response, an impulse to requite it, and, it may be, an expansion of your own generous feeling towards others. All this is a very agreeable reflex experience. But if no answer had been vouchsafed to your petition, or if you had received a stone when you asked bread, would you have enjoyed an experience of this precious and happy character ? We may well be disposed to ask, whether there be men who set themselves deliberately to test practically the value of a theory so adverse to human reason ?

We learn also from these illustrations, that prayer or petition from man to man is the same in nature as from man to God, and that prayer belongs to the natural life of man as necessarily as to the spiritual. And we learn the function of prayer in the natural life, and prove its efficacy directly and reflexly before we have any experience of the spiritual life. We are natural men before we become spiritual. We are conscious of our natural relations before we become conscious of the spiritual. We are conscious of natural wants and desires before we are conscious of those which are spiritual. "That was not first which is spiritual, but that which is natural, and afterwards that which is spiritual." It is within the natural relations we test our powers and become acquainted with their action, and in which we observe their phenomena and deduce their laws. And when their action is transferred to the spiritual sphere, we find their laws unchanged, and all their phenomena similar. That which is changed consists in the deposing of the former objects from their place of influence, and in yielding to God the supreme rule and authority. It is He who now engages their action, not to the exclusion of the natural, but to their subordination. Our relation with God we call a spiritual relation; and the action of our powers within that relation we call spiritual. Our experience is then a spiritual experience; and every term which denotes it has first served to denote a natural experience, so that the natural and the spiritual have a common language. Love, joy, peace, long-suffering, gentleness, goodness, faith, meekness, temperance, are natural experiences of the human soul before they become graces of the Spirit. In like manner the principles and acts of worship have their basis in nature, and their natural action in our human relations. We reverence parents and magistrates, and others whose superiority we acknowledge; and we express that reverence by speech, and by various forms and symbols of homage. We praise men for their gifts and excellences; for their wisdom, their benevolence; for their fidelity and fortitude. We supplicate men to help us; we entreat them to bestow favours upon us, to guide and counsel us, to have mercy upon us, and to forgive us. All worship, reverence, homage, praise, prayer, has its place in nature, and finds its earliest expression in our natural relations.

II.—PRAYER A LAW OF NATURE.

Our position, then, is this, that prayer is an original
element in the constitution of nature, a law of nature, co-
ordinate with every other law, and of co-ordinate necessity
to the order of nature.   It belongs to the sphere of life,
to living organisms and their relations, and is necessary to
the maintenance and government of those relations.   The
laws of life are wholly different from those of matter.   Life
does not submit itself to sense-perception ; it is invisible,
intangible.   It cannot be weighed nor measured.   It is the
great mystery of science, to the elucidation of which no
approach has yet been made.   It occupies a place in nature
single and alone. It is a class by itself. It cannot be compared
with anything known.   It proves its superiority to matter
and to its laws, by framing and building up the particles
of matter into the infinitely diversified organic structures
which it inhabits, and by the marvellous and mysterious
instincts by which it rules the organisms which it constructs,
controlling their action, their growth and reproduction.
The relations among living organisms, also, are altogether
different from the relations of particles or masses of matter
amongst each other.   Amongst organisms so low and
diminutive as to be readily overlooked, polypes, "when
aggregated into groups, severally catch food for the common weal."   This implies a power of communication, and
of entertaining a common end.   There is nothing similar to
this in the relations of matter.   Even amongst merely sentient beings, the laws which rule man's sentient life are
found in action ; and asking and receiving, seeking and
finding, belong to this class of laws.   Something like this
must take place by natural instinct, in such a class of beings
as has just been referred to, in order to their carrying out
a common end.   But, passing by the lower organisms, the
natural instinct to ask manifests itself, in those species of
animals with which we are most familiar, in a perfectly
conspicuous way.   The fundamental condition, out of which

the necessity for asking and receiving arises, is a state of dependence. Living beings are dependent upon one another to a greater or less extent, for food, for care, for combined action, for mutual help and defence. For such ends the several species have their necessary associations, from pairs up to numerous individuals in herds and flocks. To a state of dependence there necessarily attaches the incidence of want. A being which has not the resources of its continued existence and well-being within itself, is exposed to want. As a general rule, the young of all the higher classes of animals are dependent upon the female parent in their early days for their necessary nutriment. The ever-recurring feeling of hunger awakens the desire for satisfaction ; and the desire is ever supplied with a suitable means of expressing itself, by which the want is made known to the being possessing the supply. That being infallibly interprets the suppliant sign, infallibly knows herself to possess the needed supply, or where to find it ; and by an infallible instinct hastens to yield it, and the desire is satisfied. Here are all the elements of effectual prayer, asking and receiving, seeking and finding. And this ever-recurring order is necessary to the preservation at least of the highest species of sentient beings known to man. When the want is thus satisfied in response to the expression of desire, we have an example of the efficacy of prayer as a law of sentient nature, necessary to the order of nature. And nothing farther than this can be said for any other natural law whatever.

This law acts upon the sentient nature of man with the same force and to the same effect as in the case of other sentient beings. The human infant is dependent upon the mother like the young of other animals. It is necessary, therefore, that he should be able to express his sense of want, and his feeling of desire ; and that the expression shall reach with influential force the source of supply, and unlock it. The little murmur, the sharper cry, the motion of the lips, are suppliant signs which the mother reads and interprets without a teacher ; and which summon up, by night or by day, in sickness or health, the prompt

response from the depths of her nature. And this act of
supplication is of constant repetition and recurrence, and for
a longer period than in the case of the young of any other
animal. The law of prayer begins to act upon man simultaneously with the feeling of infant want and desire ; and
he proves its efficacy from the very beginning ; for God
has made the mother to be, like Himself, a willing hearer of
prayer. Within the department of sentient existence, therefore, we perceive prayer to be an original instinct, a law of
nature ; and that the answer to prayer is provided for in
the same infallible way. And the bearing of this line of
observation upon our main question is this, that prayer by
the constitution of nature is inseparably connected with the
relation of dependence amongst living beings. And that
dependence, which is a law of the existence of all living
beings, must ultimately rest upon one point of support—
the will of Him "by whom all things consist." And to
Him, therefore, with poetic beauty, the Scriptures represent
the beasts and the birds as crying for their food—" Who
provideth for the raven his food ? when his young ones
cry unto God, they wander for lack of meat."* " The young
lions roar after their prey, and seek their meat from God." †
" He giveth to the beast his food, and to the young ravens
which cry." ‡ But our main concern is with man ; and let
it be observed that there is a foundation laid in his sentient
nature, which makes him, by the resistless necessity of
instinct, a praying being.

Consider man when he has passed the stage of infancy,
when his nascent curiosity manifests the dawn of intelligence. He is now as dependent upon others for knowledge
and wisdom as for food and care. So soon as he attains
the first stages of the power of articulate speech, his prattle
is a running stream of request and inquiry, ever asking and
seeking. As he grows, his wants grow in number and
variety, and his desires and inquiries are importunately
addressed to all around him. This is not now merely the
means of keeping his bodily wants before those who might

* Job xxxviii. 41.   † Ps. civ. 21.   ‡ Ps. cxlvii. 9.

not always anticipate them ; it is also the means of his earliest lessons in knowledge. What is this? what is that? Why is this? why is that? How is this? how is that? His inquiries determine the order in which his first lessons come ; and the more clear and satisfactory and prompt he finds the answers to be, with all the more rapid succession will the inquiries come. And alas for the child whose ignorant parents cannot, or those who in their selfish impatience will not, satisfy the thirst of his natural curiosity at this early period ! When the more systematic course of his education has fairly commenced, it is the aim of the intelligent teacher to take advantage of this law to train it to his purpose, to direct it, and to make it the most active instrument of all the youth's acquisitions in wisdom and knowledge. Teaching would be a hopeless drudgery without this spirit of inquiry, and the development of the human intellect would be impossible. If a mother observed, when her child had come to a suitable age, that it never asked questions, never inquired the names or uses of objects, never asked for information, would not her sad heart tell her that her child was an imbecile? When you ask for information, when you open a book, you are seeking for the thoughts and judgments of others to help in the guidance of your own. The nutriment of the mind is secreted in the works of creation and providence, discovered and gathered thence by the skill and toil of many labourers, and deposited in the great reservoir of human literature from age to age, that every new generation may seek and search and learn, and add its own contribution to the ever-enlarging store. It is not now the mere instinct of sentient life which impels to ask. Prayer has now assumed its intelligent form, and manifests itself to be a law of our rational nature ; and the order of our rational nature is as dependent upon it as is the order of our sentient nature. To suspend its action would be to arrest the development of the human mind, and speedily to lose the gain of all the ages. The other laws which rule our mental nature would be inoperative without this law, so essential is its action as a constituent element in the life and government of thought. It exercises a controlling influence over the acquirement of knowledge, over its distribution and conservation. Prayer, then, belongs constitutionally to our nature, and the condition of intellectual dependence of man upon man renders its action constant and imperative as any law of thought. It is a necessary constituent in all intellectual fellowship, necessary to the life of intellect. As an intelligent being, man is a praying being.

Let us now consider man in society, man as a subject of moral order, and we shall find prayer holding a place of commanding influence in his social life and relations. Man is a social being, a being with a constitutional capacity for union with his fellows, and with a tendency to union strong with the resistless force of necessity. The individual cannot live alone ; he is not sufficient for himself. Fellowship is a necessity of his nature. But this is to say that he is dependent upon society, and that this dependence is constant. He possesses a constitution, physical and mental, which renders personal independence, in any absolute sense, impossible. His constitutional endowments are not self-acting. The co-factors which are necessary conditions of their action are supplied by their external relations. This is true both as regards body and mind. He is dependent upon his social relations for life and well-being. But those relations necessitate asking and receiving. Even in respect of those things which are necessary to bodily sustenance and support, they are so distributed in kind and measure that no individual possesses them at all times. When he rises in the morning, the things which he shall require throughout the day are in the hands of many persons as their own proper possession. How are they to become his ? There may be the condition of utter poverty, when no equivalent can be offered or given. In this case the only course, consistently with the order of society, is to appeal to the benevolence of the possessor—that is, to ask or beg for gratuitous relief ; in other words, to pray. And this is the natural impulse. Suppose this natural law of prayer did not come into action,

or that it was without efficacy, the destitute must perish, or
take by force or fraud, to the grievous disturbance of social
order.   But it is not to the condition of destitution alone
that prayer is necessary to preserve the order of society.
Even though you have an equivalent to give for what you
want, that fact does not entitle you to seize upon the property of another, and to deposit your equivalent in its place.
You must ask before you are entitled to receive in exchange.
The transactions of human society could not be conducted
without this process, nor its order maintained.   The condition of mutual dependence necessitates the observance of
fixed and recognised laws and regulations for its right
adjustment.   There must not only be recognised rights of
property, there must also be recognised modes and terms
of transfer from one to another.   Now whatever other terms
and conditions may enter into the necessary transactions of
exchange, there is ever present one indispensable condition
—asking with a view to receive.   No negociation could be
conducted among men without this condition.   Suppose
this practice of asking suspended, as we have just supposed,
in the case of sheer destitution ; men's wants are imperative ;
the supplies they need are in the possession of many persons
as their proper rights ; you may not ask, you cannot want,
for that would violate the natural law of self-preservation.
What, then, would be the alternative, to rich and poor alike,
but to seize by violence or stealth whatever they needed,
wherever it could be found.   That violent aggression would
provoke violent resistance ; and what becomes of social
order ?   What existing law of our social life could supply
the necessary cohesive and flexible force of the repudiated
law of prayer ?   This law of social life is necessary to the
exercise of benevolence.   You cannot know or anticipate
the special and pressing wants and troubles of others.   To
obtrude your benefactions might often be felt to be offensive,
or your tenders of assistance insulting or mortifying.   Your
nearest neighbour may be in deep distress for help, which
you would gladly relieve if he would make his want known ;
and the simple statement of his case would imply supplica-

tion. Not material wants only prompt men to request favours from each other ; we want counsel and consolation, and mental and moral support ; and we ask these favours from one another, and readily yield them to entreaty. Benevolence, not less than justice, is necessary to the order of society, and prayer is necessary to benevolence. And when we consider the place which it holds in those minor forms of benevolence which' pervade the intercourse of society in its fairest and happiest conditions, its amenities and courtesies, it is impossible to withhold our admiration of its wondrous influence. It is like a fragrant oil that perfumes while it lubricates the hinges of social life. We entreat as a favour where we have a right to demand. We substitute the language of request for that of command, the optative for the imperative mood, greatly to the advantage of our social placidity. We are constantly asking gratuitous services from others, the most trifling assistance from their courtesy and good-will, in our own households, from equals, from inferiors, from strangers casually met—services rendered because they are asked for, and rendered in the same courteous spirit in which they are asked. All this is of constant recurrence. And prayer proves itself, in those forms of it, to be the ever-ready minister of kindness and good-will. Let anyone observe the effect produced in a company of persons of fairly cultivated habits, when one, in some unsatisfied mood or momentary thoughtlessness, snatches what courtesy required him to request of another, or disregards a request made to him, and he will see how it jars upon the sensibilities of all, disturbing the social harmony. And let anyone observe the state of society where the absence of these forms is the rule, and not the exception, and he will hear harsh and imperious commands met with cowed or surly compliance, or defiant resistance. Whether, therefore, it be in great things or little, this natural law is essential to the harmonious action of social life. The numerous synonyms, with equivalent phrases, in constant use in human intercourse, and which occur to everyone's mind, show how indispensable it is to the cultivation of human fellowship. Every form of interrogation, of question and answer, of invitation or inquiry, by word or letter, all come under the same category. Social intercourse could not be maintained without it.

Thus far, I think, within the natural relations of human life, we are entitled to say that prayer is necessary to human welfare, physically, intellectually, morally—nay, that it is necessary to the continuance of man's existence. It is an instinct of his sentient nature, inseparable from his intellectual and moral nature, as necessary to him as food and thought and conscience. It is deeply and permanently seated in the constitution of his nature ; and the laws of all nature around him are in such correspondence with it, as to contribute their action as a necessary element in securing its efficacy. To render prayer ineffectual would be a violation of man's nature, and of the order of his correspondence with his environments. I believe I am warranted, from what has been said, in affirming that prayer is a law of nature, and that prayer, within the relations we have reviewed, does not disturb the order of nature, but is an element of its stability. But in order to all these beneficent issues, this prayer-force must possess objective efficacy. The value of the subjective influence depends upon the confidence entertained in the reality of the objective efficacy. And this confidence is a natural instinct of the human mind, as firm as that entertained in kindness, or justice, or any other bond of social life. It is an element inseparable from man's relation to man, kept in constant action by the necessities of his condition, and exercising a controlling influence in his schemes of life and conduct. In his intellectual life, in his moral and social life and relations, man is, by his mental and moral constitution, a praying being.

III.—PRAYER IN RELATION TO OTHER NATURAL LAWS.

Still confining ourselves to the sphere of the natural relations, we have next to inquire *whether prayer exercises any modifying or controlling influence over the action of other natural laws.* The order of nature, it is well known, is maintained, not by each law acting out its own proper tendency to its own proper results, by its own inexorable and inflexible force, but by having its own proper action modified by the action of other laws ruling within the same sphere. No one of them possesses despotic sway. We have the most conspicuous and grandest instance of the reciprocal control of natural laws in those of gravitation and motion. These laws meet on the great arena of the planetary and stellar worlds, like gigantic athletes, contending, amongst other prizes, for mastery over this fair earth of ours. Should the law of gravitation prove the victor, our world would be precipitated upon the surface of the sun, to the great disturbance of the present order of nature. Should the first law of motion prevail, our earth must rush from her orbit, and be eventually dashed against some other world, equally to the disturbance of the order of nature. But the well-matched force of these great wrestlers compels a compromise ; and because neither is inflexible, but each controlled by the other, our planet is borne in stately equipoise in her magnificent orbit, to the well-being of her teeming population, and to the conservation of the order of nature. If, then, prayer may be found to exercise, in any measure, a modifying influence upon the action of other laws, and be in turn modified or limited in its action by them, it would be in accordance with the order of nature, and not a violation of it. Let us instance the physiological laws. The cry of the hungry infant, inarticulate though it be, is rightly interpreted by the maternal instinct as a prayer for the bland nutriment secreted in her frame. The natural force of that natural prayer stirs into activity a whole cycle of physiological function in the bosom of the mother, and immediately after, as by a reflex action, in the frame of the infant. Suppose no direct effect followed from the infantile prayer, what would be the effect upon the nutrition of childhood ? But not in infancy only, and in maternity, are such effects produced by the natural power of prayer. Very strong emotions may be excited by requests, by urgent and importunate solicitations, painfully

B

unwelcome. And the emotions thus excited will stimulate physiological action. Professor Bain says, "It may be doubted if any considerable emotion passes over us without telling upon the processes of digestion, either to quicken or depress them. All the depressing and perturbing passions are known to take away appetite, to arrest the healthy action of the stomach, liver, bowels, &c. A hilarious excitement stimulates those functions." All these effects may be produced by asking questions. It will stir passion, love or resentment, desire or indignation; and the responsive emotion proves the force of prayer.

Prayer in the natural relations is necessary to man's control over matter, and to his dominion over the earth. Mind rules over matter through the organism of the human body. The body is the only portion of matter over which the mind's executive power, the will, acts with direct and immediate effect. The mind, in ruling the body and controlling its motions, is ruling over matter, and modifying the action of its laws. There are two forces in existence which successfully assert their superiority to matter, by their power of resisting and controlling the force of its laws— life and mind. The living vegetable organism possesses the power of assimilating mineral substances, changing their forms, imparting new qualities, and employing them in new functions, wholly alien to their nature and laws, under their original forms. The tiny sporule of the moss, a microscopic speck, is endowed with this potency. The grass, the flowers, the stately trees, are the mineral substances of the earth, wrested from the grasp of material laws, transformed and organised by the power of life. The meanest thing that crawls, by that very motion proves its superiority to the law of gravity. The stone offers no resistance, but lies immovable, passive in the power of that mighty law. It cannot exercise the same absolute force over the insect; the insect has life. A living man disputes the force of gravitation by his power of free, voluntary locomotion. In the morning, in fresh vigour, with elastic step, he spurns the heath and breasts the hill, knowing that he has entered into conflict with this mighty force.   As the sun declines, he is conscious that the material law is gaining upon him. By the evening he drags his limbs wearily.   As the vital force abates, the physical force gains, and by night he yields the struggle, laid passive on his couch.   But he is not con-quered.   He has been visited by "tired nature's sweet restorer, balmy sleep," and he renews the contest with the morning light; and he wages this war from day to day, from year to year, until life's tired servants, worn out with the weary conflict, crumble amongst the clods of the valley, and gravitation is the conqueror.   No ; not the conqueror of life!   Life has defied it ever.   And its seeming conquest is not final.   Another morn shall come ; and the body which has obeyed the Divine law of gravitation, and has been rested in obeying, shall rise, unimpeded by its force, "to meet the Lord in the air."   Life is superior to matter.

And mind is superior to mere sentient life, and therefore superior to mere physical force.   Man is able to interfere with the order of nature within certain limits, and is obliged to do so for his own well-being, even for the preservation of his life.   This is a very obvious fact in respect of the food by which he is nourished.   The plants upon which he so much depends are not provided, in the order of nature, in the form adapted to his natural constitution.   By our pro-cesses of cultivation we interfere with the natural order of their production, and change their qualities, replacing those which, in their natural state, are injurious, by qualities which are nutritious and healthful.   It is an interference with the order of physical nature to disturb the surface of the earth by spade or plough.   It is the order of nature that plants shall bud and grow and decline and die.   It is not in the order of their nature to have their processes violently arrested, and destruction to visit them in the freshness of their young beauty, or in the maturity of their prolific fertility.   Yet wherever man rules, he disturbs the order of vegetable life to promote the order of his own.   In a similar manner does he deal with animal life.   Animals are not provided in the order of nature in a condition to satisfy his appetite or

nourish his life.   Man cannot be nourished otherwise than
by organic matter; yet not while it lives, but after it has
been put to death.   What more firmly established order in
nature is there than the law of animal as well as of vegetable
life—that it develop from the germ, grow and mature, re-
produce its kind, and decline and die ?   And what more sig-
nal instance of interference with the order of nature can be
imagined than to lay violent and instant arrest upon any
given life, at any stage of its development, by a single volition of man, human life itself not excepted ?   And this takes
place in the highest department of natural order and of
natural law.   And this interference with the order of life is
practised on a still larger scale amongst the lower animals,
in one kind preying upon another, one class in conflict with
another; the order of nature in one class interfering with
the order of nature which obtains in another, that the
general order of nature may be preseved.   Every death by
violence, every premature death, is a violation of the order
of nature.   That children die before their parents is a violation of the order of nature.   Man, by his mental power,
is able to subject the order of nature to his own purposes,
within the limits of his own interests.   But as the only
portion of matter subject to the direct volition of his own
mind is his own body, with a very limited portion in contact
with his body, the power of the individual over matter is too
limited to serve fully his own interests.   I may want a book
which is now in London or New York, but it will not obey
my volition ; but a request, addressed to a person in either
place by letter or by the electric telegraph, will place it in
my possession.   Prayer, as a natural law, is essential to the
formation and maintenance of such combinations of men as
are necessary to man's dominion over the earth.   Prayer
has power to prevail with other minds, to bring their bodies
to act upon matter beyond my reach, and to transport it
for my service wherever I desire.   I have acted upon it by
prayer, and so moved other wills and other hands to accomplish my desire.   Whatever other influences may be brought
into action, asking is ever a necessary element to secure co-

operative labour. It is thus the busy work of human life goes on. Streams of urgent petitions are flowing in from man to his fellows, streams of ready answers ever flowing back ; mutual help and support maintain social order and action, and man makes good his dominion over the earth.

It is surely a significant fact that God, in His government of the inter-relations of mankind, and in His government of man's relations with the material world, has made prayer to be a law of His government, of necessary and constant action, indispensable as a vital, mental, and moral force, to the stability of this economy, and to the facile and harmonious adjustment and action of its parts. Man is by nature a praying being.

IV.—LIMITATION OF THE EFFICACY OF PRAYER.

Within those limits, then, within which prayer acts, is it of invariable efficacy? Does the desired answer follow so necessarily upon the petition, and in terms of the petition, that it may be counted upon with entire certainty? No. Both the asking and the answering are subject to limitation by the action of other laws. It is like all other natural laws in this respect. In our human relations, if prayer were of invariable efficacy, it would be destructive of social order. If a man were compelled, by the inexorable efficacy of prayer, to give to every petitioner whatever he chose to ask—his property, his labour, his time—he would speedily be despoiled of his liberty and means of life, and be driven, in his turn, to despoil others by his importunate entreaties. For the safety of society, there are certain natural as well as moral and conventional restraints placed upon asking in the intercourse of human life. Our deliberate reason and our common sense impose a limit upon the expectations we form from others, and upon the desires which we address to them. And there is a corresponding limit to granting petitions on the same grounds of reason and common sense. The law of conscience, the sense of propriety, our self-respect, forbid our seeking favours from others, or benefits and advantages, which our own efforts may achieve for ourselves. And a man's prudence and sense of right may constrain him to refuse a petition, having a better knowledge of his means and resource, and of the prior obligations resting upon him, than the petitioner. And petitions may be refused on public grounds by those who dispense the patronage of empires. And very many petitions are rejected by the very categoric and decisive conclusion, "I will not." Your pleadings may address a man's reason, his benevolence, or his conscience; you may use all importunity, and bring all influences to bear upon him, to move him to will as you desire; but his will is the court of last resort, and is entitled to determine the issue of your request. It is obvious that if will did not impose a restraining force upon the efficacy of prayer, no man's liberty of action would be secure. That prayer possess efficacy is essential to its proper nature, but unlimited efficacy would be destructive. It is equally essential to the order of nature that prayer be efficacious, and that its efficacy be limited. And this is a characteristic of all natural laws.

We have now seen, by a sufficient induction, that prayer is natural to man, an original element in his constitution; that he is placed under conditions of life which necessitate its habitual exercise, and that he is thus trained from his infancy to be a praying being. We have seen that its exercise is necessary to the existence and well-being of human society; and therefore it is a constituent element of the Divine moral government over the human race. In truth, it is quite evident that no moral government would be suited to man, or could take effect upon his social relations, which did not make account of this principle and recognise its action. It is inseparable from his intelligent and moral nature; and he is incapable of sustaining relations with any intelligent being from which prayer, as an element of fellowship, were necessarily excluded.

V.—Prayer in the Spiritual Relation.

I have considered it necessary, by all this line of observation, to show that there is a foundation in nature to render it *prima facie* probable that God recognises the efficacy of prayer in man's relation with Himself; that as surely as He has designed him for a life of dependence upon Himself, so surely has He designed him for a life of prayer, and has provided that the conditions of its exercise shall never be wanting. And we are now sufficiently familiar with the natural operation and efficacy of prayer to be prepared, in some measure, to illustrate its place and power in the spiritual sphere. "That was not first which is spiritual, but that which is natural, and afterward that which is spiritual." · In point of fact, we have no new principle to deal with when we come to consider our relation with God. We carry with us into the spiritual relation the same powers of mind, the same constitutional tendencies, the same moral faculty, the same affections, which are in constant action in the natural sphere. And the spiritual relation is maintained concurrently with the natural, and without confusion to either; because the same natural powers consciously act in the same natural way when the spiritual is superadded to the natural. And our relation with God is conducted, both on His part and ours, on the same moral principles which rule the inter-relations of mankind. No other classes of such principles are known to us, or could be known by us, unless there were imparted to our nature corresponding faculties. Justice, goodness, and truth are determining principles of God's conduct towards man. These same principles He has implanted in the constitution of man, and they are the principles which of necessity rule all his moral relations, human and Divine. Our relation with God is a personal relation, involving the reciprocation of personal feeling, the interchange of thought, intelligent fellowship, benefaction on the one side, veneration, trust, gratitude on the other. Justice, goodness, and truth are sufficient for all moral relations. Our relation with God involves the condition of

dependence on our part, with every experience incident to
dependence. Every dependent being is subject to want.
The feeling of want excites the desire for relief, and the
desire is naturally directed to the known source of supply.
All this applies to our relation with God, and with similar
effect, as in the analogous case of our relations with man.
We must, therefore, have respect to the laws of giving and
receiving. Now the law implanted in our nature, and
coming into thought whenever the sense of dependence and
the feeling of want arise, is, "Ask, and it shall be given you."
And the impulse of suffering nature is to pray. I know
there is to be found in many such an insensibility to God's
right to His own, that they violate all righteousness in their
treatment of what is His, laying hands upon it, appro-
priating it without leave asked, and withholding it from the
Divine service; just as there are many who have lost all
sensibility to the distinction between mine and thine, and
freely appropriate their neighbour's goods. Every one who
believes in God the Creator of all things, believes also that
He is the Sovereign Proprietor of all, and that all is at His
sovereign disposal, to give or to withhold. Now we know
that "ask, and it shall be given you" is a law of His moral
government, as authoritative as any other moral law implanted in our nature. We are dependent beings, and our
nature is constitutionally adapted to a condition of dependence; and nothing in our nature can suggest to us the
possibility of becoming independent—that is, of possessing
within ourselves all the sources of our life and well-being
and perfection. That prayer shall for ever constitute an
essential element in conducting our relation of dependence
upon God, is a conclusion absolutely necessary from the
nature of the case. But prayer implies answer as its
necessary correlative. The natural disposition to ask is
inseparable from our dependent nature, and is itself a proof
of the existence of a corresponding disposition to answer;
otherwise our nature would deceive us, prompting us to
fruitless effort. Every thoughtful man contemplates with
admiration the correspondences between the nature of man,

mental and physical, and the nature that surrounds him. There are suitable objects for the perception of all the senses. For every desire of our nature there are appropriate objects ; for every affection, and for every faculty of the mind, the necessary conditions of their action are freely provided. Now prayer engages in its exercise our intellectual and moral powers, our will and emotions, prompted by our want and desire; and it is unphilosophical to suppose that no response is possible. It would be contrary to the whole course of nature. *Dependence* implies *support.* A *dependent being* implies a *supporting Being.* *Want* implies *fulness ; human want, Divine fulness ; human dependence,* a *Divine supporter ; human prayer, Divine response.* The native intuitions of man apprehend these pairs of relations simultaneously. Besides, it is rational to believe that the exercise of our powers in our human relations is designed to fit them for the cultivation of our relations with God. "That was not first which is spiritual, but that which is natural, and afterward that which is spiritual." Every mental and moral exercise which is necessary to the social order of human life is necessary to the cultivation of our fellowship with God. Every affection which binds us to man is designed to rest upon God as its supreme object. We are dependent upon our relation to Him for the highest, for the only satisfying object of every mental and moral power we possess, and for every affection of our heart. Our dependence upon man is partial only, and it is only in a partial measure he can yield us support and satisfaction. Our dependence upon God is total, and all the treasures of wisdom and knowledge, and all the fulness of the earth, are His, and His dominion extendeth over all. He can support us, and satisfy every want and every desire to the uttermost. We ask of man for the measure of help he can render, and he responds to our asking ; and our asking and his response are alike natural tendencies, inseparable from the nature of our relations with each other. I ask, Is it rational to believe that while God has made it obligatory, by the very constitution of our nature, that we should respond to one another's petitions yet that He Himself, by a rigid system of ordinances, which we denominate "the course and constitution of nature," has rendered prayer to Him wholly without efficacy? This would be to destroy the correspondences between external nature and the nature within us. In our felt dependence and want, the law of our nature prompts us to pray to Him upon whom we depend ; but it is alleged that the laws of material nature oppose all response. Even Mr. Spencer regards external nature as a manifestation of his First Cause ; but the hypothesis of fruitless prayer would interpose the order of nature to hide God from our view, and, indeed, to make it of no consequence to us whatever, whether there be a God or no. In truth, the hypothesis is altogether atheistical. A being that could not answer prayer, from whatever cause, could be no object of trust, nor of love, nor of reverence. We could have no ennobling intercourse with him, no loving, holy fellowship. We would be confined to the low level of our fallen humanity for our fellowships, and men in their best state are too nearly on a level with each other for one to bear his fellows upward to the perfection prophesied by the possibilities of our nature. We need for this habitual fellowship with a perfection above us—to help, to allure, to guide us onward. It is the belief of the supernatural which has been the basis and spring, and which continues to be the living support of our civilisation, and that because of being the root and support of our moral life. But this belief is not in the supernatural as an abstraction, but as a personal God. And even this would be ineffectual to elevate man's life, without the belief that personal intercourse with Him was a possible privilege, open to the enjoyment of every one who will. And in conducting this intercourse with God, there is a special suitableness in prayer, because it is the expression of our dependence. It is therefore, at the same time, an expression of our homage to God as Sovereign Lord and Proprietor of all things, the only source of all power and wisdom and goodness. It is an expression of our trust and confidence in Him. But then the question

may arise—All this is natural on the human side, but what
of the Divine? Has God given any intimation of His
willingness to communicate with man, in such form that
man can certainly interpret it? Is there any medium of
communication? Yes, in nature; for our argument does
not, at this stage, admit of reference to the inspired Word.
Nature, as the work of God, is a communication from God
to man, a vast system of significant symbols, symbols of
Divine thought addressed to the human senses, and intelligible to the human understanding. It is here that man
finds the treasury from which he stores his own mind with
all the opulence of thought. What are these terms so
familiar to our minds—law, order, proportion, fitness, design,
adaptation, means and ends, equality and inequality, force,
equilibrium, cause and effect, beauty, sublimity? They are
thoughts, conclusions of mind. Whence do we derive them?
They are not original creations of man. He finds them
in nature. They obtrude themselves upon him; he learns
them and appropriates them. Let him treat them reverently, they are Divine thoughts; they have their source in
the mind of God. Then man himself belongs to nature, and
he finds in himself another class of Divine thoughts, richer
and more precious still—justice, goodness; truth, holiness,
love; and these, he rightly infers, pre-existed in God Himself, attributes of His nature; and man exults in the consciousness, that as he can read Divine thoughts in their
symbols and make them his own, his mind bears affinity to
the Divine, and is capable of fellowship with God. Realising this relation to God, and "God's conversibleness with
man," prayer becomes as natural and as necessary as to
breathe. And it is not until sin has made man *unnatural*,
that any controversy could have arisen upon the subject.
That God cares for man is abundantly evident in the provision made for the continuance and well-being of the race,
and in the way in which He has subordinated nature to His
will and use. And let it be kept in mind that I address
myself only to those who believe that there is a God who is
the Creator and Lord of all; for only on that assumption is

there any ground for discussing the subject of prayer at all. By the very fact that He has brought us into existence, He has brought us into relation with Himself; and thereby also intimates His will that we shall have intercourse with Him. And by making us dependent upon Himself, He has made it a necessity of our condition that we should "feel after Him, if haply we may find Him, though He be not far from every one of us." God thus manifests, in the symbols of nature, the power and the will to hold converse with man. But that converse can only be conducted on the part of man by the use of his natural powers. His desires are inseparable from his nature, and the expression of his desires is as natural as the desires themselves. The sources and means of their satisfaction are external to themselves. No desire contains the object of its satisfaction within itself. It must seek for it outside of self; and it seeks that it may find, it asks that it may receive. Prayer is attached to desire by necessity of nature as surely as desire springs from want. If man recognises his dependence upon God, he will be conscious of wants in his life's experiences which neither man nor nature can supply. Intense desire will be born of urgent need, and will prompt importunate entreaty. This is the order of human nature. Has God made the order of external nature to be antagonistic to the order of human? Is the constitutional tendency to prayer, of which man is conscious, made to be abortive when the urgencies of human need are the sorest? Is prayer a bond of union between man and man, and a necessary means of mental and moral advancement? And can it serve no similar purpose to man in his relation with God? The elevation and refinement of his mental and moral nature depends upon intercourse with God; and he has been trained to prayer, that he may instinctively feel that the end of that training is prayer to God.

VI.—ARE THE LAWS OF MATTER ANTAGONISTIC TO THE LAW OF PRAYER?

I believe the considerations thus adduced are quite sufficient to prove that prayer is a necessity of our nature in
conducting our relations with God; that God is Himself
the Author of that necessity; that it is a law of our nature
and of our relation to Him. Are the laws of matter, then,
antagonistic to this law? and is their power sufficient to
nullify its action? This is the averment of modern science.
There are surely strong presumptions against this conclusion. He that ordained all these laws must have designed
them all to be effectual for their end; and His power and
wisdom are sufficient guarantee that they should not be
mutually destructive, neither that one should be destroyed
and the other survive. And surely, least of all, the presumption is, that the law which affects the highest interests of
man should give place to the laws which maintain the order
of the material world. In point of fact, we see and experience that the interests of man are the superior interests in
the world; that all animal life, if it endangers his interests,
may be destroyed. Now animal life is more valuable than
dead matter, as it serves a higher purpose in the economy
of God. We may, I think, conclude that, *a fortiori*, if
matter and its forces were found in the way, impeding the
mental and moral progress of man, there would be found in
the infinite resources of the Sovereign Ruler the means of
effectual counteraction. But as the laws of matter and the
law of prayer meet on the plane of human life and of human
interests, I believe the rational conclusion to be, that they
all, under Divine control, work together for good. It is
surely possible to believe that prayer and the physical laws
were pre-ordained, with their mutual adjustment, in the
original design of the great economy; so that, when they
met on the same plane, they would, like the physical laws
amongst themselves, act and re-act upon each other, to the
stability and harmony of the order of all departments of
nature. And it is surely manifest that in the adjustment of

the economy of the world every element must be taken into account. Human wants, human desires, human affections, and the human will, would find a place and occasion for their action. Now we know and feel that these experiences of mankind are indefinite in their variations—varying in their objects, varying in their intensity, varying in the conditions of their actions. Does the economy not provide for these variations? Are these variations less to be considered than the variations of the atmosphere? Are the ever-shifting forms of its clouds, the flashes of its lightning, the roll of its thunder—the changes of temperature, from that of the frozen north to that of the torrid zone—the changes, through all degrees of its motion, from the gentlest zephyr that fans the cheek to the tornado that roots up forests, that overthrows cities, and wrecks proud navies—of more account than all the diversified experiences of human souls? Our experience teaches us that there is a place for the play of the human will in the order of nature. Mr. Huxley says that "our volition counts for something in the course of events." It is necessary to our life and mental progress that within the limits of our interests the course of nature shall obey the control of our wills. The course of nature does not supply food in a condition fit for human nourishment. It does not provide clothing ready for use. It does not hew blocks from the mountain, nor transport them to the site you have chosen for a house, nor will it by its natural action construct it and prepare it for your habitation. You might perish in the midst of the opulence of nature if your own volitions did not count for something in the course of events. Nature produces the materials, but you must transform them by the agency of your own hands, under the direction of your own designing mind, and impelled and controlled by the determinations of your will. But in order to the desired results, it is absolutely necessary that the forces of nature shall, within the limits required by human well-being, obey the human will. It is by directing the forces of nature man stores up light in the form of gas; imprisons the mighty force of steam, graduates its action,

and compels it to perform his will and do his work; and
by the control of his will he guides the force of electricity
through thousands of miles to any spot on the earth, and
there compels it to utter his mind and express his desires.
By this control he is transforming the face of the earth, and
subjecting it to his dominion. The superiority of man over
all else that belongs to earth, the importance of his interests
above all other earthly interests, his mind, his will, his
conscience—all proclaim his superiority to all materialism,
that it is not his master, and that its order is subordinated
to him and his interests. Truly, "his volition counts for
something in the course of events."

But it would seem rational to suppose that there is also
some place for the volitions of the Divine will, and that they
too would tell for something in the course of events. This,
however, is denied by some who believe that God, having
set the mechanism of the material universe in motion, leaves
it to the automatic action of the laws impressed upon it;
and that these laws are so fixed and invariable that no
interference is possible, and that the Divine will no longer
acts within the sphere of matter so as to interfere with its
action; and that, therefore, God cannot answer prayer for
physical changes. Now this might be granted on one
assumption—namely, that the physical universe was to be
regarded simply in itself. But this is not the view in which
alone it is to be regarded. It is the abode of intelligent
beings, with free wills, capable of being influenced by the
materialism, because partaking of its nature and qualities;
and therefore also capable of re-acting upon it. The element
of will is thus introduced into the materialism, acting upon
it, and yet not a law of it; influencing its order, and yet
not of its order. In man's connection with it, it is a necessary means of his mental discipline and training. It contains
stores of knowledge, courting his research and investigation,
affording constant exercise for the powers of his mind, and
therefore for their continual improvement. Besides, the
human body exercises a very important influence in the
moral training of mankind. Its susceptibility of pleasure or

pain forms a test of moral power and of moral principle.
The bodily wants, deriving their supplies from the organic
and inorganic matter of the earth,—property, that is, the
means of bodily sustenance and support as a *right*, becomes
a necessity of the individual. And the acquisition and use
of property become very important elements in the moral
training and discipline of the race. When the material
world is regarded thus, as acted upon by free wills through
a material organism, and that it is thus brought into relation
with life and mind and morals, and as having an influence
through its laws upon man's life and character and experience, physical, mental, and moral,—I think there is good
reason to believe that a God showing so much interest in
man's welfare will not abandon His immediate control of a
world and its laws freighted with such interests ; but whenever the occasion arises in the lives of His worshippers
needing His interposition, His will shall prove a power to
determine controversies between man and matter. We
cannot but believe that in all His works God had moral
ends supremely in view. His greatest, His noblest work
is a race of mortal beings. They are created in His image,
and are His special care ; and we may very well believe that
when they specially need physical help which the order of
nature does not supply, He will modify that order for their
relief, and yet the universe shall never feel a shock. May
not God act upon matter in ways unknown to us ? Men of
science do not claim to have discovered all the properties
of matter. Dr. Tyndall says he has not even a theory of
magnetism. Do they not often observe phenomena to
which they cannot assign a cause ? The laws of nature
obey the human will, within circumscribed limits indeed,
yet sufficiently for man's need. They are surely as pliant to
the will of God. And because of the ineradicable tendency
to pray, under a sense of dependence and of obligation,
whenever God is recognised, we may undoubtingly infer
that this law of our nature shall be as effectual, within the
conditions of its action, in attaining its end as any law of
matter. Not only so, but as mind is superior to matter,

and the interests of mind of more value than the order of
material nature, we may rationally infer that if conflicting
claims shall arise between them, the order of nature shall
not prevail against the interests of man. Those who believe
miracles to be historical facts, have satisfying proof that
no order of material nature shall be allowed to stand in the
way when moral interests are to be advanced. And one
end served by miracles undoubtedly is, that it may be
demonstrated to man that God is present in nature, and
exercises power over all its laws, whether in the line of
their natural order or against them ; that from this also
man may be assured that the order of nature presents no
obstacle to the efficacy of prayer.

VII.—How does God Answer Prayer ?

Still the question is pressed, How does God answer
prayer ? Is it by interfering with the order of nature, by
suspending the action of its laws, or by compelling them to
a course of action contrary to their nature ? That prayer
is not answered by disturbance of the order of nature, the
continuance of the order of nature through the historical
period, and its continuance by the testimony of all men's
senses to-day, is sufficient to prove ; men have been praying
through all that period, and from generation to generation
have believed that their prayers were answered in the forms
of material good as well as spiritual; and yet the ordinances
of nature bear no trace of change. And in this present
generation, and at this day, multitudes assemble, not only
from Sabbath to Sabbath, but also from day to day, besides
in secret and in the family, with earnest and importunate
petitions for every form of temporal and spiritual blessings
for themselves and others; still the order of nature proceeds
in grand procession undisturbed. The praying people, therefore, are not looking for disturbance in the order of nature.
The presumption, then, is that the answer comes in the
order of nature, and by the silent ministry of its laws.
When I ask for my daily bread, I expect it to come, and I
find it does come, through the ever-recurring ordinances of

C

seed-time and harvest, as the fruit of forethought and skill and toil of man. For it is manifest that God, in making prayer to be a law of man's nature, designed it to act with the constancy of a law, neither fitfully nor at stated seasons, nor on special occasions only, but that it shall be habitual and persistent as our dependent condition is ; and that we shall have the confidence in its efficacy of operation and fruitfulness of result, according to its proper nature, which we entertain in every ordinance of nature.

But if it is thus the answer comes, how can it be distinguished from the action of natural law ? If the two things are strictly coincident in their course of action and result, is there any test by which the share of the result contributed by prayer may be marked off from that produced by human labour, by rain and sunshine. This is the demand of the men of science. They say every physical effect is susceptible of scientific verification. But it is quite evident that, if the physical answer to prayer were observable, it would require no scientific process to verify it. All men's observation would verify it, and neither doubt nor controversy could arise upon the subject. But as it does not, as a rule, submit itself to common observation, I think good reason can be shown why it cannot be detected by any scientific process. Dr. Tyndall represents prayer as an appeal to a Power, "under pressing circumstances," which "produces the precise effects caused by physical energy in the ordinary course of things." "Forced," he says, "upon his attention as a form of physical energy, or as the equivalent of such energy, he claims the right of subjecting it to those methods of examination from which all our present knowledge of the physical universe is derived." It may be observed respecting these statements, first, that prayer is not confined to "pressing circumstances," for Christians not only pray for their daily bread, which they expect to come under ordinary circumstances, but when it is on their table, they pray that the Divine Giver may bless it—that is, that by some energy competent to Himself alone, He may give the full designed and desired effect to the conditions of nutrition which He

Himself has ordained. Our dependence knows no intervals and no exceptions; and we seek that our prayers shall cover the whole extent of our dependence. When, therefore, we ask our food to be blessed to us, we do not know in what manner the Divine energy may influence the "physical energy" to the desired result. Even "pressing circumstances" may be met and adjusted according to our desire, by means whose natural adaptation we shall recognise in the welcome result; yet not the less shall we ascribe the issue to the interposition of Divine energy. But, again, observe the remarkable expression in the sentence I have quoted from Dr. Tyndall—"A form of physical energy, or the *equivalent* of such energy." What does Dr. Tyndall mean by "an equivalent of physical energy"? It can only mean an energy not physical, yet capable of producing physical effects. But such an energy would not submit itself to his "methods of examination." We would regard a Divine volition to be such an energy; nay, more than an equivalent for physical energy, as being the cause of physical energy, its efficient cause. And, strange as it may seem, Dr. Tyndall appears to acknowledge the reasonableness of supposing such a non-physical energy acting upon physical phenomena. After saying that "he contends only for the displacement of prayer, not for its extinction," and that "physical nature is not its legitimate domain," he adds the following beautiful passage:—"The theory that the system of nature is under the control of a Being who changes phenomena in compliance with the prayers of men, is, in my opinion, a perfectly legitimate one. It may of course be rendered futile by being associated with conceptions which contradict it; but such conceptions form no necessary part of the theory. It is a matter of experience that an earthly father, who is at the same time wise and tender, listens to the requests of his children, and, if they do not ask amiss, takes pleasure in granting their requests. We know, also, that this compliance extends to the alteration, within certain limits, of the current of events on earth. With this suggestion offered by our experience, it is no departure from scientific method to place behind natural phenomena a universal Father, who, in answer to the prayers of His children, alters the currents of those phenomena."* Dr. Tyndall has here conceded the legitimacy of our position—a universal Father altering the currents of natural phenomena in answer to the prayers of His children. It may be legitimately asked how he would discover, by his scientific method of examination, the action of the universal Father in the altered phenomena, and show the share contributed by His agency as distinct from that contributed by the physical forces? The alteration of phenomena is a physical effect; will analysis of it disclose the distinction? One observes with pain that Dr. Tyndall does not adopt the theory which he states with some nice feeling; but he acknowledges its scientific legitimacy. By this acknowledgment Dr. Tyndall bars the claim he had just advanced to "the right of subjecting prayer to those methods of examination from which all of our present knowledge of the physical universe is derived;" or he must confess that he is bound by his hypothesis to take his place by the side of the believers in prayer; for that hypothesis, which he affirms to be legitimate, is the Theist's theory of prayer. It is wholly inconsistent with his views of prayer as its most conspicuous opponent. But the claim he makes to subject the alleged physical effects of prayer to the test of physical analysis is not merely unreasonable; it is irrational. Dr. Tyndall, with his unsurpassed skill in physical analysis, is not able, in every experiment, to appropriate to each physical force its own proper share in every physical effect. I present for his analysis a grain of wheat. I ask him to separate by actual experiment, with scientific accuracy, and to label the several parts of that physical effect respectively due to the several ingredients in the soil, to the several elements of the atmosphere—to light, to heat, to electricity, and other forces exhaustively. And as the grain of wheat is a cultivated product, he is required to show in the analysis the exact portion due to the human will.

* " Contemporary Review," Oct., 1872.

This demand is the parallel to that of Dr. Tyndall himself. He claims that if there be real efficacy in prayer, it should discover itself in a physical analysis of its effect, as distinct from the forces of nature. The answer to prayer is from the will of God. The will of man combines with the order of nature in the production of the grain of wheat. Let him show the effect of human volition as a distinctly recognisable element. He will then have a more plausible claim to demand that the will of God, in answer to prayer, shall discover itself in the crucible of physical analysis. Now we hold that the prayer-force is an efficient agent in the production of the grain of wheat, acting with and by every other force; not because we can separate its effect from that of the other forces, but because, on the theory of prayer, its influence is present everywhere, wherever human interests extend. Its range of action is co-extensive with the human race; it pervades all human interests of every kind, and connects itself with everything by which human interests may be effected. When we pray for the success of our sowing, there is comprehended under that prayer the full natural efficiency of every force which contributes to the germination of the seed, to its growth, to its maturity and its ingathering, together with the skill and labour of man. Prayer is persistent as any other law; it never ceases. There never has been wanting a praying people on the earth; and their prayers are for all men. And because the order of nature affects man's condition—his health, his comfort, his prosperity—prayer acts upon the processes of nature by its efficacy with God. And Dr. Tyndall assures us that "it is no departure from scientific method to place behind natural phenomena a universal Father, who, in answer to the prayers of His children, alters the currents of those phenomena." And he adds, "Thus far theology and science go hand in hand." It may be asked, Why, then, do they part company? According to Dr. Tyndall, it is on the question of verification by experiment. And he instances how decisive experiment is as a test of the truth of theory—the test applied to Newton's theory of the

emission of light. But the cases are not parallel. In the
experiment upon light there were physical elements only
to deal with. In the case of prayer, the element of will
enters, and will acting with the physical forces to the desired
result. And Dr. Tyndall's theory of experiment must
embrace all the facts. In every instance in which human
will acts concurrently with the physical forces in producing
physical effects, as in the cultivation of plants, if Dr.
Tyndall's theory be right, the portion due to natural forces,
and the portion due to will, ought in every case to emerge
from the experiment with the distinction plainly marked.
No one will pretend to effect such a separation as this.
Our theory is that prayer does not produce a distinct and
separable portion of these effects, but that by its own efficacy
it secures the efficacy of the physical forces, according to
the good pleasure of God. It is impossible, therefore, in
the nature of things, to separate by any analysis known to
science the effect of prayer in changing the currents of
natural phenomena from that of the natural forces. And
the demand is unscientific.

Then prayer acts at all distances ; it embraces the whole
sphere of human life. And no man could insulate himself,
by any non-conducting medium, from partaking of some of
the forms of its influence. Prayer rests upon the field of
the prayerless, when the supplication of his praying neighbour for a bountiful harvest ascends to God. Not even Dr.
Tyndall could devise a non-conductor that would ward off
its influence. Thousands of prayers are being offered every
day for the increase and wide diffusion of all useful knowledge—for seats of learning, for colleges and schools, for
professors and teachers. Prayer-influence enters the lecture-
rooms and laboratories and observatories, where the princes
of science are exploring the wonderful works of God, and
revealing the boundless treasures of wisdom and knowledge
which they conceal, unconsciously to the operators. And
what indeed would the great body of the Christian people
know of the works of God but for the researches and discoveries of such men ? And let us thank God they are not

all prayerless and unbelieving. Well may Christians pray for the success of their labours, for they are illustrating the power and wisdom and goodness of God in a way incompetent to any who do not spend their lives in observation and experiment. The most sceptical amongst them are doing service to religion, helping the faith of the intelligent Christian, supplying ever-fresh grounds for adoration and praise to the glorious Creator. They are daily bringing to light facts sufficient to discredit their unbelieving theories. They are "hewers of wood and drawers of water for the house of our God."

When, therefore, we ask for changes in our relations with nature, beneficial to health or safety or prosperity, for ourselves or others, it is in the faith that God is able so to control the agencies of nature that they shall simply satisfy the desire expressed by the prayer, and that then their intensity shall exhaust itself; or when the desired effect has been produced, the forces may generate other sequences which shall find their place in the current of events without disturbance to the order of nature. We know that by methods known to science it is possible to localise, in increased or diminished amount, some of the great forces of nature; and when the desired effect has been produced, they are liberated to follow the law of their dispersion. To to this fact we owe not only interesting scientific experiments on electricity and magnetism, but also most important economic results, as in telegraphy and other instances. And it is conceivable that God may, by means in His own power, or by His mere volition, locally control the intensity of any physical force within limits sufficient for the special end, without any appreciable change in the surrounding phenomena. And the effect might appear in connection with the prayer in a manner so marked to the immediate suppliant, that it would be thankfully recognised as due to the efficacy of prayer, while that element would still elude all methods of scientific verification. On Dr. Tyndall's own interpretation of prayer as "a form of physical energy, or as the equivalent of such energy," what is to be expected but physical effects!

Man is comprehended in the order of nature. He is a being with wants and desires, with mind and will. The course of nature does not supply, as has been already noticed, his wants in the forms required by his constitution. What would be the value of his will in his connection with the system of nature, if it can do nothing in changing natural phenomena, either through the agency of man's own body or through his supplications to a higher power, when even his own life is concerned? His wants arise out of the course of nature; his volition must affect the course of nature, and transform its products to satisfy them. And nature is found pliant to his will within the limits necessary to his life and well-being. It is no extravagance of faith to believe that nature is pliant in the hand of its Creator, and that He can employ its ordinances in answering prayer. Those ordinances are the vehicles of His will in conducting His relations with man. They are the agents of His benevolence. Is it not conceivable that He may, under conditions of special need to His children, increase or diminish the intensity of the action of natural law, and affect the productiveness of a harvest or the course of a disease, without disturbing the equipoise of nature? A tornado in China produces no sensible effect upon the atmospheric phenomena of our own country. A thunder-storm in the next county shall have spent itself, but no atmospheric disturbance intimates the fact to us. If rain shall fall over a limited area, it does not disturb the order of nature. If that rain fell in answer to prayer, by a special volition of God, would the effect upon the order of nature be different? We do not ask for miraculous interpositions; but we believe that there are possibilities within the order of nature which lie beyond the discoveries of science, which God holds in His own power, from the resources of which He can supply healing and help as His children require. But it is sufficient for us to know that as man is able to "alter" the phenomena of nature within certain limits, but which are daily expanding, and without disturbing the order of nature, we are amply warranted in believing that nature is plastic in the hand of Omnipotence, that God may rule the relations between man and nature for man's good. And in settling the stability of nature, it is evident that He reserved a margin with sufficient mobility to allow of the play of free wills, and for the efficacy of prayer.

VIII.—PRAYER NOT OF INVARIABLE EFFICACY.

Another reason why it is not possible, by any scientific process, to detect the physical effect of prayer as distinguished from the effects of the physical forces, is this— namely, it is not of uniform and invariable efficacy.

In the former part of this lecture I showed that prayer, as a law of our social relations, is limited in its efficacy ; and this limitation is necessary to the order of society. And it is a proof of the identity of the law in the natural relations with that in the spiritual, that in both it is of limited efficacy. Of course there are limits to our asking. We cannot ask what we know to be morally wrong. We cannot ask what our natural reason teaches us would be unreasonable, and what our observation of the course and constitution of nature shows us to be fixed and unalterable. We cannot ask that past time be recalled, that accomplished facts should cease to be facts. Even within the limits of possibility there are many things which we feel we could not ask without feeling ourselves chargeable with folly.

But apart from such classes of things as these, it is necessary for our own good, and for the general good, that there should be a limit placed upon the efficacy of our prayers, even when we ask for things lawful in themselves. Nature teaches us, not less than Scripture, that we know not what to pray for as we ought, in relation to the things of this life. We might ask for some temporal advantage to our condition which might seem to us perfectly right to ask ; but things are so linked together in the course of nature that this good thing could not come alone, but would, by some natural necessity, bring other things in its train which might become the dead fly in the box of ointment. Considering that changes run in

series, and that series cross series at all angles, we are altogether incompetent to calculate or to imagine how many
changes, nor of what character, may, by necessary physical
action, follow upon the one which we desire.   The whole
interests of man and of the universe are under the government of God, and it is necessary that He should, both for
the good of the individual and for the general good, impose
a limitation upon the efficacy of prayer.   Our narrow vision
fixes itself upon some purely personal interest, the whole
form and colour of which may be changed to us in a day.
and it shall have lost all value in our eyes ; but the consequences of our change of mind begin a new series of phenomena, running on we know not whither, nor to what issues,
Were there no limits to the efficacy of prayer for physical
effects, physical phenomena would be undergoing ceaseless
abnormal changes.   The invariable efficacy of prayer would
be absolutely destructive.   Even the interests of praying men
are often antagonistic, therefore in their prayers asking for
opposite and contradictory physical effects.   The sequences
of some desired change disappoint us; we ask for its rever-
sal, and so on from day to day ; and the destruction of the
course of nature would result from the prayers of men.
And this would be the end of a system of prayer whose
physical effects were capable of scientific verification.   But
the will of God counts for much in controlling the current
of events, by controlling the efficacy of prayer.

    These necessary limits imposed upon the efficacy of
prayer render its uniformity impossible, and therefore renders it impossible for science to discover its law, so as to
bring it within the reach of scientific verification.   The
reasons of the volitions of a Being infinitely free are beyond
the scrutiny of man, and will not subject themselves to his
methods of examination.   But from the fact that the Divine
will is free to determine when any given prayer shall be
effectual, all Christians learn never to ask for any physical
effects unconditionally.   They know that the relation between prayer and the answer is not the relation of cause
and effect ; the sequences are not invariable.   The will of

God is supreme in the matter ; and they know that to ask a
favour is not to assert a right.   Therefore, with every petition for temporal good they present an alternative prayer,
" Thy will be done."   They are prepared, at whatever cost,
to forego any form of physical good, that the Divine will
may be done.   Their great aim is to have their wills conformed to the will of God ; then if His will is done, so is
theirs.   Temporal good is not the main end of their prayers.

No method of verification known to science is applicable
to the efficacy of prayer.   Although involving physical
effects, it cannot be tried by physical tests.   Nothing less
than the subversion of the present economy of the world
would supply facts sufficient to satisfy Dr. Tyndall, and
men like-minded, of the reality of the efficacy of prayer ;
and then the proof would be destroyed in the method.   It
would be impossible, by any scientific method, to test the
reality of the prayer of any individual.   No human mind is
naked and open before any other.   No man, therefore,
could with any certainty connect any event with any other
man's prayer.   Even the occurence of the event sought for
would not always be certain evidence that it came in answer
to the prayer.   It might be a mere coincidence.   How could
any man prove to another that it was not ?   If, then, the
efficacy of prayer eludes the test of science, and if even
uncertainty may rest upon the connection between an event
asked in prayer, and the prayer that sought it, is there any
evidence by which the efficacy of prayer may be tested and
known ?

IX.—The True Test of the Efficacy of Prayer.

I by no means deny that in special cases, of a public kind,
the event may be so marked that believers in the efficacy
of prayer will be fully persuaded that it has occurred in
answer to prayer.   But if the answer came unmarked by
startling phenomena, it would not satisfy sceptical men ;
nor even then, for they would still believe that the phenomena, although unusual, were still the effect of natural
causes.   And if the desired event occurred in the course of

nature, it would be ascribed to natural causes alone. And as prayer for physical effects is accompanied, as a rule, by physical effort, it is always open to men to ascribe the effect to the observed effort alone. And even those who have no speculative doubts about the efficacy of prayer, may show less confidence in it practically than in the efficacy of their own effort. The evidence is not overwhelming of the efficacy of prayer, or there could be no scepticism on the subject. If proof of the existence of God and religious truth possessed all the force of demonstration, no man could be an unbeliever ; but then his faith would have no moral value. It would not be moral at all. Then, again, in the case of individuals ; they may have the highest moral evidence that their prayers have been answered, but they cannot make others partake of their conviction by any evidence they can impart. Those who have similar experience will believe their statement, knowing it to be altogether credible. But it is wise and right to acknowledge that no evidence of the efficacy of prayer for physical effects, sufficient to compel the credence of sceptics, is forthcoming. But I believe there is a form of evidence sufficient for the Christian, which, though it will not bear a physical test, will bear the test of reason. Let it be kept in mind that all along we have been speaking of prayer for physical effects. But then all Christians know that they do not pray for such effects to come alone. They pray that spiritual benefits may accompany them. If they ask for restored health, they ask at the same time that it may be sanctified to themselves and others. The prayer itself is a spiritual action ; they ask for a physical good. The spiritual and the physical are combined in the prayer, and they desire that they shall be combined in the answer ; and the answer would not be according to the prayer if it did not convey both. The test of the efficacy of the Christian's prayer would not be the physical benefit, if it actually came to him in the form desired, if it came alone. With what feeling and with what state of mind is it received? This is the test. Is it received merely with the natural satisfaction of a desire accomplished, and with self-gratulation in the enjoyment of a valuable possession? This is a natural state of mind, and not a spiritual. On the other hand, is it received with solemn, cheerful thankfulness—with more joy in it as a token of the favour of the Giver than in the gift itself? Then the prayed-for gift has not come alone, presenting only its own proper value. It has brought something better than itself—a happy sense of God's regard penetrating the whole soul, until it is bright with the radiance of gratitude. What, then, can follow but a revived faith, a warmer love, and a renewed dedication? Then arises the sense of obligation to use the gift according to the clearly indicated design of the Giver. Now these feelings and states of mind are spiritual, but they are not less natural and rational, considering the relations between the Giver and the receiver ; and they are in entire accordance with the nature of the human mind. Such an experience as this, coming with the material gift asked in prayer, would be a proof to every believer of the efficacy of prayer, strong enough to turn aside any sceptical argument. And this experience is repeating itself daily with the prayed-for gift of our daily bread, sustaining the strength of the Christian life.

But there are other physical effects of a painful kind which also issue in spiritual benefit to the children of God. There are bodily sufferings, and adversity of circumstances, and trying bereavements. But do we pray for these? Not specially. But we present petitions which we know will involve these afflictions in the answer. The Christian prays, "Father, glorify Thy name," in me, in my heart and life ; and that may imply fiery trial. And there is a second petition like unto the first, "Sanctify me wholly ;" and according to the law of the Father's house, this necessitates chastisement by various forms of calamity, for "what son is he whom the Father chasteneth not?" We pray for physical good, and spiritual good comes in the answer. We pray for spiritual good, and physical suffering is combined with it in the answer. And the soul learns to say, "Good is the will of the Lord." The will of the Lord is the rule and measure of the Christian's prayer. He gives it the first place, therefore.

The test here named offers itself to the judgment of mental science ; and a thoughtful examination of consciousness would, I think, show to even a sceptic that, grant there is a God, and that He holds converse with men, and the experience we have noted would seem not only possible to the mind, but also to be the logical consequence of the relation.

X.—THE MAIN END OF PRAYER.

Asking and receiving even amongst men are not the main ends of prayer. The bestowal of material help, the transfer of material good from one to another in response to asking, are not the main ends of prayer. These are signs and symbols of states of feeling, the cultivation of which is the grand end of our mutual dependences. And these mutual dependences are the conditions out of which our desire of association springs, and which make society a permanent necessity. And we are dependent upon society for the exercise and cultivation of those sentiments and affections upon which our moral perfection and happiness depend, more than upon any amount of adjustment between our nature and its material environments. When asking and receiving are the symbolic language of kindness and good-will, the whole intercourse of mutually dependent life moves on with tranquil and harmonious action. And the main end of prayer in our relation with God is not the receiving the bountiful supplies of His providence, nor restoration from sickness, nor protection from calamities, nor length of days; but the cultivation of a right state of mind toward God—love, trust, reverence—and thus to enjoy His fellowship. But if He never answers our prayers—never extends His help in weakness or danger—never consoles a sorrow, what could we believe but that He was indifferent to our happiness? And would it reconcile us to all this disregard to be told that He had bound Himself by inflexible laws never to answer a prayer—never to respond to the

cry of beings, the prime law of whose existence is dependence upon Himself? What state of mind would this beget
but estrangement and aversion? But the impulse to pray is
so natural to man, and in such constant exercise in all our
social relations, that in spite of the sophistry of unbelief, our
nature teaches us that He who has made us dependent and
praying beings is Himself the hearer of prayer. And as
prayer belongs to our mental and moral nature, the inference is irresistible that it has a higher end to serve than is
required in the inter-relations of mankind—that it is necessary to maintain our relations with God. And this is its
pre-eminent distinction—that it keeps the spirit of man in
contact with the mind of God, in the consciousness of
dependence, in the faith of His kindness, in the happy confidence of His never-failing and ever-present help. It
secures a constant enquiry after His will, a watchful observation of His providences, and a jealous guarding of our
desires, that we cherish none which may not be formed into
prayers, and be presented with confidence to God. Then
there is a constant alternating between prayer and thankfulness for prayer answered, ever ministering to the health,
the vigour, and the cheerful content of the spiritual life.
And the crowning result of this nearness to God by prayer
is the accordance of our wills with the will of God, and the
consequent assimilation to the Divine character. In this
is fulfilled the perfection of man. This is the main end of
prayer.

Concurrently with this highest end, there is the cultivation
of the unity and fellowship of the praying brotherhood
throughout the world. They are ever praying for one
another. It is most pleasant and grateful to think of being
comprehended in the prayers of all believers. Millions are
praying for you. Their prayers compass you about in your
daily life, falling upon your fields and homes and hearts as
imperceptibly, yet as really and beneficently, as the dew at
eventide. And you are reciprocating their prayers, bearing
the interests of all the brethren on your heart before the
Lord; and the whole household of faith, in spite of all

dividing influences, realise their common relation to the
Father. But this is not all.   The whole body of the faithful
unite in supplication for all men, in relation to all interests
which are common to man—bursting the narrow bounds of
self-interest, expanding our human sympathies, and testi-
fying to the brotherhood of man.   Every thoughtful believer
in the efficacy of prayer, therefore, realises the fact that
prayer is a power in the world, an established law of its
order, indispensable to order, co-operating with every other
law in the production even of physical effects.   And there
is no more reason to believe that health will be restored
without prayer than without medicine ; nor that the harvests
of the world shall be less indebted to prayer than to sunshine for their ripeness.   Prayer is as widely diffused over
the earth as the sunshine, and is as much an ordinance of
God as the sunshine, or as man's labour, in promoting the
fertility of the earth.   It is a power over the human mind,
a power in social life, a power in the world's politics, in
science and philosophy, and, above all, in the spiritual life
of man.   But its power is not being fully proved, through
the want of the strong faith to which the greatest effects
are promised.   And we often ask amiss, and are therefore
not heard ; and at the best our prayers are imperfect.
And we need the Spirit of grace and of supplications to
purify our desires, that we may ask in faith, nothing
doubting.

But prayer has its perfection, under perfect conditions,
conditions so pure, so perfect, that whatsoever is asked is
given in terms of the asking ; and in this case there is no
limit to its efficacy.   It is the intercession of the Divine
Redeemer—" Him the Father heareth alway."   And He
Himself has told us what the law of effectual prayer is—
"Whatsoever ye shall ask of the Father in my name, He
will give it you."

Man's Responsibility for his Belief.

REV. JOHN MACNAUGHTAN.

17/1063.²

MAN'S RESPONSIBILITY FOR HIS BELIEF.

I N entering upon the discussion of this theme, it is necessary to define the terms of it—*Man, Responsibility*, and
Belief. By man, we understand every human being possessed of those faculties and feelings that are proper to
humanity—not man as a mere sentient creature, nor man as
a higher animal endowed with intellect, and enabled thereby
to observe, to reason, and to judge ; but man as an intellectual and moral being, with mind and conscience, with
affections and emotions, combined with a will whose volitions
enable him to determine and decide—in short, man as we
find him in the everyday walks of life.

Responsibility is a term imported into the English
language from the Latin tongue—its root is the verb
(respondeo) " to answer"—and describes an existing relationship to some Superior, who has a right to question, and to
require a reply.   Terms of similar import and significance
are found in all known languages, and seem to indicate, from
their use, an almost universal belief that the transactions of
human life will one day be reviewed and inquired into by
the Governor and Lord of all.   The prominent idea involved
in " answerableness," or responsibility, is that of a judgment
throne—a future great assize—presided over by some One
who has the power and the right to supervise the life of
man, to sift his every motive, to analyse his most complex
actions, and adjudge such penalty or reward as justice may
demand—in short, the very existence of the term, implies
the belief that man is not independent, that he is the subject
of moral government, and must give an account of himself
to God.

It is interesting to find such terms in all languages;
for if language is the reflection of the facts and feelings of

human nature, the image of existing ideas, the use of such terms originates the inquiry, How came they to find a place in the vocabularies of earth ? Not certainly as the result of education, or of domestic training, though these expand and enforce the ideas which such terms convey ; they seem to be inwrought with the feelings and the instincts of humanity, and to crop up with the earliest manifestations of our reflective powers. The use of such phrases as—*I ought, you ought not, you should have done, it was your duty to act differently*, seems to be the natural outcome of the innate or underlying thought, that responsibility to the Creator and Moral Governor of the universe is a very part of the nature He hath bestowed upon us.

There is a beautiful passage on this subject in Taylor's "Natural History of Enthusiasm." When arguing that the terms found in language must have their archetypes in nature, and applying this argument to the subject of man's responsibility, he says :—"If man is not a moral agent, and if his sphere in this respect does not immeasurably transcend that of the sentient orders around him, how came he to talk as if he were a moral agent ? If, in regard to a moral system, he is only a brute of finer form, born of the earth, and returning to it again, whence is it that in respect of virtue and vice, of good and evil, the dialect of heaven rolls over his lips ? whence was it, and how, that he stole the vocabulary of the skies ?" We need not go far for an answer to the general question—Am I a responsible being ? Our own consciousness furnishes the reply ; and such acknowledgments as—*I ought* not to commit sin, *I ought* to love my neighbour, *I ought* to love and fear God, are echoes from the depths of man's constitution, proclaiming that his freedom to think and act and will has its limits. For, as the apostle saith in the Epistle to the Romans, "Every one of us shall give account of himself to God."

Belief includes all opinions, thoughts, and sentiments, whatever the subject of these may be—social, political, scientific, or religious ; all the various conclusions to which the human mind may come on facts, on questions, on doctrines, when it has sources of information and capacity for weighing the evidences by which such sentiments seem to be sustained. But when belief is associated with responsibility, there are many limits to be observed which greatly narrow the question. There are entire classes of beliefs to which no moral character can be attached ; and these, of course, are excluded from the discussion. I believe that a stone is hard, that a ball is round, that a box is square, and so forth ; but there is nothing moral in such opinions. I believe the axioms that form the bases of all mathematical conclusions, and I hold the accuracy and correctness of the solutions they enable me to arrive at ; but there is nothing in the results of exact science that involves merit or demerit. The process followed out is a purely intellectual one ; and there is neither moral excellence nor guilt in the reception or in the refusal of the conclusions.

Again, while man is responsible to society for his actions, and is under the control of its governments and subject to its laws, he is not responsible to his fellow-man, nor to the powers and dominions of this world, for his thoughts and opinions, so long as he keeps them to himself. His sentiments may be of the most treasonable character, utterly subversive of the integrity and good order of the State ; but if he keeps these hidden in the secret chambers of his own mind, no earthly power has a right to demand that they shall be dragged to the light, be adjudicated on by any earthly tribunal, and be dealt with as if they had been published openly to the injury and detriment of the nation.

The soul of man is a little world of its own, and within that sacred domain man is as free to think as he is to breathe. God alone is Lord of the conscience ; He is the Lawgiver and the Judge in and over the heart.

This truth is the foundation of all enlightened toleration —of all true liberty. No doubt tyranny and bigotry have often attempted to invade this citadel, and by the force of agonising tortures have extracted from quivering lips the secrets of thought ; men maddened by pain may sometimes have disclosed their hidden belief, to the eternal infamy of their inquisitors. But all such processes are ineffectual to suppress that freedom of thinking which is man's birthright. Coercion in the region of opinion may make men hypocrites ; it never can be consistent with the duties of rulers of Churches or of States.

It is altogether, however, a different question—Will God, as the Moral Governor of the universe, judge of our most secret thoughts, and take account of all our opinions and beliefs ? If it be true that not a ripple passes over the wave, nor an insect hovers in the sky, nor a leaf trembles in the forest, that is not observed by the Divine All-seeing Eye, will not this exquisite minuteness of inspection penetrate the soul, range over all the thoughts, and witness the formation of opinions ? And, in the day when God judges the world, will not our thoughts and beliefs be found graven on the imperishable tablets of eternity, and rise from the grave of our memories to be arraigned and judged of in the day of final account ?

Again, when discussing the question of man's responsibility to God for his belief, we do not mean that all men are equally responsible for the opinions they hold ; the degree of accountability must be regulated by circumstances, as of position, of privilege, of opportunity. Some men are, unquestionably, without any fault of their own, at far greater disadvantage than others, as regards their means and opportunities for hearing and receiving truth ; their responsibilities must be proportionately less. Men, for example, who never could have heard of the gospel doctrine of salvation by grace, cannot be chargeable with 'unbelief, nor with the rejection of a redemption that was never offered to them. On this point the Scripture testimony is clear and explicit— a man is accepted of God according to what he hath, and not according to what he hath not ; or more expressly still, in Romans ii. 12,16—"For as many as have sinned without law shall also perish without law : and as many as have sinned in the law shall be judged by the law ; in the day when God shall judge the secrets of men by Jesus Christ."

Again, when affirming that a moral character attaches to

opinion or belief, we do not restrict our thoughts to the act of the mind dealing with a certain amount of evidence presented to it at the time when it forms its opinion ; but include all that influences the judgment, all those self-pro-duced inclinations, that bias the understanding and colour its conclusions ; in short, whatever in nature, in research, in habit, or in neglected means of information, hinders the mind from appreciating evidence, and prevents it from giving due weight to its value. Very possibly the persecuting Jews and Pagans in the first age of Christianity were sincere enough in the belief that they did right in putting Christians to torture and to death. It was the time predicted by Jesus, when every one that killed His disciples thought, they did God service ; they pleaded conscience in justification of their wicked deeds : but their minds were ill informed ; their hearts were inflamed by passion ; they should have known better, and have felt more kindly. And if we could absolve them from all criminality in believing that to imbrue their hands in the blood of the martyrs was serving God, what moral guilt could attach to the acts that were the necessary consequences of such a faith as that ?

The main point in this controversy is whether or not belief is moral in its nature, or is a necessary and unavoid-able result of evidence presented to the intellect ; is man in believing absolutely passive, so that it is physically im-possible for him to do otherwise than he does, whether he receives or rejects any specific dogma or doctrine? It is chiefly in connexion with theological truths or religious beliefs that these issues are raised ; and therefore we shall consider, first, what are the teachings of the Scriptures on the point ; and then inquire whether the lessons of the Bible are in harmony with the conclusions of philosophy, and the ascertained results of human experience.

If man is not responsible for his belief, then unbelief can-not be a sin ; for if it is not a voluntary act, no fault can be attached to the man who rejects the truth which God, in His word, has proposed for acceptance. It may be a loss to the man not to have believed, but he cannot be censured nor condemned for that mental process over which he had no control ; his believing could not have raised him in moral excellence, and his non-believing cannot involve the disapprobation of God, nor the forfeiture of any benefit or blessing which His gracious hand would otherwise have bestowed.

Assuredly this is not the light in which belief and unbelief are set forth in the inspired record. Faith is therein described as the highest and noblest virtue, and unbelief as a deadly and ruinous sin—a sin peculiarly dishonouring to God and destructive to the soul, to be followed by the direst penalties, and admitting neither of palliation nor of apology. All through the Bible, belief and unbelief are held to be *works* or *acts* of man—the subjects of praise or of censure, of promise or of threatening ; in short, they have attached to them all the responsibilities that can cleave to the actions of any free, moral agent in the universe of God.

It is not unworthy of notice, in passing, that in the New Testament the same word is sometimes translated *unbelief*, and sometimes *disobedience ;* * and as disobedience always implies the existence of a command (for where there is no law there can be no transgression), so a commandment, issued by a great and gracious ruler, always implies the existence of a will, in the subject of that order, either to obey or to despise the injunction. The whole language of the Bible is constructed on the recognition of this principle—as when we are commanded to search the Scriptures, to receive the truth, to seek for wisdom, to know God, to believe on Jesus, and to accept the message of reconciliation.

Let us examine this point a little more minutely. Faith or belief is described as a duty. God requires us to believe; our believing is an act of obedience to His will ; for God is obeyed when His testimony is believed—"They have not all obeyed the gospel. For Esaias saith, Lord, who hath believed our report?"—"A great company of the priests were obedient

---

* ἀπειθεια. Compare Rom. xi. 32 with Ephes. ii. 2 ; and again, as identifying unbelief with disobedience, John iii. 36, Ὁ δε ἀπειθῶν is contrasted with ὁ πιστευων.

to the faith." "Ye have obeyed from the heart that form of doctrine which was delivered you." "This is His commandment, That we should believe on the name of His Son Jesus Christ." Now, whatever be the nature of faith or belief (and we shall advert to that by-and-by), it is the object of a command that issues from the throne of the Eternal, an act of obedience demanded by the Sovereign Lord of all from His intelligent creatures—an obedience that can only be yielded when the will consents to believe what His precept requires.

Again, the commandment to believe is enforced by the very highest sanctions that can be attached to any law of God. The rewards conditioned on belief, and the penalties affixed to unbelief, are the grandest and the most awful to which our conceptions can reach—EVERLASTING LIFE, AND ETERNAL DEATH. "Believe on the Lord Jesus Christ, and thou shalt be saved." "He that believeth shall be saved ; he that believeth not shall be damned." "He that believeth not the Son shall not see life, but the wrath of God abideth on him." "He that believeth not God hath made Him a liar." "The Lord Jesus shall be revealed from heaven, . . . taking vengeance on them that know not God, and that OBEY not the Gospel of our Lord Jesus Christ: who shall be punished with everlasting destruction from the presence of the Lord, and from the glory of His power; when He shall come to be glorified in His saints, and to be admired in all them *that believe.*" "This is the condemnation, that light is come into the world, and men have loved darkness rather than light, because their deeds were evil." In all these passages unbelief is described as a sin, a moral evil, which not only leaves man an unforgiven transgressor, with all his guilt crushing him into ruin, but as being *itself* a heinous transgression, involving an indescribable amount of guilt, and therefore followed by certain judgment ; so that *on account of* unbelief, men are as certainly guilty before God, as they are if chargeable with murder or any other crime. Hence it is that, in the catalogue given us in the Book of Revelation of those who are finally and for ever outcasts from God, the *unbelieving* occupy a conspicuous place. "The fearful, and UNBELIEVING, and the abominable, and murderers, and whoremongers, and sorcerers, and idolaters, and all liars, shall have their part in the lake which burneth with fire and brimstone : which is the second death."

What sanctions grander than these : life, eternal life—bliss, endless bliss, in fellowship with God—happiness in common and in communion with all the pure and the holy of the moral creation of Jehovah! And woe, unutterable woe, the punishment of unbelief! Can it be that no moral character attaches to belief or to unbelief? Can it be that, where there is no moral delinquency, the Holy and the Just One will overwhelm with terrific judgment? "Shall not the Judge of all the earth do right?"

The truths of the Gospel are presented to the human mind very much as other truths are—that is, accompanied with evidence suited to man's capacity for understanding them, and sufficient in amount to induce and warrant his cordial reception and belief of them. But the evidence, however varied and multiform, is not the only element that determines the belief—it is the *discernment* of that evidence that brings about the faith.

In the evening sky, millions of stars sparkle in gorgeous splendour, lighting up the depths of night, and revealing the wondrous glories of the works of God ; but no amount of intellectual capacity would enable the mind to take in the idea of that immeasurable expanse, or picture to the soul the panorama of the skies, unless there was an eye to look upon it—that is, an actual power of discerning what the visible universe displayed. There is another heaven—the sky of Revelation ; every truth of God studs that sphere like a very sun, and each truth that sparkles in that firmament carries with it the evidence of its Divine origin ; but if the eye of the soul be closed, or if the moral vision be diseased or distorted, the evidence will fail to convince, for it will not be discerned. Just as light, though self-demonstrative, cannot be known without the eye; so Divine truth, flashing first from the heart of God,

cannot be comprehended except by the heart—that is
to say, if we merely exercise our reason about the truths
of the Gospel, they may remain to us a dead letter, or a
mass of tangled dogmas, and of strange conceptions ; and
we may turn over page after page of the written record,
and never come into contact with its grand central truth,
the key to the comprehension of all the rest.

We have said that belief depends on the discernment of
evidence, and we must here add that the power to discern
depends largely on the inquirer himself ; and hence one
source of his accountability. It is his work to collect and
examine evidence, to weigh and consider arguments, to
watch against prejudice, to inform himself of the facts that
bear upon the thoughts presented to his mind ; and surely
it is easy to conceive of this being done carelessly, indo-
lently, and partially, or not done at all, so that the conclusions will be as defective as the examinations were
imperfect. In such a case, culpability must attach to error
in opinion, when closer scrutiny would have led to a very
different judgment. For example, my understanding cannot
assent to the proposition that Jesus Christ is the Son of God
till I have apprehended what the terms of the statement
mean ; but this cannot be done if my will is so slothful, so
worldly, or so disposed towards the lusts and pleasures of
the world, as never to suffer me to think of them seriously ;
and in that sense the understanding is at the disposal of
the will.

Nor is it to be forgotten how much a man's habits influence his opinions. Let him blunt his moral feelings by
indulgence—let pride, or lust, or passion, or avarice, or
vanity, establish themselves on the throne of the affections,
and they will bend and bias the intellect ; inclination will
overbear judgment, a depraved taste will prevent the soul
from approaching truth with an ingenuous desire to know
it, and to follow it, the light will be refused because the
deeds are evil. This is the explanation of the fact that the
force of argument and the power of evidence tell very
differently on different minds. In the case of some honest

inquirers, they sweep like an avalanche all doubt and difficulty from the field of belief; while in other cases argument
and evidence come like the mists of the morning, and hide
for a little moment the rocks of error and ravines of doubt;
but these mists speedily pass away, and leave the whole
panorama as wild and desolate as before.   In all such cases
the want of belief does not arise from lack of evidence, but
from the perverted state of the heart, and the moral
influences that are allowed to overbear the judgment.

This is admitted by all who adopt the Scriptural account
of belief, and who hold that whosoever believeth on the
Lord Jesus shall be saved; nor can any objection be
reasonably taken to a reference to the history and operation
of gospel faith or belief, inasmuch as this involves the
highest interests of man, deals with the grandest and most
momentous of all opinions, brings into view our moral
relationship to God, and enables us to analyse minutely the
operation of heart and mind and conscience in the formation
of the noblest species of belief.

The grand difficulty that stands in the way of a sinner's
forming a right opinion of his moral relationship to God,
and of giving a place in his heart to the message of salvation, does not arise from any want of evidence to prove the
grand truth that "God so loved the world, that He gave
his only begotten Son, that whosoever believeth in Him
should not perish, but have everlasting life;" nor from any
difficulty about the fact that "God sent not His Son into the
world to condemn the world, but that the world through
Him might be saved;" the difficulty lies in the state of the
heart and will of the sinner.   He cannot help feeling that
the gospel truths stand on a different basis from all others—
that their admission involves a change in the life, and an
admission of responsibilities, that do not attach to any other
beliefs.   If received, he must submit his soul to God, in
contrition, in fear, in gratitude : and by personal consecra-
tion to duties that his likings, his tastes, his will, are opposed
to ; hence, in the face of evidence, he will not come unto
Christ (that is, he *will* not believe) that he may have life.

These words were originally spoken to the Jews, and were true of the great majority of that unhappy people. They had the testimony of John, whom they acknowledged to be a prophet; they had the evidence of miracles, the very signs and wonders they asked for; they had the voice from heaven, attesting the character of Jesus; and they had the testimony of their Scriptures, to which Christ appealed, saying, "They are they which testify of me." And yet they rejected the Messias as obstinately as if His claims had been supported by no evidence, or as if their duty and their interest justified their unbelief; it was want of *will*, and not lack of evidence, that kept them from believing. Will is not a mere principle; it is under the direction of reason; and yet there is a certain influence it wields over the mind. By a volition, it makes one thought take precedence of another, and one emotion command another; and in this it is free, active, voluntary. If belief is the link between a soul and salvation, it is easy to understand that a man's responsibility depends largely on whether he has anything to do, personally and actively, with its existence and operation. Is it the result of a persuasion produced by evidence addressed to the understanding? or are there in the state of the heart moral barriers that resist the light, and act like fastenings on the closed windows of the intellect? And must man be a consenting party to their removal—in other words, is gospel faith or belief a result usually attained, or in its nature possible, without the will and heart of the man being cognisant and consenting parties? Assuredly it is not. The heart, the conscience, and the will must acknowledge the power of the truth, and the grand proof of belief be given, when the sinner yields himself to God.

"In the work of believing," says Dr. South,* "the understanding is chiefly at the disposal of the will; for though it is not in the power of the will *directly* either to cause or to hinder the assent of the understanding, yet it is *antecedently* in the power of the will to apply the mind to, or to take it

* South's "Sermons," Vol. I., page 96.

off from, the consideration of those objects to which, without such a previous consideration, it cannot yield its assent,
for all assent pre-supposes a simple apprehension of the
terms of the proposition.   But unless the understanding
employ and exercise its cognitive power about these terms,
there can be no apprehension of them; and the understanding, as to the exercise of this power, is subject to the command of the will." And hence it is that the Lord Jesus
stakes the whole character of His mission on the issue, that
the evidence by which His doctrines were sustained was
adequate and sufficient, and that the withholding of assent
did not arise from want of light in the understanding, but
from the perverseness of the will, and the corruptness of the
heart. Now, just as certainly as the power to consent implies
ability to refuse the consent, accountability for giving or
withholding that assent is chargeable on man, and comes
within the range of those acts for which, as a moral being,
he is responsible to God, the Lord of all.

When we examine the features of "gospel belief," or the
reception of the grand truths about the way of life, which the
revelation of God discloses, we find that the sinner has presented to him a picture of himself as a lost, helpless, guilty
transgressor.   How is this to be believed by him ?   Not by
the force of testimony alone, apart from the acting of his
own consciousness, the declaration of his own conscience, and
the comparison of himself, as a moral agent, with the law of
God.   This sentiment, opinion, or belief, is not the mere
result of external evidence presented to reason.   Like a
large part of our knowledge, it does not flow from reason ;
for, just as in the sentient world, our belief in the properties
of sensible objects is derived from the senses, and not from
the reason ; for it is not reason that tells us that the odour of
the rose is fragrant, or that musical sounds are harmonious.
So in the moral world. We judge and form opinions
largely by the power and operation of our moral sense ; and
though the heart does not reason, yet within the limits of
sentiment it comprehends as well, if not better, than reason
does.   Hence it has been well said—" All the effects of the

most active intellect cannot give us a conception of the taste of a fruit we have never tasted, nor of the perfume of a flower we have never smelt, much less of an affection we have never felt."

Now, as lowly views of one's self, profound personal humiliation, the abasement of natural pride, the acknowledgment of sin and transgression before God, are acts that enter into the belief of gospel truth, acts that may be neglected or performed largely according to the will and liking of the man, they obviously come within the range of the opinions for which man is accountable.

Again, if belief in an offered Saviour depends on the knowledge of His character, His person and work—such a knowledge as takes possession of the soul, and leads it to trust, to confide, to cling, with all the intenseness of ardent affection, to Him and to His cross—does it not imply careful examination of the truth, and personal, patient investigation of the grounds on which the Redeemer claims our reliance? Are we not bound to test the strength and validity of the argument for believing on His name, so that we may be able to give a reason for the hope that is in us, whether we rely on His atonement, or depend on a righteousness of our own? Here, surely, there is a field for voluntary action; for while it is acknowledged that conviction must ultimately depend on evidence discerned, man, in the investigation of it, is plainly accountable for research, for honesty of inquiry, for diligence and attention, and for the honest endeavour to keep his mind free from all prejudice.

Can we hold that the Jewish priests and scribes were not chargeable with guilt in rejecting Jesus as the Messiah, when they did not go even as far as Bethlehem to ascertain the facts about His birth? They were apparently expecting the appearance of the promised Saviour. They were able to give directions to the wise men from the East as to the locality in which He might be sought, and to verify their information from the sure word of prophecy. And yet, though they heard of His star in the East, they did not make the least effort to convince themselves whether or not the King of the Jews was born.

In the field of belief, are there no powers at work but reason and evidence, intellect and argument, nothing but the powers of the human understanding, busied with logical deductions, joining together its cords of ideas, till it finds itself immeshed in a web of inevitable conclusions, and all this without allowing an inch of space for the influence of feeling or emotion? Have we not, on this field, man—the whole man—acting as a free, voluntary agent? Do we not see him pausing over *this* proof, and scanning it very minutely—carelessly or wantonly passing by *that* evidence as if it did not deserve his notice—his whole emotional nature now at work ; and now, again, his preconceptions inducing him to turn with scorn from the offered argument, his moral feeling, his will, his affection, his intellect, all conspicuous throughout the entire process—not mind alone, but the man? The *I* is prominent. The man sues for mercy, looks towards the Saviour, humbles himself before God, and expresses his new-found faith, when he exclaims, " Lord, I believe ; help Thou mine unbelief." It is the *I* who is the subject of the belief ; not that any man saves himself, but that he is not saved without his own consent ; and hence the responsibility.

This is illustrated by the figure of looking, which, in the Bible, is often used as the synonyme for believing—" Look unto me, and be ye saved, all the ends of the earth, for I am God, and there is none else"—" Looking unto Jesus, the author and finisher of our faith"—implying that, just as we have the command of our eyes, and can turn them towards or away from any visible object at will, so, in a certain sense, have we the command and control of our moral vision, and can direct it towards the great object of faith. This is, indeed, the history of the act of belief. " We all with open face behold, as in a glass, the glory of the Lord," &c.— " Every one which seeth the Son, and believeth on Him"— that is, every one who, having seen the Son, hath believed on Him—"hath everlasting life." A single glance, unaffected and earnest—one child-like look, into which the affections of the soul are thrown—perceives in Jesus an infinitude of love and grace ; and that vision necessarily results in true belief.

Man is not passive in all this ; the discernment of the glory of Christ is not forced on him ; it is with an open face he beholds the glory—dimly, it may be, at first, but becoming brighter and clearer as the result of thought and contemplation—till at the foot of the Cross he lifts up his eyes from the dust to the crucified Redeemer, and in the earnestness of a true belief exclaims, "My Lord and my God !" In fine, on this part of the subject, if we receive the Bible as a revelation from God, there must be an onerous responsibility dependent on the use we make of its promises and exhortations, and on the degree of attention with which we listen to its commandments and warnings, arising from the authority of Him whose word it professes to be.   If, instead of the voice of God in the written word, we were startled from our security by that voice speaking to us, as it did to Israel, out of the fire, and awing us into silence by blackness and darkness and tempest—would not our whole being be brought under the influence of that Speaker, and a deep sense of responsibility for believing or rejecting His message take possession of our souls?   Or if, instead of quietly reading in the Scriptures the exhortation, "I pray you, in Christ's stead, be ye reconciled to God," Christ were to leave His eternal throne, leave the heavens, and come down into the midst of us, in all the glories of His Mount Tabor state, and ask us to believe in His atonement, and be reconciled to God by His blood—would we feel that we could treat this as an ordinary subject of inquiry, that our minds must of themselves inevitably act on the evidence presented, and that we would incur no special guilt if we concluded to disbelieve the proclamation, and reject the remedy offered for our guiltiness and sin ?   Nay, rather would we not feel that it would be impossible for us to escape personal accountability if we refused that offer of grace ?   And where is the radical difference between that imagined condition of things and our present position ? Can we, if we receive the Bible as from God, separate altogether the voice of authority from its requirements, or place its truths on the ordinary level of statements in books of philosophy and science ? Are not the truths the same, when enshrined in revelation and attested by sufficient evidence, as when spoken by the lips of the Lord ? And is not this Scriptural conclusion regarding the testimony of God sufficient to establish our responsibility on the matter ? " See that ye refuse not Him that speaketh ; for if they escaped not who refused Him that spake on earth, much more shall not we escape if we turn away from Him that speaketh from heaven."

We must now advance a step farther, and inquire whether the teaching of Scripture is in harmony with the conclusions of philosophy and the ascertained results of human experience. Is man in the matter of belief a mere automaton, possessed of no control over the actings of his intelligence, actuated in the formation of his judgment solely by pure intellect, and not liable to be influenced by a thousand varying feelings, nor to be swayed by strong prejudices—never subject to fitful passions, nor to powerful inclinations that influence all the processes of his intellectual life ? Is there no element at work, when he forms his opinions, but facts and evidences ? and do these, by hard and fast lines, shut him up to inevitable and unavoidable conclusions, so that he can no more be held accountable for his opinions, than a watch is accountable for the figures on the dial at which the pointers stand ?

It is granted that facts and evidences must be the bases of all belief—that they are essential elements in the formation of all opinions. No man believes anything as a mere act of his will, in the absence of all real or supposed evidence. The wish may be father to the thought, but there will always be the interposition of a something besides the wish, that is made the warrant for the conviction, or for the alleged belief. Hence it may be conceded that, if man was nothing more than an intellectual being, if he had not a moral as well as a mental nature, it might be difficult to prove him responsible for his opinions. If an arithmetical proposition be presented to us, so that we understand it, we *must* acccept it ; that two and eight make ten is a truth not in the least dependent on our being willing to receive it —the belief is imperative ; and so, if pure intellect was supposed to be dealing with perfect evidence, it must always arrive at one conclusion, and there would be no responsibility. But this is not the constitution of man, else there never would occur an instance in which error would be espoused, in the face of abundant evidence to establish the rejected truth ; nor would there ever be occasion to say of any man's belief, it is his heart, rather than his head, that misleads him ; meaning thereby that a man's latent feelings, and hidden inclinations, or wayward habits, had more to do with his sentiments and opinions than he himself was aware of, or would allow. "Is there," says Dr. Wardlaw, "no reciprocally influential connection between the understanding and the affections ? and, more especially, has the state of the latter no influence on the exercise of the former ? Who that knows anything of even the most ordinary phenomena of human nature—phenomena which, so far from being recondite, are open to everyone's observation—is not aware how weighty is the power of the desires and inclinations over the operations of intellect ; to what a vast extent, both in the number of instances and in the degree of force, opinion and belief are affected by predisposition by the previous bent of the will !" If this be accurate—and all experience confirms it—then, in so far as any opinions are influenced by disposition, by the affections, by the inclinations, they are the subjects of responsibility.

The whole question might be discussed from this point— Does man exercise any power in the formation of his belief ? and, if so, what is that power, and how is it put forth ? To such questions we answer, man largely chooses and selects the subjects of his thought, and acts with perfect freedom in collecting the evidence, for and against the question on which his opinion is to be formed. He may shun all inquiry

on any subject of which he is ignorant, or on which he is
ill-informed ; and, if so, this is an act of his will.   True, his
volition could not create satisfactory evidence, but it could
lead him to investigate the nature and amount of the
evidence that is available, and give it all due attention.   If
that is not done, is it not his act that keeps the windows
closed, and thus excludes the glorious light of attainable
knowledge ?   On this subject, Dr. Abercrombie has well
said—" There are laws of evidence as absolute and immutable in their nature, as the laws of physical relations.
But for the operation of them a state of mind is required,
and without this, even the best evidence may be deprived
of its power to produce conviction ; for the result of
evidence on the mind depends on close and continued
attention ; and *this is a voluntary process*, which every one
may be able to perform.   It is on this ground," he adds,
" that we hold a man to be responsible for his belief, and
contend that he may incur deep moral guilt by his disbelief
of moral truths, which he has examined in a frivolous or
prejudiced manner ; or which perhaps he indulges in the
miserable affectation of disbelieving, without having examined them at all."   In fact, it is well known that, as regards
every opinion to which there are two sides, there will be
arguments, more or less cogent, for and against it.   These
should be sought out by a candid inquirer—be examined and
weighed by him.   Man's action in this is wholly voluntary,
and therefore it can be the subject either of praise or of
blame.   He can neglect this duty entirely, or he can
perform it partially, or he can do it candidly and earnestly.
He may lean to the one side, so as not to see the argument on the other, striving to find out everything which
strengthens his preconceived notions, and through negli-
gence or design overlooking or refusing to consider all that
favours a different sentiment.   Surely, in this most common
procedure, there is a moral wrong done, and culpability
incurred.

Who does not know that the influence of argument or
evidence, in creating belief, does not depend altogether on

its own force or weight, but largely on the degree of attention that is given to it; so that, if calm and deliberate
reflection is paid to one statement, while little attention is
given to the other, the inevitable consequence will be this—
the mind will lean to the side to which the attention has
been given, and a very erroneous judgment may be the
result.

All who are acquainted with the laws that regulate the
human mind, are aware that a man's self-interests and prejudices, his appetites and passions, his pride of consistency,
or his repugnance to acknowledge former error, will often
drive him pertinaciously to cling to opinions in the face of
evidence to the contrary, which everyone sees but himself.
In such cases, the beliefs are warped to that side where
inclination points, and swayed as humour, or pleasure, or
passion direct, so that the belief seems true that is pleasant
and grateful. Would it not, then, be plainly absurd to
assert that the man has no control over his opinions, or
that he was wholly passive as to the impressions made on
his understanding? *

The error on this subject arises largely from overlooking
the structure of the human mind, and from forgetting that
conscience and moral feelings are integral parts of the constitution of man. It is in virtue of this constitution that
moral feelings alter and modify, direct and control, the
actings of the intellect, and thereby attach to them their
responsibility. All through the processes of thought and
the attainment of belief, it is *the man* who acts—never
ceasing to be a moral agent, and, as such, ever accountable
to a higher power—not in one department of life or action
only, but in all. It would be a hard, I believe an impossible

* "Whatever may be thought of belief or unbelief, it can never be
questioned that there may be a contracting of guilt by the refusal or
the neglect to attend to evidence. The degree of this guilt must be
in proportion to the intrinsic magnitude of the subject, the authority
under which it presents itself, and the importance of the consequences
depending on the determination of the question at issue. Now there
is a host of unthinking sceptics, or uninquiring infidels, who have never
considered, never examined. They are without excuse."—*Wardlaw*.

task, to separate, by any process of analysis, what is purely mental from what is purely moral, in any jndgment or conclusion on moral questions ; for the workings of our mental and moral nature are so interleaved and interwoven, that we cannot extricate the one completely from the other, nor absolutely prevent our feelings from entering into the chamber of our thoughts.   Take, for example, the case of a man who is either judge or juror in a case of trial : his earnest desire is to decide and determine according to evidence, and to keep his mind free and uninfluenced by any prejudice, either for or against the prisoner.   Can he be as impassive as the bench on which he sits—as calm and cool, and as free from the influence of all environments, as if he were reading in his study, the history of a trial that had occurred a hundred years ago ?   Will the appearance of the prisoner, the knowledge of his previous life, the very character of the crime with which he is charged, the greatness of the issue as concerns the accused, and the impassioned appeals of the counsel to his heart and conscience, import no feeling into the case? and will he retire to form and frame his verdict with as little concern, and with as little emotion, as he would sit down to a question in arithmetic, or to solve a problem in Euclid?   The thing is impossible.   The fact is, that the union of heart and conscience, of will and mind in man, carries into all mental transactions a moral character, and thereby involves the element of responsibility.

Nor would this statement be complete if we did not add that the conscience takes cognisance of opinion and belief ; and wherever conscience judges, there must necessarily be accountableness.   What more common, in the intercourse of human life, than the expressions—I am conscientiously of opinion; or, I hold this opinion conscientiously; my belief is a matter of conscience, I am bound by it, I cannot change it.   And if this language be correct, it admits all that is contended for ; for conscience deals with voluntary actings, and is indissolubly associated with them exclusively.   " It has never, perhaps, been observed," says Sir Jas. M'Intosh, in his treatise on Ethics, "that an operation of conscience precedes all acts deliberate enough to be, in the highest sense, voluntary, and does so as much when it is defeated as when it prevails. Conscience has no object but a state of the will; and, as as an act of will, is the sole means of gratifying any passion. Conscience is co-extensive with the whole man; and, without encroachment, curbs or aids every feeling, even within the peculiar province of that feeling itself. It seems, therefore, clear that conscience takes cognisance of all voluntary acts, and must be universal and independent." It is not at all necessary, here, to discuss the question—Are reason and conscience separate faculties of man; or are they different names for one attribute of mind, acting on distinct objects, and under different circumstances? As a part of our moral nature, the mind recognises a distinction between good and evil, between right and wrong; it pronounces as certainly on these two qualities as it does on two quantities, where the question is one of number or of magnitude. It may be that we cannot explain the ground of the conclusion thus arrived at—that it belongs to the intuitions of the heart, and must be traced back to the moral nature of God, the impress of which was originally enstamped on man's being. It might, therefore, be said, without entering on the metaphysics of the subject, that conscience is the capacity to perceive the right, and to be affected by the moral emotion which accompanies that perception. Now the state and condition of a man's conscience depends largely on himself. He can render it frigid, inactive, perverse, or tender, acute, and sensitive; and, according to its state, so will be its influence over the mental and emotional state of man. A right state of the conscience admits of the understanding being free and unfettered, and therefore allows it to form its opinions more correctly. This mutual influence of the moral sense on the mental economy is part of our constitution; for as far as observation extends, every rational creature has a conscience;* and

* Each animal has its instincts implanted by nature to direct him to his greatest good. Man has his—an instinctive approbation of right

every creature endowed with conscience is a rational being ; the conscience in all men intuitively recognises some law superior to itself, the force and authority of which it can neither evade nor modify. Under the influence of that law, conscience takes note of all the free actings of man in the world of thought, in the world of motive, in the world of desire, as in the world of overt acts, and of fulfilled purposes. At the same time, it must be remembered that reason and conscience act together ; that there is not within man one *thinking* engine that works by itself, and another *moral* engine that takes up the products of the thinking, and weaves them into new forms and fashions ; the conscience always acts with the reason, and gives the moral colouring to its fabrics.

Now, while it is true that the conscience is not an unerring guide, and is not invariable, nor infallible, in its judgments, any more than reason is in its conclusions, it is, nevertheless, true that in society, where the members have different degrees of mental culture, and are endowed with different sensibilities, and hold different opinions, we do conscientiously judge of the sentiments and beliefs of each other, and, without any hesitation, pronounce this to be right, and that to be wrong ; we must do so, standing on our own moral convictions, and maintaining the honour and authority of our consciences. And if we can deal thus with the sentiments and beliefs of other men, have we not greater facilities, and much more reason, for dealing thus with our own ? and, in approving or disapproving of them, do we not recognise our responsibility ? If we can meditate on the errors in opinion of other men, and conclude that, if we had been in their position, we would have judged differently, why may we not sit in judgment on our own beliefs, and

and abhorrence of wrong, prior to all reflection on their nature or their consequences.—*Warburton.*

Every bias, instinct, propension within, is a real part of our nature, but not the whole ; add to them the superior faculty, whose office it is to adjust, manage, and preside over them ; and take in this, its natural superiority, and you complete the idea of human nature.—*Butler.*

acknowledge that we have often neglected evidence, have often avoided the perception of truth, because we did not wish to see it; or, if we did look at it, interposed the coloured glasses of strong prejudice, and therefore could not be convinced, because *we would not?* This propensity has embodied itself in the well-known proverb—"None are so blind as those who won't see."

It does not follow from this that all men must think alike or judge aright—that the consciences of all men will arrive at one and the same conclusion on all subjects. As it is in nature, so it is in life. All flowers do not grow alike—all do not assume the same forms, nor exhibit the same shades of colour, nor do they all make the same impression on the beholders ; the varieties are infinite, but that adds to the general beauty of the landscape. So, in the human soul, you will scarcely ever find two judgments absolutely the same ; the minds are not of the same calibre, nor the moral senses equally tender and delicate ; and, therefore, while it is the duty of every man to cultivate an enlightened conscience, and to be fully persuaded in his own mind, he should make allowance for the conscientious convictions of others. But that whole process involves the idea of responsibility for opinion, though, of course, it is a responsibility to God, and not to man. "Through the conscience," says Dr. Lee, "we behold that which is the most august aspect of the Divine nature, and the noblest attribute of our own. Resistance to that law which speaks through the conscience, is, therefore, as much rebellion against human nature as against the Divine government; and where there is rebellion, there is assuredly responsibility." Very likely it will be replied to all this—There is nothing in this argument ; for the utterances of conscience are very different in different men, and among different nations, and therefore the distinctions between right and wrong are altogether arbitrary. But surely the fact that the moral sense may be corrupted and vitiated by sin, till a man, imbruted by vice, feels no more the pangs of remorse over his brutality, than the lion or the bear do when gloating over the mangled remains of their victim, is no proof that conscience does not exist ; it would be just as wise and correct to say that man is not a rational being, because cases can be produced in which the lower and more debasing appetites have so broken up the reasoning faculty, that it is hard to dig out the fragments of it from the *débris* and desolation with which vice has overlaid it.   The machine is all in ruins; but the broken wheels and dislocated connecting-rods are sufficient to prove the original purpose of the great Architect ; in short, there is enough, even in the ruins of man's moral nature, to show that conscience is a part of his constitution, that it judges his opinions, informs him that he is a free agent, and therefore responsible to God for what he thinks and believes.

Finally, philosophy and experience attest that there is a necessary and uniform connection between belief and practice, and that to absolve a man from all responsibility for his belief would render him to a large extent unaccountable for what *he did or said*.   The entire life of man is composed of these three things—thought, feeling, action.   Knowledge supplies the food for thought, and feeling provides the motive for action.   Belief is consequently an active principle that displays its power in all the walks of life ; and more especially in the highest walks, wherein deeds of moral heroism have mantled with dignity the memories of the illustrious.   Take the case of two nations.   In the one there is a general belief in the existence and perfection of Jehovah, in the rectitude of His laws and in the benevolence of His government, in the duty of obeying His statutes and of glorifying His name ; in the other there is a general belief in false gods—in Jupiter, or Juno, or Venus, or Shiva, or Vishnu. These are to be worshipped and served with sacrifices and offerings agreeable to their nature.   Are these beliefs harmless ?   Will they remain dead and stagnant in the intellect ? or will they, must they be operative in and over the life ?   Let history and experience tell.   In the one nation they produce a certain amount of holy fear, of virtue and morality ; the worship that is practised and the lives that are led are somewhat in harmony with the ideas that have been formed ; they run out in the same plane with their thoughts of Jehovah, and, in proportion as they accord therewith, we call them virtuous or good, for the opinion and the practice are inseparable in their character. In the other case, the belief in false divinities leads, and always has led, to demoralised actions, which we term sinful and evil. The Hindoo drowns his aged parent in the Gunga; the Moabite makes his child to pass through the fire to Moloch; the worshippers of Venus indulge in unmentionable licentiousness; the Indian leaves the aged and infirm to starve to death in the woods; the altars are stained with human blood; infanticide becomes a duty, and is elevated into the rank of a virtue. Now if man has no control over his opinions and beliefs, he can have none over the actions that necessarily result from them; and we are not warranted in pronouncing any condemnation on those who commit such or similar crimes. The world is not old enough yet to have forgotten the triumphs of infidelity in France in the end of the last century, and the actions resulting therefrom in the terrific scenes of the revolutionary period; nor is it so courteous as to allow that there is no moral evil in holding communistic and socialistic opinions, and no risk that society would be convulsed to its centre if such opinions were entertained by the masses of the people.

If the principle that man has no control over his opinions in morals and religion be true, it is equally true that he has no control over his opinions in the common affairs of life; and if opinion be the basis, the guide, the spirit of action, irresponsibility would become the law of human life; the distinction between virtue and vice would soon be lost sight of, and disorganised society become the curse of the earth. It was not a forced nor a necessary conviction, but one to which the free consent of a man's whole soul was given, that inspired and led to the noble deeds that stand emblazoned in records human and Divine. The men who have done honour to their race have been the first and foremost to recognise the connection between their belief and their actions. The belief led to the action, and carried them to the triumphant issue of their conflicts, in the face of a thousand perils, and of all but insurmountable difficulties.

Look at that intrepid man who, year after year, besieged the courts and crowned heads of Europe, beseeching them to send him forth on a voyage of discovery. He believed in the existence of an unknown country; he had formed the strong opinion that it could be reached, and it became his life-work to reach that land; and not the dangers of unknown seas, not the mutinies of his sailors, not the thought of starvation and death, could deter his noble spirit. His belief was a power within him; it made him victor in the end; and the name of Columbus will never be forgotten till the time has come when there shall be no more sea.

But why speak of deeds like his when we have illustrations nobler far. In that record of heroes in the eleventh chapter of the Epistle to the Hebrews, we have the story of the men who subdued kingdoms, wrought righteousness, obtained promises, stopped the mouths of lions—the men of whom the world was not worthy, the grand pioneers in the noble army of martyrs. There, see belief in action. The faith within is clothed upon with visibility—heroic wills, powerful to endure all the world's malice; for the men knew in whom they believed; and that faith, with its acknowledged responsibilities, led them to their sacrifices, and animated their hearts to dare and endure all things for their Lord. And what do their lives and lessons teach us but this, that belief is an energetic principle of action, and Christian belief the most powerful and energetic of all?

But when we say that opinions necessarily develope into actions, as seed developes into a plant, and that accountableness must follow the process all through; that if a man does not believe in a world to come, in a state of future and final retribution, his life will be very different from that of a Christian, who thinks and walks, as seeing God who is invisible; we are met by the reply—We can produce men who deny all the cardinal doctrines of Christianity; yea, who dispute the very existence of God and of a hereafter; who are as amiable and gentle, as loving and upright, as the best among those who speak most freely of having believed in God, and of loving Him with all their hearts. It may be so, but where are they found ?—in the midst of Christian society, surrounded with all the indirect benefits of Christian nurture and education, largely fashioned and moulded by the very beliefs they now reject or vilify.

Look at the atheist, when he is separate from the indirect influences of Christianity, in his native dress, with all the surroundings that his own opinions have called into being, or have failed to control. See him in Ancient Rome in the days of the Apostle Paul, and in the history and character of the vices and crimes that disgraced the imperial city, as recorded in the first chapter of the Epistle to the Romans ; see the spawn which that philosophy spread over the waters of life, and the pollutions which, if it did not produce, it at all events failed to remedy or remove. See him in Ancient Greece, in Ephesus, and Corinth ; and learn that Epicurus and his Stoics could not bear to be placed on the same platform with the humblest followers of Jesus, and have their moralities compared and contrasted even by the philosophic atheists of modern days. The practice in both cases would be at once the result and the exponent of the faiths.

No responsibility for opinion ! Call up the spirits of the persecutors of the Church of God—the men who slew the saints for the testimony they held, and against whom the souls of the martyred cried from under the altar, " How long, O Lord, holy and true, dost Thou not judge and avenge our blood on them that dwell on the earth ?" and tell those spirits that society, which now execrates their opinions and their crimes, has done them great injustice ; that in believing that it was for the honour of God that heretics should be tortured, hunted like wild beasts from the earth, and put to the cruelest deaths, their opinion was wrong, but as they held it honestly and sincerely, they are not condemnable for having entertained it, and that the practical carrying it out was as inevitable as the opinion itself ; and if they could believe you, it would mitigate the

anguish of their remorse, and help to quiet a little their
terrible forebodings of the coming judgment.

Not responsible for belief! Will the British Government
teach that doctrine to the Thugs of India, who believe that
in murdering the unwary traveller they are guilty of no
crime? Not responsible for belief! Will humanity permit
the young widow to mount the funeral pile, and be consumed
with the body of her deceased husband, because she believes
such sacrifice is required, and is her passport for heaven?
Not responsible for belief! Will a parent preach that
doctrine to a prodigal son, who has wasted his substance
with riotous living? Will he address him thus—I think
you have acted sinfully and shamelessly, bringing disgrace
on yourself and on your father's house ; but knowing that
you believe that the course you are pursuing is the most
pleasurable—that you do not see the evil of it as I do—that
you believe that there is more happiness to be had in the
companionships you have chosen than in the peace and
quietude of home, I pity you, but I cannot condemn you,
because you have no power over the belief in which you act?

Not responsible for belief! Will a judge teach that
to a convicted thief at his tribunal? Will he say—The
evidence against you is full, clear, and undeniable ; I must
pronounce you guilty ; but I cannot blame you ; you don't
believe in the rights of property ; you cannot see any reason
why some men should possess wealth and comfort in abundance, and you should want both ; and you see no harm
in filching a part of their superfluous store, if you can do it
without detection—that is your belief ; it is a very erroneous
one, but you cannot help it ; and it is very sad that law,
with its austerity, compels me to pass a sentence upon you
for an act which was the necessary and the natural result
of opinion and belief you could not control? Would
common sense, would the interests of society tolerate such
jargon? Reason and philosophy might not be able to
solve the connection between opinion and practice, and
yet both would maintain, at least in all the ordinary affairs
of human life, that man is responsible for his deeds. Any

other sentiment would arrest all social improvement, sap
the foundations of all morality, and enable the wicked to
find a justification for every crime ; for if a man's opinion
is to be his standard of honesty and his test of virtue,
religion might at once spread out her snow-white wings, and,
soaring off to a world of purity and love, leave the earth a
prey to darkness and to death.

Perhaps it will be said that, in all cases where the opinions
result in criminal practices, the beliefs formed were not warranted by evidence. But if the man is not responsible, who
is to judge? The question is not how the evidence would
affect *your* mind, but how it has affected *his*, and determined
his procedure ; for the power of evidence varies immensely
according to the men and the minds it is presented to.
Argument, cogent and apparently irresistible, is no evidence
to a man whose soul is vitiated by sin, or whose understanding is clouded by superstition. Even facts are not
evidence to a man who does not perceive them, and whose
non-perception is due to the state of his own heart and will.
The conclusion of the whole matter is this—What we
believe determines what we do, and thus the responsibility
covers the whole area of opinion and of practice.

These are not the times in which there is occasion to
lessen man's sense of accountability to God. Men's wits
are sharp enough to frame excuses for their sins, and to fancy
that they cannot avoid thinking and doing what they wish
to think and delight to practise. What is needed in these
eventful days is the plain and forcible teaching of the fact
that man has a conscience, which will one day awake, and
from its tribunal in the soul judge of thoughts and deeds, and
prove in the bitter experience of the condemned that that
silent monitor, like a bird of prey, has followed him in all
the walks of life, with its terrible retributions and indescribable forebodings of wrath. Vain, vain will ever be the
task of trying to divest man's mind of the thought of a
coming day of retribution ; for the idea of that future
judgment, which is to vindicate the moral government of
God, and explain all that seems anomalous in the workings

of His providence, flashes upon us every hour of our existence. The lessons of history, the aspects of society, the prevalence of evil, the depression of the godly, the long-continued and God-dishonouring sentiments that have prevailed in the world, demand a day of trial—a day in which the claims of *truth* will be vindicated as certainly as the claims of righteousness, and a judgment be passed that will include all error, as well as all criminality. Oh, blessed thought! before that hour arrives, knowledge will have spread over the earth as the light of day spreads over the world, false opinion will have lost its foothold in time, human thought will have achieved its noblest triumphs, right beliefs, in union with piety and charity and love, will be commanding influences in all climes and kingdoms, and all the ends of the earth be found rejoicing in the faith that saves, and in the truth that sanctifies.

The Life and Character of Christ.

REV. JOHN MORAN.

LIFE AND CHARACTER OF CHRIST.

THE evidences of the truth of Christianity are manifold and varied, addressing themselves not only to different types of mind, but also to different parts of our mental and moral nature. One of the strongest and most convincing of these is to be found in the life and character of Christ as portrayed in the gospels. To set forth the nature and value of this evidence is the object of the present lecture. In the time at our disposal it will not be possible to do more than give an outline of the argument derivable from this source.

We have in our hands four writings or compositions, generally known as "The Gospels;" and according to the present results of criticism, the first of these was in existence before A.D. 70, the second and third some few years later, and the fourth about the close of the first century.* We do not assume the truth of these writings, for that would be to take for granted the matter in dispute, but simply that they now exist, and that they can be traced back to the dates that have been mentioned.

When we examine these compositions, we find that they are memoirs or biographies of a remarkable person called Jesus Christ, and that they represent him as possessing a character transcendently excellent and beautiful, faultlessly pure and perfect, unique and unparalleled in history. They do this, not by any formal description or delineation of his character—nothing of that kind is attempted—but by the simple record of what he said and did. Our limits forbid anything but a mere sketch of the character thus set before us ; and no such sketch can do it anything like justice. Indeed, no delineation or description can—nothing but the gospel narratives themselves.

These memoirs introduce us to this remarkable person

* Christlieb's " Modern Doubt and Christian Belief," p. 395.

in his infancy.   After intimation, by an angel, to his mother of his birth and of the name by which he should be called, he is miraculously conceived through the power of the Holy Ghost (such is the representation), and is born a " Holy Thing."   He is born in a stable and laid in a manger, yet an angel from heaven announces his birth to men, and a multitude of the heavenly host praise God for his appearance in our world.   And thus we meet at the very commencement of his earthly life that combination of greatness and lowliness, dignity and abasement, which marks it throughout and distinguishes it from every other life.

The child Jesus is not a prodigy, displaying superhuman wisdom and doing wonderful things from his very infancy. He is a perfectly natural and truly human child, but pure and holy, without any taint of evil or any stain of sin.   He grows like other children, both physically and mentally, in stature and in intelligence.   He attracts the affection of all who come in contact with him, and has favour with God, whose grace is upon him.

This is the picture given us of his infancy.   Of his boyhood we have but a glimpse—one recorded incident, but it is in harmony with the childhood that has preceded. When twelve years of age, he goes up to Jerusalem with his parents, and is left behind there at their departure. When they return to seek him, they find him " in the temple, sitting in the midst of the doctors, both hearing them and asking them questions "—the impression made upon all who hear him being one of amazement " at his understanding and answers."   There is nothing in his conduct or bearing to offend—no pertness nor forwardness, no want of modesty or humility ; yet he shows a measure of intelligence and an interest in Divine things so far beyond those of an ordinary and merely human youth, that those who hear him are " astonished."   His mother gently reproaches him for having remained behind his father and herself without their knowledge, and thereby caused them anxiety on his account : and then we have that first recorded word of his—"Wist ye not that I must be about my Father's business?"—the "solitary floweret plucked out of the enclosed garden of the thirty years," which shows us that he had come to know himself and his relation to the Father—a knowledge which surprised his mother, and which, not understanding, she carried away to meditate on and ponder.

Now it has been well shown by Bushnell that, whether fact or fiction, we have here the sketch of a perfect and sacred childhood—that, in this respect, the early character of Jesus is a picture that stands by itself—that in no other case has a biographer, in drawing a character, represented it as beginning with a spotless childhood. He adds—"If any writer, of almost any age, will undertake to describe not merely a spotless but a superhuman or celestial childhood, not having the reality before him, he must be somewhat more than human himself, if he does not pile together a mass of clumsy exaggerations, and draw and overdraw, till neither heaven nor earth can find any verisimilitude in the picture."* This is strikingly exhibited by the apocryphal gospels in their portraiture of Christ's childhood. While the writers of the gospels we are considering say so little of the infancy and youth of Jesus, and expressly tell us that he did his first miracle at Cana of Galilee when entering upon his public ministry, the apocryphal gospels fill his childhood and youth with all manner of grotesque and absurd miracles and prodigies, showing us what it was in the power of that age to invent, and in what a contrast it stands to the naturalness and reserve of the canonical gospels.

When we pass from Christ's childhood to his manhood, and consider his character as it is then presented to us, we find that it is just the development of his pure and spotless youth, to which it stands in the same relation as the flower does to the bud from which it has expanded.

As we survey this character, the first thing that strikes us is its perfect innocence and sinlessness. According to the representation given of him in the gospels, Jesus Christ is a perfectly innocent and sinless being. During his whole life, he neither does wrong, nor gives just cause of offence to

* " Nature and the Supernatural," p. 280.

any one. He never injures any one, by word or deed. Many, no doubt, are offended with him, but it is with what is good in him that they are offended—with his faithfulness and truth, his purity and holiness, his compassion and benevolence. The Scribes and Pharisees are offended with his humility because it rebukes their pride, with his benevolence because it reproves their selfishness, with his holiness because it contrasts so strongly with their moral turpitude and vileness. But this is their blame ; he is blameless. The idea of Christ, in this respect, conveyed by the gospel narrative, is that of a perfectly innocent and harmless being, one whose life is altogether inoffensive, and to whose heart every feeling of hatred and unkindness is a stranger. And, while thus innocent and harmless, he is so without sustaining any loss of dignity—without giving any idea of feebleness or weakness, such as we often associate with mere innocence—nay, while conveying the strongest impression of greatness and power.

Nor is Christ innocent and harmless merely; he is sinless. This, we are aware, is denied by some ; but we contend that it is the representation of the gospel narrative. There is no act attributed to him that can, with any show of justice, be regarded as a sinful act. His driving of the traffickers out of the temple, especially when taken in connection with his claim as Son to rule in his Father's house, is an act not only compatible with sinlessness, but positively holy and even godlike in its character. And the fact that so many retire without resistance before a single man, implies a consciousness of wrong-doing upon their part, and shows the majesty of reproving holiness. As to the charge of injustice and unreasonable resentment, founded on his smiting a fig-tree with barrenness, it is almost unworthy of serious refutation. There was no injustice and no resentment in the case. It was a warning expressed in symbol, an admonition given by an act. It was Christ's taking an inanimate object—and, therefore, one that was incapable of suffering—and using it to reprove the people of Israel for their unfruitfulness, and warn them of impending doom.

Then we have most important testimony on this point borne by Christ's enemies. Pilate washes his hands before the multitude, in token of his freedom from all participation in the crime of putting an innocent man to death ; and says, " I am innocent of the blood of this just person." Judas, who knew what Christ was, not only in public but in private, so far from having anything to allege against him that might have excused him to himself and others for what he had done, testifies to his innocence, and says, " I have sinned in that I have betrayed the innocent blood."

And what shall we say of Christ's own declarations respecting himself? That he claims to be a perfectly sinless being is undeniable. His challenge to his enemies is, " Which of you convinceth me of sin ?" Of his invulnerability to the assaults of Satan, he declares, " The prince of this world cometh and hath nothing in me ;" and of his obedience to the Father, he says, " I do always the things that please him." And not only does he make this claim ; he carries it through without faltering in its assertion, or abating it for a single moment. During his whole life he never makes a confession of sin, drops a tear of penitence, nor offers a prayer for forgiveness. He has no remorse, no regrets, no sense of having failed in any duty— no feeling that he should have done anything different, or in a different manner, from what he has done. " It is clear," as Dorner says, " in the most decided moments of his life, that he is conscious of no sin. That his self-consciousness was really of such a sort that his conscience never accused him of any fault or error, is the firmest and most indisputable historical fact, explain it as we may. That he imposed upon himself as his life-task the salvation and reconciliation of the world ; that he was conscious, too, of being occupied with the solution of this problem, in suffering even to the cross ; and that he died in the full consciousness of having solved the problem, as well as of unbroken communion with God, is just as undeniable as that it would have been an insane and absurd thought to wish to redeem and reconcile others, if he had been conscious of needing redemption himself. How, then, can the phenomenon be explained, that he, to whom even sceptics do not deny the rarest measure of purity and clearness of mind, stands before us without being conscious of a single sin, or of the necessity of conversion and amendment, which he requires of all others ; if not in this way, that he was *conscious* of no sin because he *was* not a sinner." This is the only adequate explanation of it : for as Bushnell has well said, " If Jesus was a sinner, he was conscious of sin, as all sinners are, and therefore was a hypocrite in the whole fabric of his character ; realising so much of Divine beauty in it, maintaining the show of such unfaltering harmony and celestial grace, and doing all this with a mind confused and fouled by the *affectations* acted for true virtues ! Such an example of successful hypocrisy would be itself the greatest miracle ever heard of in the world."

No ; Christ lived in a world where he was exposed and tempted to evil, but the purity of his nature constantly repelled it. As he touched the leper, and no uncleanness followed, so he mingled with sinners and received no con-tamination from them. He had evil suggested to his mind by Satan, but his holy soul did not admit it. " He did no sin, neither was guile found in his mouth." He was " holy, harmless, undefiled, and separate from sinners." And in this sinlessness of Jesus, in the midst of a sinful world, we have something that separates him from all other men, in which he stands solitary and alone, the one sublime exception to a universal sinfulness.

But not only is Christ free from all stain of sin ; he is distinguished by the highest positive moral excellence, even perfect love to God, and pure, disinterested, self-sacrificing love to man. This love is the groundwork of his character, its grand distinguishing peculiarity. He shows his love to God by a regard to His will in all things—a constant, cheer-ful, devoted obedience. At twelve years of age, as a matter not more of duty than of delight, he must be about his Father's business. As he fulfils his ministry, it is his meat, the joy and invigoration of his soul, to do the will of Him

that sent him, and to finish His work. And when his earthly
life is closing, he contemplates it with satisfaction, because he
can say to the Father—" I have glorified Thee on the earth ;
I have finished the work which Thou gavest me to do."

And what shall we say of his love to man, but that the
world has never witnessed anything like it before or since.
His whole life on earth was just the expression of that love
—the shedding of its light on the world's darkness, the
pouring of its life-giving and healing waters on the world's
barrenness and drought. This love showed itself in his
tender sympathy with all human woe—with the deprivations
of the blind, the heart-sorrows of the bereaved, the infatuation
of the erring. How he pitied the widowed mother of Nain
in her bereavement, the sisters of Bethany in their grief,
his disciples when they sorrowed in the prospect of his
departure, the inhabitants of Jerusalem in their sinful and
infatuated rejection of himself!

Nor was his an empty and barren sympathy, but one
accompanied and made efficacious by an active benevolence.
" He went about continually doing good, healing all manner of sickness and all manner of disease among the people."
He declared that he " came not to be ministered unto, but
to minister, and to give his life a ransom for many." And
he fulfilled this, his own high ideal, at once of his mission
and of true greatness. His whole life was one constant ministry of self-sacrificing love. He ministered to man in his physical and earthly wants, healing the sick, cleansing the lepers,
opening the eyes of the blind, comforting the sorrowing,
restoring the dead to life. And he ministered to man in
spiritual wants. He did so by the gracious words that proceeded out of his mouth, his words of compassion and
tenderness and absolving love. He ministered thus to the
paralytic, when he said, " Son, be of good cheer, thy sins are
forgiven thee ;" to the woman who was a sinner, when he said,
"Thy faith hath saved thee, go in peace ;" and to the woman
of Samaria, when he revealed himself to her as the Messiah, and gave her the true water of life. And the crowning
act, the climax of this ministry of love, was when he

ascended to Calvary, and there, by a voluntary death of agony and shame, gave his life a ransom for many. " Herein, indeed, was love"—greater than ever man has shown.

To the highest active benevolence Christ united the passive virtues. It has been justly remarked that, by his life and teaching, Christ has revolutionised the world's estimate of these as an element of greatness. Before his time, men associated greatness almost entirely with the heroic virtues, and regarded meekness under injury, patient endurance of wrong, forgiveness of enemies, as little more than weaknesses. But Christ, by his example, has taught the world not merely that true greatness is compatible with the passive virtues, but that they form an important element of it. He exhibited these not only in the greater trials of life, but also in what are said to be their severest test, its commoner and minor trials. During his life he was a man of sorrows and acquainted with grief. He was so poor that he had no dwelling he could call his own. He knew what it was to hunger, to thirst, and to be weary. He was misunderstood by his friends, and misrepresented and maligned by his enemies. His good was evil spoken of, and his works attributed to Satan. His disciples clung tenaciously to their mistaken views of the Messiah, and were slow to believe all that the prophets had spoken, and all that he taught respecting his sufferings and death. His words were often watched for ground of accusation against him, and plots were formed against his life. But amid all this privation, misconception, and opposition, so fitted to discourage and provoke, he is never ruffled or chafed in spirit, never manifests fretfulness or impatience, displeasure or discontent, never complains or murmurs, but holds on his way with an unclouded serenity and a sublime and undisturbed composure. He is not insensible either to physical or mental ills. Exquisitely sensitive both in soul and body, he feels these acutely ; but in virtue of his perfect unselfishness, his devotion to the Father, and his love to man, he rises above them and possesses his soul in a celestial patience.

When we view him in the closing scenes of his earthly life, in what is specially called his passion, he presents a spectacle of meek endurance of wrong, and of undeserved, yet patient and uncomplaining suffering, such as the world has never seen. None ever suffered as he did ; but, although innocent, he is an uncomplaining sufferer. He is silent in the hall of judgment when the mockery of a trial is conducted for his condemnation—silent when he is blindfolded and buffeted, spit on and scourged, ridiculed and crowned with thorns—silent when he toils with his cross along the road to Calvary, the only word that he utters being one not of self-lamentation, but of pitying regard for others, " Daughters of Jerusalem, weep not for me, but weep for yourselves, and for your children." Well might it be said of him, " He is brought as a lamb to the slaughter, and as a sheep before her shearers is dumb, so he openeth not his mouth." If, therefore, to suffer even to death uncomplainingly, being innocent, manifest greatness of soul, none ever exhibited such greatness as Jesus of Nazareth.

Then think of his forgiveness of injury ! When Peter came to him on one occasion, and asked, " Lord, how oft shall my brother sin against me, and I forgive him ? till seven times ? " his reply was—" I say not unto thee until seven times, but until seventy times seven." And what he thus preached he practised. He forgave Peter for denying him, Thomas for doubting him, all the disciples for forsaking him at his apprehension. Nay, he forgave those who crucified him. As they drive the nails into his hands, he raises his meek eyes to heaven and prays, " Father, forgive them ; for they know not what they do." No wonder that even Rousseau felt constrained to say that if Socrates suffered and died like a sage, Christ suffered and died like a god.

And not only did Christ combine the different *classes* of virtues in his character ; he united in himself *all* the virtues. Unlike any other great man of whom we read—of whom the most that could be said was that he possessed one or more virtues in a high degree—Christ possessed every virtue in its perfection, so that it is not possible to name any·

moral excellence that did not belong to him. He possessed these virtues, moreover, in such just proportion, that his character was not only complete and full, but in perfect equipoise and balance, exquisitely symmetrical and harmonious. His love to God was in beautiful accord with his love to man. The one of these virtues did not outrun the other, or develop itself at its expense, but wrought harmoniously with it. And what was true of these fundamental elements of character was true of the various virtues into which they resolved themselves. In him, love for the race co-existed with love for the individual. Shepherd of the whole family of man, he could leave the ninety-and-nine in the wilderness, and go after the one that was lost. With a world upon his hands, he could stand and call one blind man to him for healing, converse with and lead to faith and repentance one erring woman by the well of Jacob, receive one anxious inquirer who comes to him by night, and make known to him the way of eternal life.

The heroic and the gentle virtues met in him. To the highest manly virtue, the courage that could stand undauntedly against an opposing world, he joined " the highest characteristics of womanly virtue—infinite devotion and singleness of purpose, the unruffled serenity of a calm and gentle spirit, pure and modest feeling in the maintenance of the finest moral distinctions, and the power peculiar to women of passive obedience—power to bear, to suffer, to forego in unspeakable loyalty." *

Never were contrasts so blended, and apparent contradictions so reconciled, as in him. He is grave without being gloomy, unworldly without being unsociable, self-denied without being austere, spiritual without being ascetic, intolerant of sin, while gentle and tenderly compassionate to the sinner. His dignity is wedded to humility, his zeal guided by wisdom, his enthusiasm joined with calmness and self-possession. He is in harmony with himself, with nature, with duty, with everything but sin ; and he is so because he is in harmony with God—because the law of God is

* Martensen's " Christian Ethics," p. 252.

within his heart, and he is filled and pervaded by love to him. And in virtue of this inner harmony he does all things well. He is never taken by surprise, nor at a loss what to do. He is never unprepared for the occasion, or unequal to the emergency, but always does the right thing, at the right time, and in the right manner.

He is truly a perfect character, "fairer than the children of men." Whatever he may have been in bodily person, he is altogether matchless in the beauty of his character. His life is a picture, not only without a blot, but without a defective line. It is a majestic anthem, running through the whole scale of love and service, sounding every chord of thought and feeling, and rising to heaven without a discordant note.

If we view Christ as a teacher, all admit that none ever taught as he does. He has not learned in the schools of the Rabbis, and yet he speaks with a wisdom which amazes those who hear him, and leads them to ask in wonder, " Whence knoweth this man letters, having never learned ? Whence hath this man this wisdom and these mighty works ?" He has had no training as an orator, and yet from the first moment he opens his lips to teach, he shews himself to be a perfect master of human speech.

His teaching is not after human methods, but after a manner of his own. He does not speculate, nor make guesses at truth. He does not reason and infer, build up and prove by elaborate process of argumentation or induction. He announces rather, and reveals. He speaks that which he knows, and testifies that which he has seen. The truth lies before him—is within his mind and heart—and he simply utters it ; and it is seen and felt to be the truth by those who hear.

His instructions are not imparted in an artificial and formal system, but in precepts and statements of truth, each of which has often a kind of completeness in itself, and which, as they fall from his lips, might be likened to the stars as they drop one after another into the evening sky and light up the heaven with glory. He teaches, moreover, not in the language of the schools, but in that of the com-

mon people, so that all can understand ; and often in para-
bles which are pictures of Divine truth, drawn from nature
and every-day life, and which come home to all hearts, and
live in the memory for ever.

When we consider the matter of his teaching—confining
ourselves at present to his ethical system—we find it to be
the highest and purest morality—a morality which even
sceptics and unbelievers acknowledge to be the noblest and
most perfect that has ever been propounded, and before
which the world has bowed down for the last eighteen
hundred years.   It is to this effect—" Whatsoever ye would
that men should do to you, do ye even so to them ;" "Love
your enemies, bless them that curse you, do good to them
that hate you, and pray for them which despitefully use you
and persecute you ; that ye may be the children of your
Father which is in heaven : for he maketh His sun to rise on
the evil and on the good, and sendeth rain on the just and on
the unjust.   .   .   .   Be ye therefore perfect, even as your
Father which is in heaven is perfect."

And this teaching is with authority.   He speaks not as
if there was any doubt of the truth of what he says, but
with the manner of one who is assured and certain, who
speaks what he knows, and who has a right to declare the
laws of the kingdom.   His teaching is after this manner—
" Blessed are the poor in spirit, for their's is the kingdom of
heaven;" "Ye have heard that it hath been said, An eye for
an eye, and a tooth for a tooth : but *I say* unto you, That ye
resist not evil ; " " Heaven and earth shall pass away, but
my word shall not pass away ;" " The word that I have
spoken, the same shall judge him in the last day."   Well
might it be said, " Never man spake like this man."   And
well might we ask, and leave the sceptic to reply—" Whence
hath this man this wisdom ?"

Closely connected with Christ's teaching are his claims.
When we examine these, we find them to be such as have
never been advanced by any human being before or since.
Time will permit us to do little more than mention some
of these.

First of all, then, he declares his humanity, and again and again calls himself "the Son of man." But by this designation, as applied to himself, he intimates not merely that he is a possessor of our nature, a member of the human family; but that he is something more than this— that he stands in a peculiar relation to the race—that he is the Son of man as no other is—the ideal, the representative man—the second man, the head of a new humanity—the "Son of man" spoken of by Daniel, the destined possessor of universal kingdom and dominion.

But while thus calling Himself the Son of man, he claims no less emphatically to be the Son of God. He calls God his Father. "All things are delivered unto me of my Father." "My Father worketh hitherto, and I work." When the High Priest adjures him, by the living God, to tell whether he be "the Christ, the Son of God," his un- hesitating and unequivocal reply is, "Thou hast said." And when he claims to be the Son of God, he claims to be so in a high and peculiar sense, a sense in which no mere creature can aspire to the title, and which implies the possession of the same nature with God. This is clear from the distinc- tion which he always makes, in speaking to the disciples, between *their* relation to God and *his*. He never places Himself on a level with them in this respect—never says of God *our* Father, but *my* Father and *your* Father. The opening words of the Lord's prayer are no exception to this; for he is there teaching the disciples to pray, and does not include himself. His language is, "After this manner pray *ye*."

In accordance with this lofty claim he speaks of himself as being "from above," having "come from God," having "come out from the Father." He places himself on a level with the Father, as when he says of the Jews, "They have both seen and hated both me and my Father," when he com- missions the disciples to baptize in the name of the Father and of the Son and of the Holy Ghost; and when speaking of the Father and himself, he says, "We will come unto him and make our abode with him." He claims co-ordi-

nate authority with the Father—"My Father worketh
hitherto, and I work." And when the Jews take up stones
to stone him because he called God his Father, and
thereby, in their view, made himself equal with God, he
says nothing to intimate that they were wrong in the inference they had drawn from the claim which he advanced.
He declares himself "Lord of the Sabbath;" asserts his
power to forgive sins and to enact the laws of the kingdom ;
claims to be honoured equally with the Father ; declares
that the dead shall hear his voice and come forth to life—
that, as the appointed judge of all, he will come in glory
and judge all nations—and that men will be accepted or
rejected according as they have shown love and attachment
to him as represented by his people, or have disregarded
and neglected him. He proclaims himself to be "the light
of the world," "the way, the truth, and the life," by whom
alone any one can come to the Father—the only one who
knows the Father, and can make him known to men. He
invites all who labour and are heavy-laden to come to him
that he may give them rest—bids all men follow him, and
forsake everything that they may do so—declares that he
will draw all men to him. He demands the highest affection of the human heart, and avers that whosoever loveth
father or mother more than him is not worthy of him, and
cannot be his disciple.

Such are some of the claims of Christ. Every one will
admit that they are the most wonderful ever made by any
being. If any man, any merely human teacher, even though
he were a prophet or an apostle, were to make such claims,
would he not cover himself with ridicule, and excite either
the world's pity of his fanaticism, or its indignant scorn of his
unfounded and arrogant imposture? Imagine any man, even
one "charged with a special, express, and unique commission from God to lead mankind to faith and virtue,"* standing forth, and saying, "All power is given unto me in heaven
and in earth," "I and the Father are one," "He that hath
seen me hath seen the Father"—holding out hands to a

* J. S. Mill's "Essays on Religion," p. 255.

world of sinners, and saying, "Come unto me, all ye that labour and are heavy laden, and I will give you rest." Imagine, I say, any man doing this, and what would be thought of him and his pretensions? Well, Christ, the meek and lowly in heart, makes these pretensions. He makes them again and again; not more distinctly when "the world is going after him," or when he rides in triumph into Jerusalem, than when he stands at the bar of Pilate, and when he hangs in agony on the accursed tree. He makes them not ostentatiously nor in high swelling words, but modestly and calmly, yet with the most assured confidence, and without faltering in their assertion for a moment. And he not only makes these claims; he supports them, so that they excite neither pity nor ridicule, neither scorn nor indignation, in the readers of the gospel narratives. On the contrary, his pretensions sit gracefully upon him, are felt to be in keeping with his wonderful life and works, and in no wise incongruous even with his lowliness and humility. We may add that these claims have been acknowledged by men of every country, of all classes and conditions, of the highest culture and of the lowest, and that in ever-increasing numbers for the last eighteen hundred years. Here, surely, is something wonderful.

In keeping with Christ's claims is his undertaking. This is to establish a kingdom that shall embrace the world, and, by redemption and new creation, to make all men members of it. He announces it to be the object of his being sent into the world—"that the world through him might be saved." He declares that if he "be lifted up from the earth, he will draw all men unto him." And when he sends forth his disciples, it is with the commission—"Go ye, therefore, and make disciples of all nations."

Such is the colossal work which he sets before him— even to found a universal spiritual kingdom—to reign in the hearts of all men—to draw all men to him, and through him to the Father; and so to knit anew the broken friendship between heaven and earth, and replace our apostate race in its original sphere of loving allegiance to its God and King.

B

In the grandeur of this his undertaking, Christ is indeed
" the unparalleled in history."   None of the great men that
we read of, no founder of any state or of any religion, ever
attempted or even conceived such a thing.   None of these
ever attempted to found a religion or an empire that would
embrace the world.   Every one of them, however liberal
his education, and however enlarged his views, was more or
less limited in his aim and influence to his own age or nation.
But Christ proposes to set up a kingdom that shall extend
to all nations and all ages, that shall not merely be one
among the kingdoms of the world, but shall embrace them all,
and unite them in one loving brotherhood.   He proposes to
enter into relation as Redeemer and Restorer, Teacher and
Example, King and Head—not with a portion of humanity,
but with the whole of it—not with one nation or people, but
with the race, that he may give it a new form and course
of development—may form it into a new community or
kingdom—a kingdom of redeemed and sanctified men—a
kingdom of God upon the earth.   He, the humble carpenter of Nazareth, brought up in the rudest village of
the rudest and most obscure province of Palestine—who has
never been out of his own country, except when he was
carried as an infant into Egypt—who has had no learned
education—who is without wealth or power, without friends
or followers, save a few fishermen and tax-gatherers—he
conceives this mighty project, and addresses himself to its
execution with a calm and assured confidence of success.

And if this scheme of Christ is so grand and wondrous
even in idea, what shall we say of the plan by which he
proposes to accomplish it, save that it is grander and more
wondrous still! he does not expect to see his undertaking
carried to completion, and his kingdom fully established,
during his earthly life.   He knows what is in his people, and
what is in man, too well for that.   He foresees and lays
his account with opposition and rejection on the part of
those whom he would redeem and save ; and he forms his
plan so that these, instead of hindering his work, shall help
it forward—instead of thwarting and defeating it, shall con-

tribute to its success. Though his miracles, his teaching, and his example should all fail to impress and win men's hearts, as he knows they will, he has still another and a mightier power in reserve—the power of his self-sacrificing love—the power of a death voluntarily endured out of love for those whom he came to save, and at their hands. And such is the grandeur at once of his conception and of his self-sacrificing love, that he contemplates making his death at the hands of men the great instrument of their conquest. He says to himself in effect, "I will reveal a love of such greatness, self-forgetfulness, and self-sacrifice, that men shall not be able to resist it—that it shall overcome their enmity, awaken their contrition, and take captive their hearts." Such is the wonderful and loving thought of Christ. And thus out of apparent failure he will bring success, and out of men's very hatred and rejection of him he will extract the means of overcoming them, and subduing them to himself. Surely we may say, alike of the sublime project and of the plan for its accomplishment, "This is not the manner of men—is not human, but Divine." "For scarcely for a righteous man will one die ; yet peradventure for a good man some would even dare to die. But God commendeth his love toward us, in that, while we were yet sinners, Christ died for us."

Such, though in meagre outline and most inadequate delineation, is the Christ of the gospels. May we not say with truth that there never was such a character ? There is no parallel to it either in history or in fiction. In stainless purity and holiness, in perfect unselfishness and disinterestedness, in grandeur of aim and greatness of self-denial, in sublime devotion to God and self-sacrificing love to man, it stands solitary and alone, without anything equal or even like to it.

This is admitted even by those from whom the admission could scarcely have been expected. "It was reserved for Christianity," says Lecky, in his " History of Morals," " to present to the world an ideal character, which, throughout all the changes of eighteen centuries, has inspired the hearts

of men with an impassioned love ; has shown itself capable
of acting on all ages, nations, temperaments, and conditions ; has not only been the highest pattern of virtue, but
the strongest incentive to its practice ; and has exercised so
deep an influence, that it may be truly said that the simple
record of three short years of active life has done more to
regenerate and soften mankind than all the disquisitions of
philosophers, and all the exhortations of moralists. This
has, indeed, been the spring of whatever is best and purest
in the Christian life. Amid all the sins and failings, amid
all the priestcraft and persecution and fanaticism that has
defaced the Church, it has preserved in the example and
character of its Founder an enduring principle of regeneration."

Now the question comes, How or whence have we this
remarkable portraiture of character? And to this we at once
reply, We have it, because Jesus Christ, the person spoken
of, lived and acted as here described. We have his life in
the gospels, because that life was lived; his portrait, because
he sat for it.

No doubt there are other supposable ways of accounting
for the character, some of which have been actually tried.
It is supposable, for example, that the character of
Christ has been invented—that it is a fiction, pure and
simple, as much so as any of the characters in a novel or a
drama—that he never really lived, and that his disciples or
other authors of the gospels drew his character from their
own imaginations. Now it would be easy to show the
insuperable difficulties of such a view—the moral impossibility, in fact, of the disciples or other writers of that age
conceiving such a character as that of Christ, and not only
conceiving but portraying it, and keeping it consistent and
congruous with itself over such a wide field of action as that
described in the gospel history. But it is needless to do
this. No one now holds this view. No sceptic of any name
maintains that the Christ of the gospels is a purely fictitious
character. Another way of accounting for the existence of
this character is what is called the rationalistic theory.

According to this view, Christ lived as the gospels state. He was a very remarkable man, and did wonderful things, chiefly cures wrought on the sick and the diseased. He performed these cures partly by his medical skill, and partly, according to some, by a magnetic influence put forth on the bodies of his patients ; according to others, by a psycological influence exerted on their minds in inspiring them with hope and confidence. His disciples, viewing these acts of his through the magnifying glass of an intense admiration and an excited fancy, honestly mistook them for miracles, and so described them ; hence the account of him that we have in the gospels. The gospel narrative is real history, but history so coloured by the imagination of the narrators that natural events are transformed into miracles. What we need to do is to sever between the mistaken views and colouring fancies of the narrators and the underlying facts. The way to do this is to remove everything that is miraculous, because nothing such can be true. The great propounder and champion of this theory was the late Dr. Paulus of Heidelberg. And here is a specimen of his so-called rational interpretation— " The glory of the Lord that shone round about the shepherds on the night of the Saviour's birth was probably a meteor, or perhaps the rays of a lantern that happened to pass by. The tempter in the wilderness was a clever and cunning Pharisee, mistaken by the disciples for the devil. The changing of the water into wine at Cana was a harmless wedding joke ; the disciples had provided the wine beforehand, and the twilight helped to deceive the guests. Christ's walking on the sea was a misapprehension on the part of the spectators ; he only walked along the shore. He stilled the storm on the lake merely in the sense that by his calmness he quieted the frightened disciples, and by a happy coincidence the winds and the waves ceased from their raging at the same time. He healed the blind by means of an efficacious eye-salve, whose application escaped the notice of the disciples. The daughter of Jairus, the young man of Nain, and Lazarus were raised, not from real death, but from a deathlike trance or swoon.   The agony in the garden was a sudden indisposition caused by the damp night-air of the valley.   The resurrection of Christ was the return to life of one who had been in the grave, swooning from the effects of crucifixion, and who was only apparently and not really dead. The angels at the head and foot of the tomb were the linen clothes, mistaken by the excited women for celestial beings. The ascension of Christ to heaven was only his disappearance behind a cloud which came between him and his disciples."

It will appear, I think, from these specimens, that the so-called natural and rational interpretation becomes very unnatural and irrational indeed; and that, while we are denied true miracles, we are furnished with something like miracles of another kind, even miraculous feats of exposition.   This theory, supposing it accepted, only accounts, even after its own manner, for some of Christ's miracles.   It fails to account for the cures wrought by him while he was at a distance, and it gives no explanation of all his other mighty works, save the stupidity and mistakes of his disciples.   It does not explain how even the Pharisees, who certainly did not view Christ's works through any medium calculated to give them an unduly favourable colouring, were constrained to admit his miraculous power, which, unwilling to acknowledge as Divine, they attributed to Satan.   It proceeds on the unfounded and arbitrary assumption, that in the gospels we have the facts magnified and coloured by the excited imagination of the writers—the truth being that the narratives are of the calmest and most sober character, altogether unlike the products of heated fancy or fanaticism ; and that there never were historians who gave less of their own judgments and opinions, and so contented themselves with a simple record of occurrences.   It requires us to believe that these men—who, according to the theory, were so stupid that they could not report accurately what they saw, but made the greatest blunders in doing so, and so fanatic that they mistook natural events for miracles—have yet drawn the finest character that ever was depicted, and written the most simple, the most sober, and the most beautiful of all histories. Verily the faith of miracles were easy compared with this. The character of Christ cannot be thus accounted for. The miraculous is part and parcel of the gospel history, and cannot be eliminated without its destruction. It is interwoven with the character of Christ, and cannot be removed from it without rending the character in pieces. Hence even Strauss admits that, if we accept the gospels as historical, miracles cannot be banished from the life of Christ; and boldly maintains that they are not historical, but legendary.

This leads us to consider yet one other way of accounting for the character of Christ presented in the gospels. This is what is called the mythical theory of the life of Christ. According to it, the character of Christ is the result of imaginative invention and legendary embellishment on the part of the early Christian disciples, whereby a wise and holy Jew was gradually transformed into the Divine Christ.

In the reign of the Emperor Tiberias, according to this theory, an austere teacher and reformer, called John the Baptist, made his appearance in Judea. He preached repentance, and baptized those who professed it and confessed their sins. Among those who were baptized by him was one Jesus, from Galilee. When John was cast into prison, he carried on the work in which his master had been engaged. He sought to reform the people by means of his wise and holy teaching ; hoping for a Divine interposition by which the kingdom of David would be restored. This was so much in accordance with the Messianic expectations of his countrymen, that they began to think and hint to him that he was the Messiah. He was hardly able to believe this at first, but gradually brought himself to do so. Going up to Jerusalem, he opposed the ecclesiastical authorities there, the chief priests and scribes, and through their hatred and machinations was put to death by crucifixion. This was a great shock to the faith of his disciples. How were they to reconcile this ignominious death with his being the Messiah? They called to mind passages in the Old Testament, in which servants of God were spoken of as suffering even to death; and applying these to the Messiah, they brought themselves to believe that he was to suffer and die, that thus the death of Jesus was in accordance with prophecy, and that, therefore, he was not lost to them, but must have risen from the dead and ascended to heaven. This belief once entertained, it would have been strange if some enthusiastic members of the community had not persuaded themselves that they had seen him. Mary Magdalene, seeing him with the mind's eye, or mistaking the gardener for him, converted this into a bodily appearance; and hence the fable of the resurrection. As the disciples proclaimed that Jesus was the Messiah, and that he had risen from the dead, the question would inevitably arise whether he had done miracles such as Messiah was to do. This led them to persuade themselves that he had. As he was the Messiah, and the Messiah was to work miracles, he must have wrought miracles, though they had failed to observe and estimate his acts aright. And thus, not intending to deceive, but resolved on keeping Jesus as the Messiah, they invented the necessary miracles for him, and so *made* him what they *believed* and *wished* him to be. Words and sayings of his, in which they had seen no miracle before, were now regarded as miraculous. His promise to certain disciples that he would make them fishers of men became the miraculous draught of fishes; and his declaration that every tree that did not bear good fruit would be cut down became the withering of the fruitless fig-tree. All that, according to their views, the Messiah was to do is attributed to him as actually done by him. As he was the prophet like unto Moses, he must have done works like those of Moses; and therefore all acts of his that bore any resemblance to the miracles wrought by the great Hebrew leader were converted by them into similar miracles. As Moses fed the Israelites with manna in the desert, Christ must have miraculously fed the five thousand in the wilderness. Thus by successive inventions and imaginative fictions, in which they bring themselves to believe, as the only way of keeping up their faith in the Messiahship of a crucified Jesus, and of sustaining the Christian cause, they transform a Galilean Jew into the Christ, a wise teacher into a worker of miracles, and a good and holy man into the God-man. In the second century, four unknown and nameless men wrought up these myths and legends into the four narratives of Christ's life that we have in the gospels.

This is the theory which is at present chiefly relied on by the opponents of Christianity, and which, with the kindred one of Baur, constitutes their great weapon of attack on the Christian faith. But, like the rationalistic theory which it displaced, it is liable to insuperable objections. We can only mention a few of these. In the first place, it has been shown by the opponents of Strauss that myths or legends belong to the childhood of nations, and not to an historic age; and that the formation of such a system of myths as is here supposed in the age of the gospels—the age of Josephus and other historians—is incredible. It has been shown, in the second place, that myths are of slow growth, and take long time for their formation; and that there is not sufficient time for the myths supposed in this case between the death of Christ and the appearance of the gospels, even if we take the dates assigned to these by the advocates of this theory, still less when we take the dates as given by the highest critical authorities. It has been pointed out, still farther, that the miracles ascribed to Christ in the gospels are not of the kind that are invented, having no marks of myth or legend ; and that there are innumerable undesigned coincidences in the gospel narratives which are altogether incompatible with the supposition of their being fabulous inventions.

Then it might well be asked, If the Messiah was to do miracles, and Christ did none, how, at the first, and while as yet no miracles had been invented to accredit him, did he come to be accepted and believed on as the Messiah ? and how, if his life was so little above what is ordinary, did it draw such a halo of mythical glory round it ? "As regards the hypothesis," says Schelling, "that the life of Christ was adorned by myths, I suppose everyone will admit that only such a life is glorified by myths or legends as has been already in some manner distinguished and moved into a higher region. Now the question is, How did this Jewish country rabbi, Jesus, become the object of such glorification? . . . . *Only if we grant that Christ passed for what we have recognised Him to be*, is it conceivable that, in consequence of this opinion, certain 'myths' may have arisen. But if we grant this, we must presuppose the dignity of Christ, quite independently of the gospels. It is not the gospels which are necessary in order that we may recognise the majesty of Christ, but it is the dignity of Christ which is necessary in order that we may be able to comprehend these gospel narratives." Yet further, if the early Christian disciples invented Christ's miracles and palmed them upon the world, how is it that they were able to do this without protest or denial on the part of the opponents of Christianity in that age? These did not deny the miracles of the gospels, but endeavoured to account for them by ascribing them to magical or Satanic influence.

But the great objection to this theory is the moral impossibility of the character of Christ being produced in the way alleged. That a character of such transcendent excellence and beauty, such superhuman dignity and majesty, such unity and consistency, was fabricated piece by piece by a succession of myths and fables invented by credulous enthusiasts, and put together by four men of like spirit, who believed and retailed these fictions, is incredible. We could sooner believe that a number of ordinary painters, acting without concert, each putting in the touch he considered necessary, had converted the likeness of some ordinary man into the Christ of Guido or Murillo, than that the common features of a Jewish rabbi were transformed by successive touches of myth and fable into the inimitable and glorious Christ of the gospels.

Such embellishment would be equivalent to invention, and even sceptics are to be found who regard such invention as impossible. "My friend," says Rousseau, speaking of Christ's portrait in the gospels, "such things cannot be invented. . . . The gospel contains so great, so astonishing and perfectly inimitable traits of truth, that its inventor would be even more wonderful than its hero." John Stuart Mill, while he holds that the miracles of the gospels might have been invented by Christ's followers, contends that his life and character could not have been so invented. "Who," he asks, "among his disciples, or among their proselytes, was capable of inventing the sayings ascribed to Jesus, or of imagining the life and character revealed in the gospels? Certainly not the fishermen of Galilee ; as certainly not St. Paul, whose character and idiosyncrasies were of a totally different sort ; still less the early Christian writers, in whom nothing is more evident than that the good which was in them was all derived—as they always professed that it was derived—from the higher source." *

This theory is at variance with other portions of the New Testament which are admitted to be genuine. It is admitted by the advocates of this theory that several of Paul's epistles are genuine—among them the epistles to the Romans and the Corinthians—and that these were written within thirty years after the resurrection. It is admitted that the Book of Revelation is the genuine production of the apostle John. Well, what do these apostolic writings say respecting the historic truthfulness of the portrait of Christ given in the gospels? In the epistles mentioned, Paul speaks of Christ in a way which takes for granted that the portraiture of him in the gospels was well known to his readers. He speaks of miraculous powers in the Church, which imply the miraculous power of the Church's Founder as their source. Nay, he expressly attributes to Christ the same dignity which is attributed to him in the gospels, designating him, among other appellations, "The Lord from heaven," and "The Lord of glory." In the Book of Revelation, John represents Christ as calling himself "The Alpha and Omega;" and speaks of him as "The

* "Essays on Religion," p. 254.

Lord which is, and which was, and which is to come ; the Almighty." These apostles, therefore, held the views of Christ's Divine dignity and power, whose origin Strauss ascribes to the credulous and enthusiastic Christians of a later period, and which, he alleges, found their way into the gospels only through their fancies and inventions.

Nay more, Strauss is obliged to admit, in opposition to his own theory, that Christ himself claimed superhuman dignity and power. He admits that Matt. xxv. is historical, and that Christ really said what he is there represented as saying. Well, Christ there declared that he would come again in his glory, and all the holy angels with him—that he would sit upon the throne of his glory—that all nations would be gathered before him for judgment, and that he would separate them into two great classes, mete out to them righteous awards, and so bring about the consummation of all things. Strauss cannot deny that Christ said these things, and in doing so raised himself above humanity, and therefore he charges him with being a visionary, and "guilty of undue self-exaltation." In other words, he admits that Christ himself claimed that superhuman dignity and power, the ascription of which to him originated, according to his theory, with the early Christian community. His theory utterly fails him at this point. It is admitted that Christ said what is attributed to him, and, on this admission, Christlieb well argues—"Either *Christ uttered these sentiments wrongly*, in extravagance and self-exaltation—and then let any man reconcile them with His otherwise perfect moral majesty ; let him explain how, from this haughty enthusiast, from this religious leader, who himself was subject to sin or error, there could proceed the religion of humility and love, and the kingdom of truth with its world-regenerating effects ; or, on the other hand, Christ was *right* in speaking these words, and did so with full clearness and truth ; *but then He was more than a mere man.* From this we see that *though all the works of Christ should vanish into myths, yet His words remain as an irrefutable proof of His Messiahship and Godhead ;* and so does

His consciousness, with the views resulting therefrom of His person and dignity as something incompatible with all mere human standards. This firm rock is to Strauss a '*stone of stumbling which shatters his whole theory to pieces.*'" He adds, in words so beautiful and convincing that we cannot withhold them, "The optical illusion of mythicism lies in the train of argument, that because in the Church herself the higher knowledge of Christ was gradually attained, therefore this higher knowledge was invented from the imagination of these primitive Christians, though, at the same time, we cannot understand how this idea should have occurred to them. From the angels' song in the first Christmas night, down to the words, 'Simon, son of Jonas, lovest thou me?' coming from the lips of the risen one, the gospel history contains a series of pictures so beautiful and grand, so perfumed with heavenly grace, that innumerable features in it must be recognised as *uninventible.* Doubtless there is a *poetry* in them; but it is not that of arbitrary fiction, it is the result of holy and divinely ordered facts. Why should legends only invent what is beautiful? Why should not the finger of God in history trace out an objective beauty of facts which exceeds all that human fancy can invent? Instead of saying that it is too beautiful to be true, each man who believes in something more than our common every-day life should say, when looking at this page of history, '*It is too beautiful to be mere fiction,*' so beautiful that it must be true. There is an ideal perfection of beauty which is itself the highest reality; or, to use the words of Göethe—

    ' The unattainable
    Is here accomplished ;'

and this beauty it is which shines in the gospels—above all, in the delineation which they give us of Christ. *Only if Christ really was what He was taken for, can we solve the enigma of primitive Christian faith—of the foundation, the spread, and the world-renewing power of the Christian Church. Christ could only live as God-man in the hearts of His followers, if He really was so. . .* We look at the *enormous revolution in the world* accomplished through Christianity ; we look at the *joyful heroism of its confessors,* braving death ; and at the *purity of the primitive Christian Church,* which is born, grows, spreads, and finally conquers the world, though placed between a thoroughly corrupted Judaism on the one hand, and a no less thoroughly vitiated heathenism on the other; and having done so, we consider the attempt to explain all this from the fact that *a certain Jew became convinced that He was the Messiah, whereupon His disciples, after His death, attributed to Him all sorts of miracles, which they drew from their imagination ;* and our final conclusion is, that *this explanation involves such an utter disproportion between cause and effect, that it is in itself the most inconceivable miracle, a pure historical impossibility."**

It will thus be seen that this theory, not less than the rationalistic one, fails to give an adequate explanation of the life and character of Christ as we have it in the New Testament. We fall back, therefore, on what alone furnishes an adequate explanation, even the faith of Christendom, that Christ lived as described in the gospels, and that hence we have this portraiture of him. This is the conviction wrought in us by a perusal of the gospel narratives. As we read them we are constrained to say, " This is not fiction or fable, but reality and truth." And this conviction is strengthened by the fact that we have four portraits of Christ, one in each of the gospels, each agreeing with itself and, in all its important lines and features, with the others. It is the same Christ that we have portrayed in each of the gospels. The attitude may be different, we may get a different profile, but it is the same countenance that is depicted, the same face that looks out on us from the sacred page. This is not denied in the case of the first three gospels, and neither can it be denied with truth in the case of the fourth gospel. It is the same Christ that is there portrayed, only in a different attitude, and from a different standpoint. The diversities and apparent discrepancies in the narratives prove that there was no collusion among the authors, but

" Modern Doubt and Christian Belief," p. 422.

that they wrote independently of one another; and the fact that, notwithstanding this, they give us each the same portrait of Christ, proves that they drew from the same original —not from fancy or imagination, but from a real historic Christ who had lived and laboured, spoken and acted, among them.

And if Christ spake and acted as described in the gospels, then he must have been what he is there represented, and what he there claims to be. The very perfection of his humanity constrains us to believe that he was more than human. His sinlessness in a world of sin compels the conviction that he was no mere shoot out of the stock of a sinful humanity, but a Divine graft inserted into it from heaven. And his claims—claims made by one who was confessedly of the highest moral excellence—leave us no alternative but to acknowledge him as the Son of God, one with the Father—the object of our supreme love and reverence.

Thus in a historic Christ, who is at once the Son of man and the Son of God, and who lived and died as described in the gospels, we get the truth of our Christianity and a Divine Lord and Saviour. Nay (for our argument may be pushed one step farther), we get what some of the scientists of our day say cannot be found, a personal and living God. The portraiture of the gospels leads us to a historic Christ as its only adequate explanation. In a historic Christ we find the Son of God, for He was the Christ that should come into the world. And the Son of God conducts us to One who is His God and Father, who knows Him and whom He knows, and therefore to a God who is not impersonal or unintelligent, who is not force or matter merely, but who is a personal and intelligent Being—One who knows and can be known, loves and can be loved—the object of trust and supplication, reverence and affection.

This view of Christ explains everything. It explains the portraiture of Him which we have in the gospels. He lived the Divine-human life there pictured, and the sacred writers have described it accordingly. It explains the miracles or the gospels. They were only what might be expected from a superhuman Being such as Christ. When He wrought a miracle, it was the falling back for a moment of the mantle of humanity from His shoulders, and a disclosure of the higher nature which it covered. It explains the existence and stability of the Christian Church, showing that it has for its foundation, not the sand of a mythical and fabulous, but the rock of a historical and Divine Christ. It explains how Christianity has triumphed over all the assaults that have been made upon it. Just as the armed men that came out to apprehend our Lord, dismayed by His simple but majestic utterance, "I am He," went staggering backwards and fell to the ground, so all the assailants of Christianity have gone down before the simple majesty of the Christ of the gospels. As the ark, when brought into the house of Dagon, cast down the idol and brake it into pieces, so the Jesus of the gospel history has discomfited and cast down all the opponents of His claims. They have fallen on this stone and been broken.

This Christ meets our wants and satisfies the yearnings of our souls. Our hearts ask for another God than the god of the materialist, even the materialists themselves being judges. They ask for a God who can know and pity, hear and help, forgive and bless—who can be an object of reverence and veneration, of confidence and love. And the Christianity which in this lecture we have sought to vindicate gives such a God. It gives us the God who was revealed in Jesus of Nazareth—a God who has an eye to see and an ear to hear, a heart to pity and a hand to save—a God who is the rest of the sin-laden, the Saviour of the soul, the Redeemer from sin and death, the Resurrection and the Life. This God meets our wants—our souls can rest in Him. We say, therefore, with Peter—"Lord, to whom shall we go? *Thou* hast the words of eternal life. And we believe and are sure that Thou art that Christ, the Son of the living God."

The Achievements of the Bible a Proof of its Divine Origin.

REV. WILLIAM MAGILL.

ACHIEVEMENTS OF THE BIBLE.

ALL natural objects are engaged in tracing a map of their movements, and in affixing their signatures. Meteors leave their track of light; leaves cast their shadows as they fall. The earth is furrowed by streams; the track of animals that roamed long, long ago over chaos is cut in stone; and even raindrops have written their history in the solid rock. What has the Bible done for men, and on man's world? Its annals—are they replete with records of good done, wrongs redressed, men saved, and God glorified? What are the facts?

1. The book itself commands attention. The Vedas, the writings of Confucius, and the Koran are modern compared with it. When it was laid in complete form on the table of the world, it was found that forty centuries had made contributions of their best things to it. Its authorship is spread over sixteen hundred years. It has been copied during thirty centuries; and survived the wreck of empires, of mythologies, and philosophies—ministering to the true needs and deepest challenges of humanity. It has been assailed by all evil things; yet, in its turn, it has borne down on them with a power that destroys them. In harmony in itself with all the laws of God's kingdoms, it moves with an energy derived from the Spirit. On opening its pages, we feel as if all around were unearthly and sublime, as if we approached the throne of its eternal Author; "while," in the language of Claude, "an unknown heaven appears opening on our meditations, in which we behold, as it were, a thousand burning luminaries, whose rays, gushing from every side, bewilder the eyes, and dazzle while they flood them with intolerable glory."

In the very constitution of the Bible there is evidence of one Divine mind, acting through and above all human agents for the production of one grand result—the eternal purpose of redemption in Christ Jesus. As the sun mirrors himself only in a calm ocean, so the living personal Jehovah mirrors Himself in the Bible as the God of providence and redemption, making the one uniform claim of faith on all men—faith in the Lord Jesus and in His kingdom. As the revelation of salvation, it is the book of life, of unsearchable wealth, of Divine fulness — a copy or manifestation of the living Saviour ; trying and judging all other sacred books in the world ; the arbiter in history, in literature, and in morals. The vigour, beauty, and purity of the ethical parts of the Bible ; the matchless simplicity and charm of its histories ; the sun of prophecy which has never set, but has rolled down a flood of light to our day ; the poetry which, in "flow and fire, in crushing force, in majesty that still seems to echo the awful sounds of Sinai, is the most superb within the breast of man"—all these have made the Bible a mighty power in the world, through its influence on the human mind. The God whom it teaches us to worship is the only absolutely perfect One in holiness and love that man has ever known ; nor heaven, nor earth, nor hell has known another Saviour besides the Lord Jesus whom it reveals ; and the religion which it brings is the only one on the earth that does not degrade man and insult God.

2. The Bible has encountered prejudice, storm, and undying hate. The Veda had no foes, the Zend-Avesta no enemies ; and the Greeks accepted with acclamation the poems of Homer. Why is not the Bible, with its power to inspire the loftiest intelligences with love and veneration, with its matchless morals and its sublime spirituality, the book of every class of men, and of all men ? Why do men of thought often look coldly on it ? How comes it that in this scientific age there is a spirit abroad of alienation from it ? The ancient classic literature, which has charmed the intellectual world for twenty centuries, is pagan in ethics and mythology, and, therefore, antagonistic to the

Bible. Modern letters, conformed in a great degree to ancient models, and derived from those fountain-heads, follow frequently the same course in depicting moral greatness ; in ignoring those moral principles and sentiments peculiar to revealed religion ; in propounding theories of life, happiness, and immortality that are not distinctively Christian ; in overlooking wholly, or partially palliating, the depraved moral condition of man, and in neglecting redemption by Jesus Christ.

In looking into the schools of ancient philosophy, we see a faithful picture of heathen thought—of the inability of the loftiest intellect to arrive at truth, and of the dimness of their light even at the best. These sages, debauched by false science, spoke in the language of gods, and in reference to morality and religion sank lower than brutes. The intelligent belief in a future state, and the knowledge of moral obligation, were alike wanting in them. Some introduce us into the dark cave of materialism ; others, like the modern sceptics, founded their freedom on the denial of every duty, and the obedience of every impulse— reason their only guide, "at one time the moderator, at another the menial of passion ;" while others, like the Stoics, gave the world "a virtue without affections, a religion without a God, and a soul without a future." The struggle between the theories and spirit of paganism and the principles of the Bible is not yet over. The infamous doctrines which prevailed in the France of the eighteenth century, notwithstanding the bloody commentary furnished on them by the Revolution, are rising again in formidable array even in our own country ; and, culminating in the atheism of Comte, they seem to aim at the uprooting of all faith in the Bible. If for twenty centuries Holy Scripture has withstood every attempt to corrupt it, every cruel effort to wrench the signet-ring of God from its finger, and every insidious war against the religious instincts of this million-peopled world—do not the hates that have pursued it, the fires that have been kindled to burn it, and the rude assaults of successions of infidels on it, prove it Divine and unconquerable. Thus they treated the Just One, and thus they treated His book.

3. The knowledge communicated by the Bible is unique, saving, and of infinite value. No other book of any age or nation gives the same view of sin—as the violation of moral law, as an evil of infinite magnitude, as involving everlasting punishment, and as mirrored only in the sufferings and death of the Son of God. This is one of the discoveries that stamp the book with transcendent power and utility. Alone in the literature of all time, it presents to men the true idea of God—in essence, self-existent ; in holiness and majesty and all moral attributes, infinite ; in wisdom and sovereignty, absolute—and this God seen in the face of Jesus Christ, crowned with a love which fills, and shall for ever fill, the virtuous universe with the lights and splendours of Godhead. And to this book alone, of all books, we are indebted for the idea of that redemptive system, of which the central figure is Immanuel—a personality so strange, new, peculiar, so suited to man in his indigence and guilt, and so suited to God for the manifestation of Himself as Rector and Father of the universe, that the mind of man or angel never could have suggested or conceived it. The speculations of Vedas, Korans, and heathen sages on theology fall infinitely short. They are rushlights held up to the sun. The religions founded on them are without morals and without evidences.

The religion of the Bible is not poetry, a code of morals, or a series of rhapsodies—it is a salvation from sin and death. The negations of Islam repudiate the divinity and propitiation of the Lord Jesus, and substitute fabulous creeds. The gods of the heathen were and are unholy ; and their worshippers, coloured and transformed by their homage, resemble them in immorality, cruelty, and misery. The sacred literature of Paganism possesses small claim to attention. It gives no reliable information. It has involved the great majority of the human race in darkness, and subjected them to a sure process of deterioration, which became greater as age succeeded age ; and history proves the inability of men to redeem themselves from idolatry, or restore humanity to its primeval purity and happiness. Let the contributions made by the Bible to human knowledge be fairly considered—let them be weighed, estimated, and compared, and they will be found to involve the recovery of man, his enlightenment by truth along the whole line of his immortality, and the germination within him of a new life, which has no superior in the universe but the life of God. The quality of this knowledge has been tested by time—by the fires of persecution, the scalpel of genius and erudition—by men in every condition, and by death-beds innumerable as the buds of spring—by the ridicule and sneer of the sceptic, and by the more perilous weapons of unscientific disbelief; and the result has proved it to be saving, Divine, infinite—possessing in itself the potency of all greatness and of all good.

4. The Bible is the mainspring of civilisation. Like the straight line of which Leibnitz speaks, which is constantly approaching the curve but can never meet it, man possesses the capacity of indefinite improvement and progress towards God. Pascal teaches that, in respect of his essence, man is thought; and he argues his greatness from his misery. Howe depicts the ruins of a stately palace, where God once dwelt, in terms of matchless force and beauty—leaving it to be inferred that the glory of humanity lay in its being the temple of Deity. Hall founds human dignity on its present probationary state and on immortality. But the real greatness of man is mirrored only in the seas of Divine love, of the blood of Jesus, and of the glory of human nature in the person of the Mediator. This fact, peculiar to the Bible, and unknown to all the sacred books of the world's religions, is the essential principle from which springs all true civilisation. Of all books, the Bible alone sets forth man in his sin and misery, and in the massive and transcendent capacities of his immortal essence.

Now experience proves that since the world began no tribe of savages from within itself civilised itself. The

growth of the natural sciences and of architecture among
the Egyptians, the progress of philosophy and the fine arts
among the Greeks, and the development of law among the
Romans, are historical results of supernatural truths regarding God and man, and remission of sin by bloodshedding
only ; which, floating down from the origin of society on the
wings of tradition, crystallised themselves in the earliest
centres of population, and, through the communion of
nations, overspread and in part moulded these great
peoples into those wondrous forms of national life which
their annals disclose.   From Babylon, through Ethiopia,
the Egyptians derived their enterprise and their civilisation.
The early Greeks, characterised by extreme simplicity and
grandeur, were indebted to the Phœnicians and Egyptians;
and the Romans formed their magnificent national life out
of elements furnished by Umbrians, Trojans, Greeks, and
Hebrews.   The civilisation of India and China has been
fossilised for twenty centuries, in the course of which there
has been a gradual deterioration of morals ; and Islam has
stereotyped society in the lust, and pride, and ferocity, and
despotism, and barbaric pomp of the seventh century.   If
these empires, which contain or command eight hundred
millions of our race, are modifying their tyrannies and approaching the verge of modern civilisation, they owe it to
the pressure of nations where the Bible is the unseen power
that rules.

As to law, more than a thousand years before Justinian
reformed Roman jurisprudence, the statutes of the Hebrew
people were published.   If, like Grecian art, the effect of
Roman law is extensive and permanent—excelling the
conquest of the world by arms—how much mightier in the
construction and regeneration of kingdoms and peoples
must have been the Divine law given in the Pentateuch?

As to freedom, more than two thousand years before
Magna Charta the rights of peoples and the powers
of princes were chartered in the Word.   The immortal
principle embodied in the Bible, that God alone is Lord of
the conscience, has done more for the emancipation of man,

for moral freedom and civil liberty, than all the efforts, sufferings, and literature of Mohammedan and pagan nations put together. How comes it that true freedom, good government, constitutional law for the protection of life, property, and liberty, hatred to despotism and political virtue, are unknown among peoples ignorant of the Bible? The Word is the author of all the heroic contendings which have won modern freedom, and erected it on an imperishable basis. Poets have sung, and martyrs have died, and patriots have fought, and tyrants have trampled out the fires of liberty ; but while the world stands, the Bible will breathe it into the soul of man.

As to marriage, let men of moral idea compare the institute of marriage—founded, hallowed, and encompassed by Divine laws and sanctions—with the polygamy, the ineffable impurity and misery, of family life in Mohammedan and Pagan nations, and they will see something of what the Bible has done for man. Where else is home found ; or woman enthroned in the sanctities of freedom, love, and purity ; or society sweetened by tenderness and moral feeling ; or culture in the arts that embellish life and multiply its enjoyments ; or the relations of life pervaded and regulated by a sense of moral obligation ; or truth made the basis of all life, of all law and commerce and institutions; or the majesty of law blended and shaded, for the public weal, with the rays of mercy—unless where the Holy Scriptures dictate the faith and morals of men.

And as to education—the birthright of every man and the greatest power on earth for good—who could tell what the Bible has done in the world ! If it has not done all, it is because its voice has been unheard amid the din of worldly interests, and its authority repelled by the depravities of men. Beyond the sphere of its beams, the culture of the disciples of Brahma, Confucius, and Mohammed is poor, unworthy of the moral and intellectual nature of man, and utterly unable to confer the peerage of true manhood. If education should reach the body, soul, and spirit of man, transforming all alike, and shed-

ding on all the radiance of highest excellence for citizenship, for virtue and happiness, it must be conformed to
the rule and breathe the spirit of the Bible.   For nations
like the Roman, who burned out the Bible—placing laws,
force, and hierarchies in its stead—have corrupted in their
own superstitions, and their remains lie entombed in history.
And nations like Spain and France, who, in their battle with
the Bible to expel it from their coasts, have shed blood
enough to make a lake, are hung up before the eyes of the
world, to teach, by their crimes, their degradation, their judgments, and their sufferings, that the Scriptures are the pillars
of kingdoms, "the parents of social order, which alone
have power to curb the passions of men and to secure to all
their rights, to nobles their honours, to the rich the rewards
of their industry, and to princes the stability of their thrones."

    5. The Bible influences and regenerates literature.   Early
in the history of the world, the mind of India embodied
itself in a literature which, beginning in theology, embraced
some science and art, and ramified into poetry, metaphysics,
and mythology.   The Chinese literature, rich in prose and
verse—in history, geography, romance, moral philosophy,
and mechanical arts—is of vast extent, and not unworthy
of the attention of scholars.   The literature of Greece,
in point of classic form, is a model, and has told powerfully on the culture and education of the world.   And not
unlike these, in some respects, is the learning of the Dark
Ages, when the Bible was imprisoned in a cell—when
Aristotle ruled the schools of thought, and the monk presided over the mind, morals, and politics of Europe.   These
literatures are continents of rubbish, into which, if the form,
which is often of exquisite beauty, could be separated from
the putrid substance which it enshrines, no scholar should
refuse to descend in search of the golden mine, from disgust
at the base alloy which mingles itself with the ore.   Compared with the literature of which the English language is
now the vehicle, all these are as night to the moon.   If
you compare, in its transcendent greatness, English literature to a globe, then, undoubtedly, if the Bible is not its

creator, it fashioned, moulded, inter-penetrated, and gave to it its substance. The Holy Scriptures furnish specimens of consummate art in history, poetry, parable, law, and morals ; and in their matter they are inspired by God. The writers are kings among men ; and their words are models for the orator, the spring of all progress, the bloom of all beauty, the charter of eternal life—having in them the seed of statesmanship, of jurisprudence, of the light and wealth of nations. From these models history has learned to criticise, to delve and hew for hid treasures, to search for the roots of things ; and even the splendid historical monuments of the genius of Mill, Hume, and Gibbon, in their relations to the Bible, remind one of the eagle whose blood is drawn by the arrow which its own wing has feathered. In poetry, too, the Bible has exerted pre-eminently its power. Here there is reason to believe Shakespeare learned to play on the human heart as on a harp ; Milton conceived his matchless epic ; the great masters of modern song got their imagery, their themes, their sweetness, their simplicity ; and even Byron, Shelley, and Burns, like Dante, are orbs belted all around, and streaked with light, and fire, and beauty, borrowed unconsciously from the lively oracles of God.

The highest meed of earthly honour, according to Bacon, belongs to the founders of empires ; does it not belong to himself, as the founder or restorer of modern philosophy, in a greater degree ? Yet the leading ideas of his system— that men ought to observe and study the works of God, and that wisdom is strength—are clearly biblical. Here Newton learned his love of truth, and his genius for generalisation gathered patience to stand peering through the lattice, till he wrested from nature her secrets, and made light paint his immortal portrait. Here Herschel and Murchison and Faraday lighted their lamps to travel over the physical universe, and lead the march of mind where the forces of matter hold their secret conclave, to the stone-chambers in the crust of the earth, where the mundane archives are stowed away, and to the throne of blue, where the centre

of creation—the Eternal—sees, rules, and wields the suns
and systems of the universe, which are but the drops of
His fulness, and the shadows of His glory. And if, beginning at the brilliant era of Elizabeth, science has been
building her pyramid for three centuries, and Christian
civilisation collecting her wonderful treasures of human
good, and poetry embellishing it with garlands more varied
and beautiful than earth ever saw before; if the sun of
freedom is shining for man with a ray almost bright, and in
an area almost as broad as the sky ; and if theology, with
its pure truth and perfect morals, its power to bless time
and light up eternity with the splendours of day, has come
to crown the edifice which three centuries have been rearing
with that wealth of supernatural life and glory which is the
tide-mark now of human improvement, and the prophecy of
yet grander things for men in God's world—all is owing to
the force, and control, and life, and spirit of the Bible.
True science, sound learning, ethical philosophy, modern
civilisation, sit down in the dust uncrowned before the
lively oracles of God, and lay their spoils on the altar of
Revelation.

6. All the powers and fruits of the Bible already mentioned are small compared with its achievements in morals.
It is Dictator here, and reigns without a rival. It alone
reveals a perfect code in the form of moral law ; it alone
exhibits a perfect pattern in the life of the Lord Jesus. As
a fallen intelligence, man is placed under sovereignty of
law, to which, in his will and conscience, he is to be subject.
And the training of a moral being belongs to God. An
ethical education makes a man true and good, pure and
graceful, faultless and benificent, the object of reverence and
love. In consequence, morality without God is impossible,
for it must have an absolute law founded in the nature of
Deity. Nor is this all. There must be reconciliation
through the Son of God, and regeneration of heart by the
Spirit—enabling the soul of man to snap the chains of its
depravity, and walk the path of ethical obedience. Without
these, men are dreaming enthusiasts, or creatures of ascetic

sentiment. Man has never discovered, never could discover, a perfect rule of duty. The Bible not only does that, but adds sanctions, asserts human responsibility, and aims at ruling the will by motives in reference to all the moral distinctions of right and wrong, which necessarily associate themselves with God. The materialistic philosophy makes morality impossible—resolving itself into the pagan scepticism which made truth falsehood, right wrong, and good evil.

In Hume's speculations the possibility of a science of morals is denied, and, proceeding from the Creator of the world by inevitable necessity, he says that "human actions can have no turpitude at all." In Rousseau and Voltaire, morality culminates in libertinism ; with Comte, in fatalism. And experience shows that atheism, morality, and government by moral law are incompatible. Of all heathen systems of morals it may be affirmed that they are fragments, broken and imperfect, handed down from hoar antiquity. The Brahmin resolves the highest virtue into asceticism, and the loss of conscious personality ; the Boodhist, into universal grief and annihilation ; the Chinese, into naturalism and politics ; while among the most enlightened of the Greeks, morality was based in knowledge, and virtue made wholly a matter of intelligence, a thing exclusively of time. We have before shown that the Holy Scriptures alone reveal the real nature of sin in the light of that eternal redemption which, glorious and stupendous beyond all thought, sets this world of our life before us as a mystic arena, in which a conflict is waged for deliverance from everlasting punishment and the enjoyment of life eternal. For the true morality for which, during forty centuries, God was preparing men, has its majestic principle in holy love—a love which is through faith ; and has introduced into the world for all time, and for eternal expansion, right views of truth, duty, justice, purity, humility, man, and God—germs of all the good that can confer distinction, and of which humanity is capable, and which even infidelity has admired for its great and transcendent excellence. Let it be remembered, as a moral axiom, that sound morals can only grow out of sound principles. The immorality of men and nations who are and were destitute of the Bible is such that no true picture could be presented of it ; and their indescribable depravation is the logical result of their pagan principles. In that morality—over every part of which, as a system, the Bible, which is sublimely ethical, sheds beauty, and to every rule of which it communicates power—every man, every household, every nation in existence has an infinite interest.

Strike down the Bible, and you will have the universal debauchery of heathenism. Exchange the Bible for the dictate of unaided reason, and for a time you may dwell in the shade of art, and play at the gymnastics of eloquence ; but come at length it will, and the glory of modern society shall go up in rottenness—introducing the reign of ignorance, cruelty, sensuality, and despair. For Deism, pure theism, natural religion, materialism, scepticism, infidelity, atheism, are the successive stages of that historical rationalism, which for the last three centuries has been at work in Europe, and reddened its annals with atrocities of crime and blood "which, for the safety of their performers, had to be enveloped in everlasting night." The Bible is the book for humanity, not only because it contains all necessary truth and a perfect moral code —things of which all other religions are destitute—but because there is a resistless energy in it to renew and purify the moral nature of our species, an energy which it has proved on a thousand fields of fame, over thirty centuries of time, in every variety of human condition, and in open conflict with all the powers of earth and hell. It has wrestled with an apostate Judaism ; with heathenism, encamped amid the pomps and grandeur of imperial Rome ; with the philosophies of the Greek schools, buttressed by all the charms of human learning and exalted genius ; with the traditional superstition of the "man of sin," whose hostility to the written Word kept Christendom for ten centuries a prison-cell for saints, for freedom of conscience, for freemen, and for saving truth ; and now, in the end of the world, when systems of specula-

tion are rising on our horizon, varied and unsubstantial as
November meteors—now linking themselves to the orb of
science, now to metaphysics, now to the spawn of an over-
weening egotism, now to the importations of German or
Indian exuviæ, and often to an intellectual sky-rocket, to
attract notice and alarm the vulgar—the Bible stands forth
in its integrity, the palladium of moral freedom, the only
true spring of individual and rational excellence, the conservatory of all the roots and fruits of Divine virtue, which
alone has power to cleanse the earth of paganism, and to
restore man to himself and to God by the science of right
and of truth.

7. But the main use of the Bible has been to originate
and sustain true religion in the world. The facts of human
consciousness prove, in opposition to the materialist, that
there is a spiritual as well as sentient and intellectual
nature in man. As light suits the eye, or water the thirsty
one, so is the Bible to the spiritual wants of humanity. An
impulse to worship is an essential ingredient in the human
soul. And it is a fixed law of mind that the character of
the object worshipped moulds the votary into its form and
likeness. If the social system of pagan lands, in every
epoch of history, has dissolved in moral corruption, idolatry
is the cause. And not only so, but, left to itself, the volume
of corruption becomes deeper and more wide-spread in proportion as the fine arts, power, and wealth increase—as in
the age of Pericles in Greece, and of Augustus at Rome.
The evidence of all time and of all the facts is that the
spiritual nature in man is supreme over the intellectual and
moral—that every effort, stimulated by human religions, to
promote happiness without heart-purity, is vain—that there
are desires and capacities in the soul which the wisdom of all
the ages cannot satiate—that the sense of guilt has such a
mastery over the soul of humanity that no form of man-
made worship has power to exorcise it—and that intellectual
greatness, apart from holiness, has never saved individuals
or converted states.

We hold it proved that the best forms of religion

which the reason of man has discovered have failed in producing, in a single instance, spiritual character. The Bible has done this in millions of cases. Employing as its only weapon, truth, it repudiates the force and despotism of other religions. It presents God in all the radiancy of an infinitely holy love ; and this suits the heart of man. It sheds light on morals, on men, on salvation, on the life to come—a clear and certain light; and this fits in to his reason. It reveals an absolution from sin which, founded on the loving self-sacrifice of a Divine substitute, does not compromise perfect rectitude or blot the Divine character and law, and that suits all the requirements of conscience. It imparts from its Divine author a new life which, consisting in love, lifts its possessor into the fellowship of the Absolute One ; and, embracing eternity in its provisions, runs up the road of perfection, scattering every gift that can make existence a blessing—thus fitting divinely in to the needs of his immortal essence. For forty centuries and more this tree of life has been wafting holiness, life, and happiness through this sinful world ; and its saving odour is still exhaustless. It has taught men all that time how to live ; it has enabled them to die. It has brought real happiness into the world ; and, wherever it has been received, it has drained the fountains of human misery. It has saved the felon in his cell, the savage in his war-paint, Paul in his harness of hate, and Augustine in his vice. It has been the pillow of the martyr's peace—the parent of humility, self-sacrifice, and hope. It has beautified whatever it touched, quickened souls innumerable, and imparted consummate finish to ideas, to taste, and to genius. The purest comfort of earth drops from its word into hearts broken by bereavement or indigence. It is the key of knowledge. It has conducted pilgrims innumerable to the celestial mansions ; for it alone possesses the secret of salvation.

Look over the dreary centuries of the past, and as you see the lights of religions and civilisations and philosophies and empires, one after another, sinking below the horizon, and perceive the holy light of the Bible flashing its rays with ever-increasing brilliance over the seas of human sin and suffering, the blessing and majesty of the book will surely grow on you. Three centuries ago it held up a torch among the Alps, in the centre of Germany, in France, and in the United Kingdom ; and to recount its fruits would be to write the annals of spiritual Protestantism in the regeneration of individuals and of nations. Its creations are peerless. Compare in moral and spiritual excellence Demosthenes with Chalmers —the death of Cicero with that of Robert Hall. The whole history of human religions cannot produce a Wilberforce, or furnish a Howard. There is not a death-bed like Haliburton's in the whole history of the world outside the Bible. Compare the last end of Hume, Voltaire, Mirabeau, and even Mill, with the death-beds of Payson and Rutherford and Knox. The heathen and Mohammedan religions never produced a Henry Martin. Among Reformers, compare Mohammed, in point of spiritual character, with Knox ; among churchmen, Hildebrand with Calvin ; among benefactors of their race, Boodha or Confucius with Luther.

Glorious book ! myriads of men have died for it ; churches live in its shadow ; commonwealths grow up under its ægis ; and the ages take their main characteristics from its sovereign spirit. It has added to the dominions of saving truth several hundred islands in the South Seas. In the might of a conqueror it has invaded Madagascar. It has planted a tree in India which shall yet cover all the land. It has belted Africa with light, and lit fires in China that shall never go out. It has robed itself in the dress of two hundred and ten forms of speech, languages, or dialects. Since the beginning of this century more than eleven millions of money have been spent by societies in its circulation ; and above one hundred and twenty millions of copies have gone out with their cargo of light and life among the nations. The wild cry—" What must I do to be saved?"— rings out in our ears as two-thirds of the human race kneel before their idols and shriek out their lament ; and the Bible alone can answer it. Another age or two of active hostility against the Bible on the part of scientists

B

and infidels, and there will not be a homestead on earth
without its copy of the Holy Scriptures.   This is our shout
of defiance—let the whole corps of sceptics show, if they
can, a man who has been made a liar, or obscene, or a thief,
or a tyrant, or proud, by the Bible.   Nay, if they will
not have this book to rule them, let them make a better.

Suppose—and they claim the highest mind of the age on
their side—that they were assembled to provide a substitute
for the Bible.   The philosopher, the atomic scientist, the
critic, and the theoretic atheist, are all there.   The Comtist
furnishes the history without a miracle or a special providence ; the scientist narrates the work of creation out of an
atom—or by development, or natural selection, or proto-
plasms—by fortuitous concourses, or by nothing ; the philosopher, who has resolved all the realities and possibilities of
existence into matter, dictates a code of ethics and law
which eliminates from human consciousness moral obligation and free agency ; the critic proudly boasts that his contributions contain a higher rule of duty than the moral law—
a more perfect model of excellence than the sinless Jesus ;
and the sceptical theorist insists that no mention or reference shall be made to God, on the ground that there is no
sufficient evidence of His existence.   Would the book, thus
formed—the magnificent product of the " illuminati," " the
highest mind of the age"—convert the world and supplant
our Bible ?   Let the papal, the material, the intellectual
forces dash themselves against the Book of God ; we cling
to it because it is guarded by the holiness and omnipotence
of its Author, throws the shield of its inspiration over our
beliefs and our prospects of eternal life, has uprooted a long
series of evils in Protestant Christendom ; and because, in
the institution of the Sabbath alone, the Bible has done
more for man—for his rest, culture, and prosperity, in all
his relations—and for God, in reference to the spread of
saving knowledge and the maintenance of true religion,
than all other religions, backed by the infidel mind of
all the ages, from the time of Moses to our own.

The Bible, which holds in custody truth so precious, has

entered on a new era of triumph, in which the mighty achievements of the past shall be eclipsed by movements deep as human thought or earth's misery, and high as the mind of the future. In virtue of its sovereign authority, it will yet settle all the questions that have arisen between the Church and the age. Flaming in the centre of the world, its beams will put to flight priestcraft, multiply education, dissipate error, and lift man into an erect posture in hope of immortality.

The infidel comes to rob us of our peace and our prospects, and to throw the shade of negation over the glory that awaits us. And for the Bible and Christ and joy and the resurrection, of which he would rob us, what does he offer? A little science, some poetry, strong negations, a sigh, and perhaps a sneer. Infidelity is poor, for it has no Divine revelation : it is narrow; for, the creature of sense, it makes the present time all : it is deaf; for it hears not the voice of God in His word : it is foolish; for it wars against the greatest, strongest, best things in the universe of God. Whatever great men may arise to reform physical science, like Newton and Pascal ; or, like Clarkson and Wilberforce, to break the fetters of the slave ; or, like the Reformers, to bring men from darkness to the light of life ; whoever they may be that shall open the mines of grace and truth to a perishing world, the Bible will be their armoury, their inspiration, their joy. Can it be that because God has not shut up every avenue by which His testimony can be evaded, that men, in their pride, "will not deign to accept His mercy?" The alternative is not the Bible or man-made religions, the Bible or materialism. No: the awful alternative for every living man that has ears to hear is, obey the Scriptures or you perish.

There is a spirit abroad which ranges over the world of thought, peers into the rocky strata of the earth, traverses space to the confines of the star-dust land—which questions light, and heat, and electricity, and force, and the structure of plants and animals, and self-evident truth, such as the argument from design—and when a fact is discovered, which may be twisted into apparent hostility to the testimony of the Bible, it is lifted up like Milton's star that "flamed in the forehead of the sky," and is compelled to do duty against the Majesty of Revelation ; the burden of which is that God hath given to us eternal life, and this life is in His Son.   Can human sin go further in unreasonableness than this ?   One would think that such good news, authenticated by myriads of witnesses, by miracle, and prophecy, and adaptation to the condition of the race and its own essential luminousness, would be welcomed by every man ; that the great masters of mind would be the first to greet the majestic dawn of inspiration, and that from their ranks armies of explorers would be ever issuing to gather from the universe confirmatory evidence for the Divine testimony—evidence assuming the form of a new "Analogy" by a new Butler ; now of a new book of thoughts by another Pascal ; and now of a series of astronomical sermons by another Chalmers.   If the sun were plucked from the centre of the system, leaving behind him death and darkness, it would be a small thing compared with the destruction of the Bible. But what—borrowing the language of an eloquent writer—if it be lawful to indulge such a thought, would be the funeral obsequies of a lost Bible ?   " Where shall we find the tears fit to be wept at such a spectacle ? or could we realise the calamity in all its extent, what tokens of commiseration and concern would be deemed equal to the occasion ? Would it suffice for the sun to veil his light, and the moon her brightness ; to cover the ocean with mourning, and the heavens with sackcloth ? or were the whole fabric of nature to become animated and vocal, would it be possible for her to utter a groan too deep, or a cry too piercing, to express the magnitude and extent of such a catastrophe ?"   For all the light that ever chased the gloom of doubt, roused dejection, or cheered the bosom of despondency ; for whatever gives confidence to faith, brightness to hope, and fervour to devotion ; for all the knowledge the world ever had of life and immortality; for whatever can tranquillise the mind in life, and minister consolation at the last hour, we are indebted to the Bible.

In primitive times theology was the chosen field of conflict ; in the Dark Ages it was the philosophy of mind, and now it is physical science.   Look forward a little, and in the temple of truth you will see all nations assembled, making offerings to the God of the Bible.   Here is freedom with her charter, and barbarism with her rudeness, and civilisation with her inconceivable grandeur, and science with her glorious dis- coveries, and the slave with his fetters, and art with her achievements, and mind with the cream of its thought, and music with its melody, and all earth with its gold, to put honour on Him whose Word has become the light of the world—a Word which, to be loved, has only to be known. And as for scepticism, what has it done ?   What immoral man has it reformed ?   What savage has it reclaimed? What barbarous tribe has it civilised ?   What wilderness has it turned into a smiling Eden ?   Over what continent has it poured out its philanthropies, to ameliorate the mass of the people ?   On what death-bed has it shed the light of a blessed hope ?   What has its questionings, its gloom, and its despair accomplished for the deliverance of the human race from sin and misery ?

Of all the facts of science, none is better established than that the mind of the natural man is enmity against God.   Let the pantheist bring his abstractions, the atheist his black cup of despair, the infidel the chemistry of his philosophical conceit, and the new school of materialists the atom of matter which possesses all the potentialities of life and mind, to dissolve that enmity, and replace it by the love of God.   " Jesus I know, and Paul I know ; but who are ye ?" will be the scornful defiance.   The Bible alone, as has been proved in millions of instances, possesses the true solvent—is able to make wise, and is the power of God unto salvation to every one that believeth.

Some one has said that a deep mathematic brings us nearer the source of all number—the Infinite One; a deep astro- nomy, a profound geology, carries us closer to the Lord of heaven and earth ; and I say that a deep philosophy draws us near that great God, around whom the Bible throws the majestic robes of light, love, and grace. When the history of scepticism, in all its Protean forms, comes to be written, it will be found that it is based in and built up of credulity ; and when the annals of Bible-work shall be completed, it will be seen that faith in the Divine testimony of the Bible, which is the seed of the world's life, and the lamp of the world's light—that God hath given us eternal life, and this life is in His Son—is a reasonable service.

8. The Bible has opened up to mankind the true springs of happiness. Every one knows that there is nothing on earth to reward the pursuit or satisfy the yearnings of man. The richest treasures of time are the glitter of the stars upon the water ; and poor is that felicity which is gathered outside the gates of paradise. Man is born to sorrow ; and all the evidence charges his suffering on his sin. The plague of misery invades the palaces of princes as well as the criminal's cell. No country or generation or order of men is exempt. The air is burdened with wailing for departed kindred. And the deepest sufferings of the soul are within —arising from the consciousness of guilt and the dread of retribution. Death, in very deed the king of terrors, projects his shadow over all the gay glories of time ; and the calm with which it is met is the torrent's smoothness ere it dash over the precipice. Now where is the fountain of comfort? Is it found in the face of nature; or in the popular religions to which the intellect, the imagination, and the conscience of men have given birth ? Does the sacred water of life, which alone has the potency to assuage human sorrow, flow from the lips of the infidel, as in his cave of gloom he spins out the threads for that net of despair which he would fain throw over creation ? Oh no ; the spring of all consolation is in that religion which has in it an expiation, a pardon as full as it is sweet, a life realising the ideal of perfection, a harmony between justice and grace, a paradise of love in light, a God in whom infinite good and right reside, an eternity made of joy. How grandly did the Divine Author

of Christianity begin His ministry by the announcement of the eight beatitudes! "If there be joy in the world," says Kempis, "it belongs to the man of a pure heart." The whole revelation of God—promise, prophecy, invitation, precept—rains joy. Great peace, deepening into something that passes all understanding, and swelling up into a joy unspeakable and full of glory, is the blessed experience of the believer in the Bible. Seeing outwardly only tears and a cross in the Christian, natural men have stigmatised the religion of the Bible as gloom. Could they pierce the breast of the believer, they would find the God of all consolation enshrined in the heart. Power, wealth, love, pleasure, are the equipage of happiness ; but they are not happiness. Whether in the abode of indigence or the palace of royalty, amid the sons of toil or the favourites of fortune, in solitude or society—wherever the broken heart clothes itself in humility and feeds on Holy Scripture, it finds delight in God, a delight which elevates and satisfies by stretching away into eternity. The Bible blesses the cradle ; it kindles a torch in the long home where the pious dead are laid. It sanctifies and diminishes every misfortune. It made Rochester say that he would not commit the least sin to gain a kingdom. It enabled Robert Hall to exclaim in death, " Very comfortable, very comfortable," while he described his body as an "apparatus of torture;" and, pillowed on the Holy Book, Payson could say, as he was departing, " The sun of righteousness has been gradually drawing nearer and nearer, appearing larger and brighter as he approached ; and now he fills the whole hemisphere, pouring forth a flood of glory, in which I seem to float like an insect in the beams of the sun ; exulting, yet almost trembling while I gaze on this excessive brightness, and wondering with unutterable wonder why God should deign thus to shine upon a sinful worm."

What gladness is brought in the tidings of a finished redemption and the resurrection-life ! And the world to come, is it not sinless—the abode of a joy at once full and eternal ? For the sum of all saving knowledge, the marrow of the Bible, is this, that man was made to glorify God and enjoy Him for ever. Take from the righteous man whatever he holds dear ; subject him to the frowns of fortune and the blasts of penury ; let him rot in a dungeon or pine away in agony ; it is the lesson taught by the annals of the world that his Bible and his Bible alone inspires him with fortitude, and in the hope of infinite riches and joy through immortal duration, banquets his soul on the happiness of God.

We challenge the whole army of infidels to produce a single authenticated instance of an intelligent man who on sceptical principles enjoyed happiness in life and peace in death. On the other hand, no fact in history is better attested than that individuals more numerous than the stars of heaven, of every nation and people—of every age, rank, and sex—of every grade of intelligence and intellect—of every age since the year of grace—of every variety of circumstance, from indigence to royalty, from the bloom of youth to the fires of martyrdom—have, through the faith of the Bible, enjoyed a happiness which the world could not give or take away, and met death with a triumphant joy, like the home-life of the better land to which they were going.

Let the present infidel crusade against Holy Scripture succeed, and what then ? We lose our civil and religious liberties —lapsing into the despotism of heathen cruelty. We lose the splendid trophies of Christian civilisation, and sink into barbarism. We lose the blessings of marriage, and exchange our happy home for the lust and life of the sensual savage. We lose the holy, just, good code of moral law, and drift on the swollen stream of depravity at the bidding of the windy speculations of the philosophers. We lose the Sabbath, which is our rest and the gospel of our salvation, and the river of life from which we drink comfort, and sink into the Dead Sea of a putrid atheism ; and upon the graves of the dead we shall see written the gospel of despair—death is an eternal sleep.

Of all the questions that agitate the human mind this is the greatest—Is the Bible an authentic and genuine revelation from God ? If the twelve hundred millions of our race were met to consider what they would do in case the sun set to rise no more, the matter would be unimportant in comparison.   If some great foe of our race poisoned the fountains of the globe, and dried up its waters with the sole of his foot, it would be nothing when compared with the sealing up of the three Bible fountains—the mercy of God, the blood of Jesus, the grace of the Spirit—from which, for sixty centuries, have issued the plentiful streams of grace and salvation.   Suppose that the solar system were turned into a gem of purest ray serene, and made over to a man, it would be a trifle compared with the Bible.

This holy book is the manna of the world.   It is the map of a river, in which whosoever washes is healed of the leprosy of sin ; and in the radiant bloom of health he comes forth to a life which soars above the highest seraph, and is ever stretching towards God.   Milton grandly described the Archangel Uriel as descending to the earth in a sunbeam.   The revelation of the Bible is a beam on which the Father of lights descends into men to dwell with them.   Sweeter than the dews of six thousand summers is the living bread which the Bible brings to a perishing world.   What though it rained gold and pearls and kings' crowns on our guilty race, it were better to give them the Bible. Salvation ! Weigh it against all created things.   Measure it by eternity.   Lay the plummet of infinity to its blessings.   Appeal to Him who weighs the mountains in scales and the hills in a balance to teach you its worth.   Climb to the throne of the Eternal, where the universe collects her glories to decorate the palace of our King, and thence survey all things that are made.   Salvation excels all you know and see ; for it makes God Himself your everlasting portion.

And if the time should ever come when it will rain infidels, there is a truth which no science can impeach, no learning undermine, no hate can annihilate ; and that truth is—oh that I could carry it round the world !—that they are a happy people who know the joyful sound, and whose God Jehovah is.   Give the revelation of the Bible in its simplicity, holiness, and majesty—the inspired Word of

God—to the mind and heart of the human race, till they
taste and see its grace and truth, its light and life ; and soon
the red dawn of that day of applied redemption for the
whole world, to which seers and saints looked forward,
will be seen on the mountains ; for very joy the wilderness
shall rejoice and blossom as the rose ; the sigh for renewal,
which this groaning creation has emitted, shall find its
response in the bloom of a new heavens and a new earth,
in which, as in a mountain-lake, heaven will mirror itself ;
man shall replace on his brow the crown of fine gold,
undimmed, that had long since fallen from his head ; this
perturbed world shall become a Beulah of beauty, the calm
home of peace, a Goshen of abundance, the worthy avenue
of an immortal Paradise ; and from the throne of His
triumphant Mediatorship, He who has the keys of hell and
of death shall look down in complacency, and the light of
His countenance beam full upon it.

MARCUS WARD AND CO., PRINTERS, ROYAL ULSTER WORKS, BELFAST.

www.ingramcontent.com/pod-product-compliance
Lightning Source LLC
Chambersburg PA
CBHW021212270326
41929CB00010B/1097